EPISODE ONE: PROTECT. SERVE. BEAT

D1306838

STORY
BILL JEMAS
JULIAN ROWE

SCRIPT
FRANK ORTEGA
BILL JEMAS

LAYOUTS
JULIAN ROWE

PENCILS
CARLOS RODRIGUEZ

COLORS
PETER PANTAZIS

CHARLOTTE GREENBAUM

EDITOR
CHARLOTTE GREENBAUM

EPISODE TWO: DEAD BADGE OF COURAGE

STORY
BILL JEMAS

SCRIPT
FRANK ORTEGA
BILL JEMAS

LAYOUTS
JULIAN ROWE

PENCILS
JOSE LUIS
BRENT PEEPLES

COLORS
DINEI R.
ROSS HUGHES

COVER
APPLE QINGYANG ZHANG

LETTERS
CHARLOTTE GREENBAUM
ELYSIA LIANG

EDITOR
CHARLOTTE GREENBAUM

EPISODE THREE: BLOOD BRIGADE

STORY
BILL JEMAS

SCRIPT
BILL JEMAS
FRANK ORTEGA

LAYOUTS
JULIAN ROWE
STAN CHOU

PENCILS
JOSE LUIS
JULIAN ROWE
BRENT PEEPLES

COLORS
CARLOS LOPEZ

COVER
APPLE QINGYANG ZHANG

LETTERS
CHARLOTTE GREENBAUM

EDITOR
CHARLOTTE GREENBAUM

EPISODE FOUR: INSURRECTION

STORY
BILL JEMAS
MICHAEL COAST

SCRIPT
BILL JEMAS
JEFF McCOMSEY

LAYOUTS
STAN CHOU
JULIAN ROWE
ALESSANDRA DIVIZIA
BENJAMIN SILBERSTEIN

PENCILS
NOVO MALGAPO
FERNANDO MELEK

COLORS
CARLOS LOPEZ

COVER
CRYSTAL GRAZIANO

LETTERS
CHARLOTTE GREENBAUM

EDITOR
CHARLOTTE GREENBAUM

EPISODE FIVE: JUSTICE

STORY
BILL JEMAS
MICHAEL COAST
JONATHAN ASHLEY

SCRIPT
FRANK ORTEGA
IAN DEMING
BILL JEMAS

PENCILS
RAPHAEL SAM
DENNIS CRISOSTOMO
JETHRO MORALES
NOVO MALGAPO

COLORS
BRETT SMITH
CARLOS LOPEZ
ROBERT NIX
LISA MOORE
JUANMAR STUDIOS

LAYOUTS
JONATHAN ASHLEY

COVER
APPLE QINGYANG ZHANG
CRYSTAL GRAZIANO

LETTERS
CHARLOTTE GREENBAUM

EDITOR
CHARLOTTE GREENBAUM

ULTIMATE TECHNOLOGY

Buyer's Guide

YOUR GUIDE TO THE BEST
TELEPHONES, TVs, CAMERAS, AND COMPUTERS
PLUS A SNEAK PEEK AT THE SMARTEST CAR IN TOWN.

HONDA

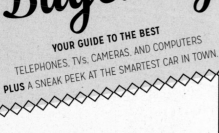

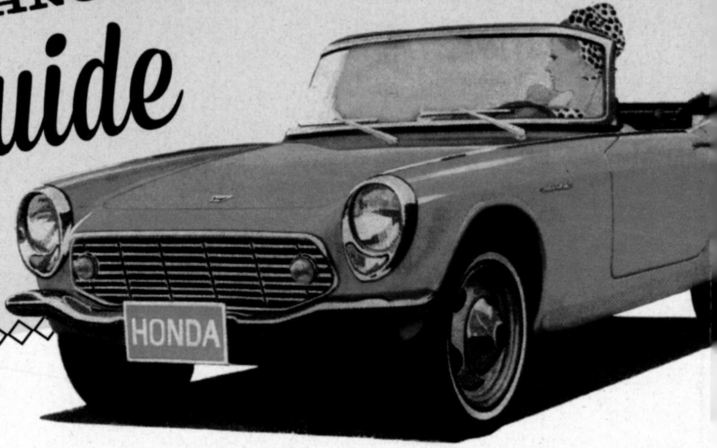

HONDA S-600

The smartest car in town for the family that has the latest high technology in their home. This car is smart in style with power to spare. It's easy to handle, easy to park, and has spacious luggage compartment for family trips.

$6500; at your local Honda dealership

MOTOROLA

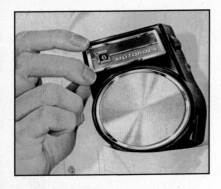

MOTOROLA POCKET RADIO

A shirt-pocket radio with the power and sound you'd expect from a larger set. A six-transistor chassis pinpoints stations and the speaker delivers sound in rich, clear lows, and crisp highs. With battery life up to 100 hours, you can take it on a trip in a custom carrying case.

$14; mail order

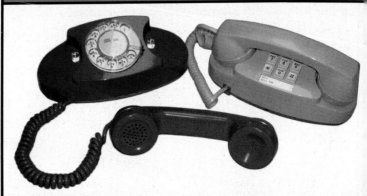

AT&T PRINCESS PHONE

America has fallen in love with the new Princess phone. It's little so it fits in those small places where you couldn't fit a telephone before. It's lovely and charms people with its graceful lines and color. It lights so you can find it easily in the dark.

$35; mail order

COLOR

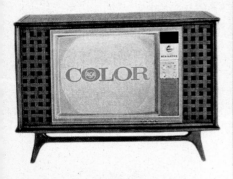

RCA COLOR TELEVISION

In living color. Get a perfectly fine-tuned picture with brighter highlights every time you watch and circuitry that won't go haywire.

$55; Kaufmann's

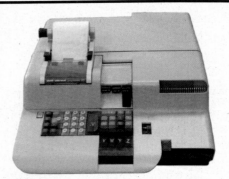

OLIVETTI PROGRAMMA 101

The first computer on your desk. Every company, university, department, laboratory, or institute can now have their own private electronic digital computer. It's only a little larger than a typewriter and doesn't require a skilled operator.

$75; mail order

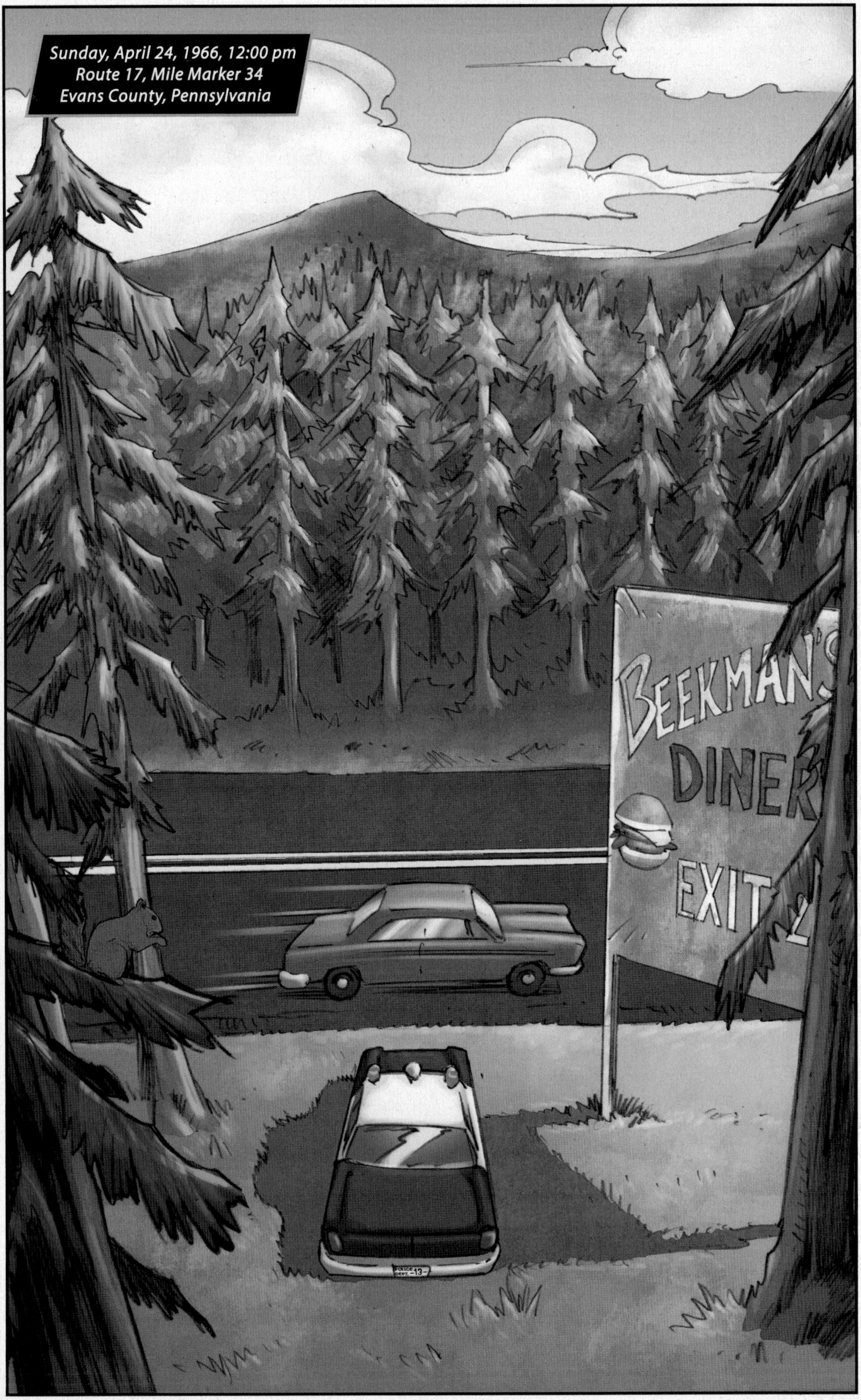
Sunday, April 24, 1966, 12:00 pm
Route 17, Mile Marker 34
Evans County, Pennsylvania
BEEKMAN'S
DINER
EXIT

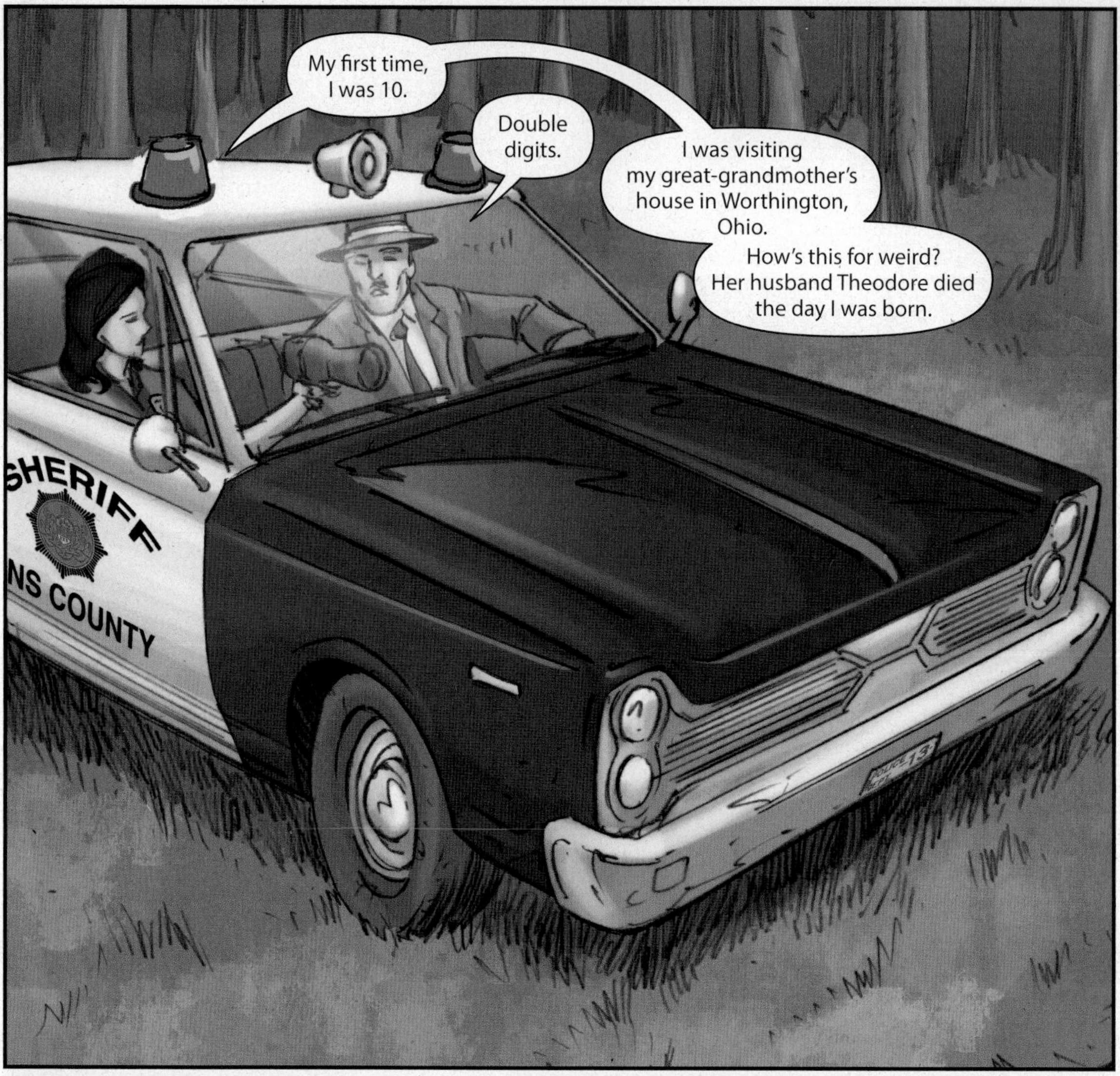
My first time, I was 10.
Double digits.
I was visiting my great-grandmother's house in Worthington, Ohio.
How's this for weird? Her husband Theodore died the day I was born.
SHERIFF
NS COUNTY

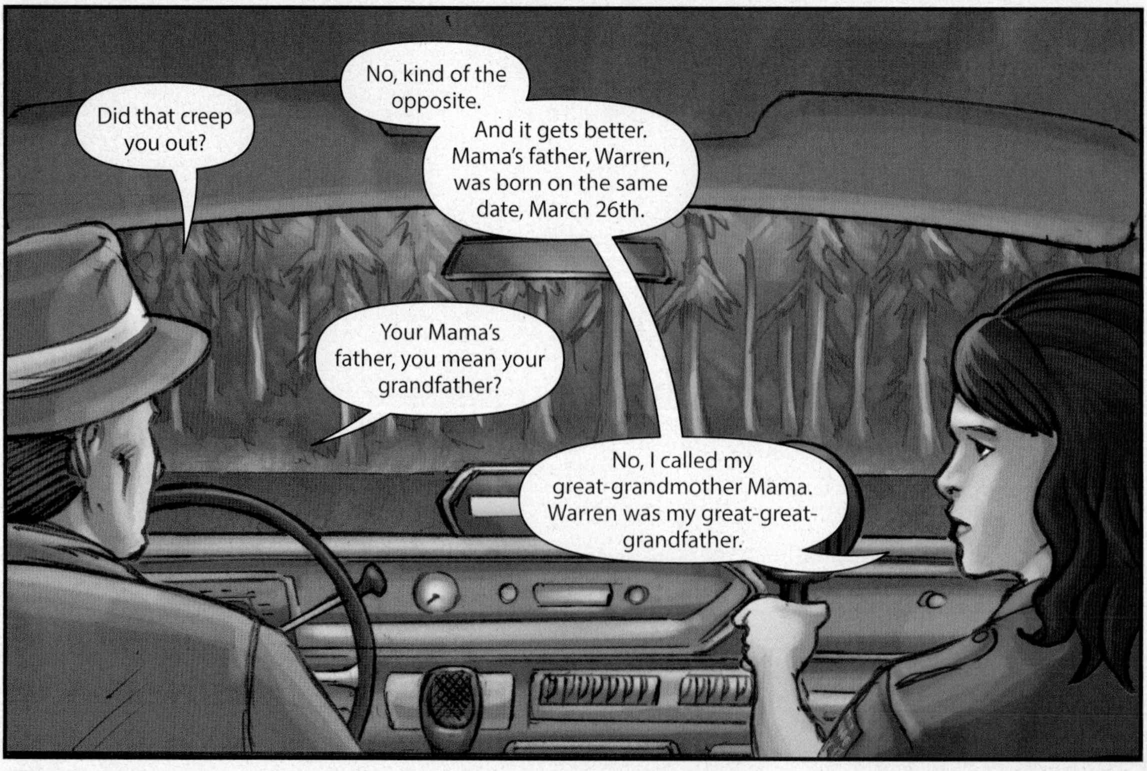
Did that creep you out?
No, kind of the opposite.
And it gets better. Mama's father, Warren, was born on the same date, March 26th.
Your Mama's father, you mean your grandfather?
No, I called my great-grandmother Mama. Warren was my great-great-grandfather.

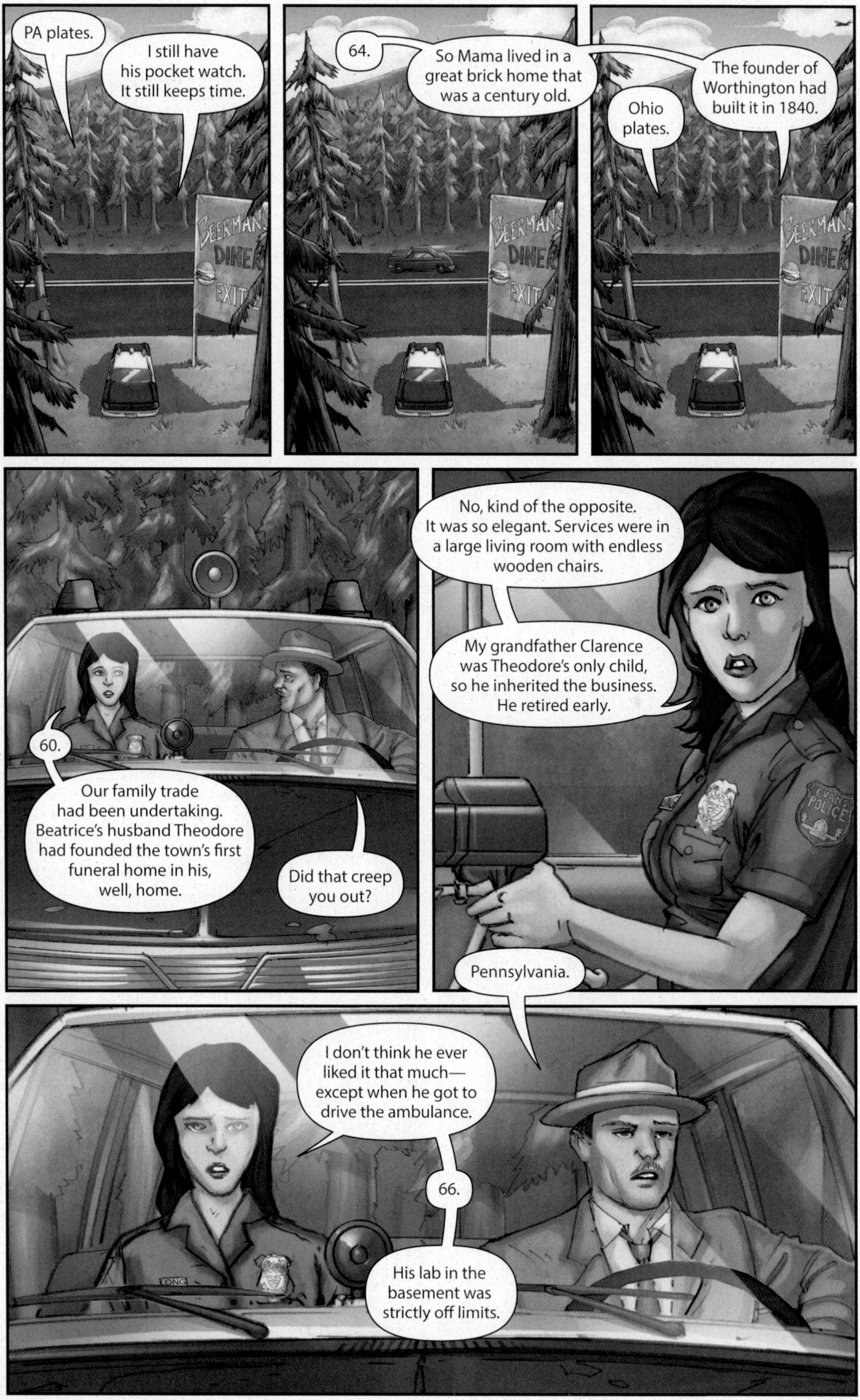
PA plates.
I still have his pocket watch. It still keeps time.
BEEKMAN'S DINER EXIT
64.
So Mama lived in a great brick home that was a century old.
The founder of Worthington had built it in 1840.
Ohio plates.
60.
Our family trade had been undertaking. Beatrice's husband Theodore had founded the town's first funeral home in his, well, home.
Did that creep you out?
No, kind of the opposite. It was so elegant. Services were in a large living room with endless wooden chairs.
My grandfather Clarence was Theodore's only child, so he inherited the business. He retired early.
EVANS POLICE
Pennsylvania.
I don't think he ever liked it that much—except when he got to drive the ambulance.
66.
His lab in the basement was strictly off limits.
LONG

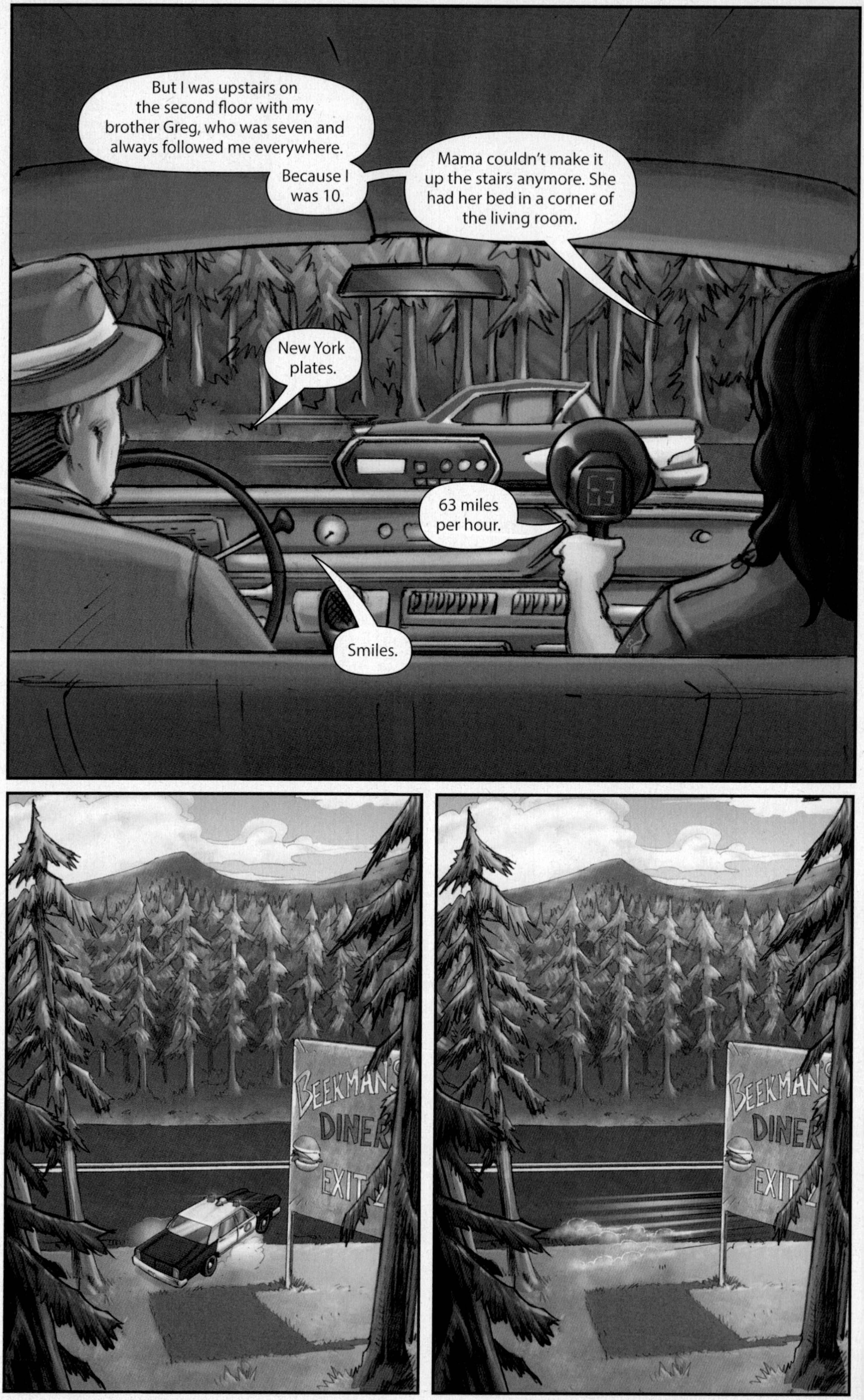
But I was upstairs on the second floor with my brother Greg, who was seven and always followed me everywhere.
Because I was 10.
Mama couldn't make it up the stairs anymore. She had her bed in a corner of the living room.
New York plates.
63 miles per hour.
Smiles.
BEEKMAN'S DINER EXIT
BEEKMAN'S DINER EXIT

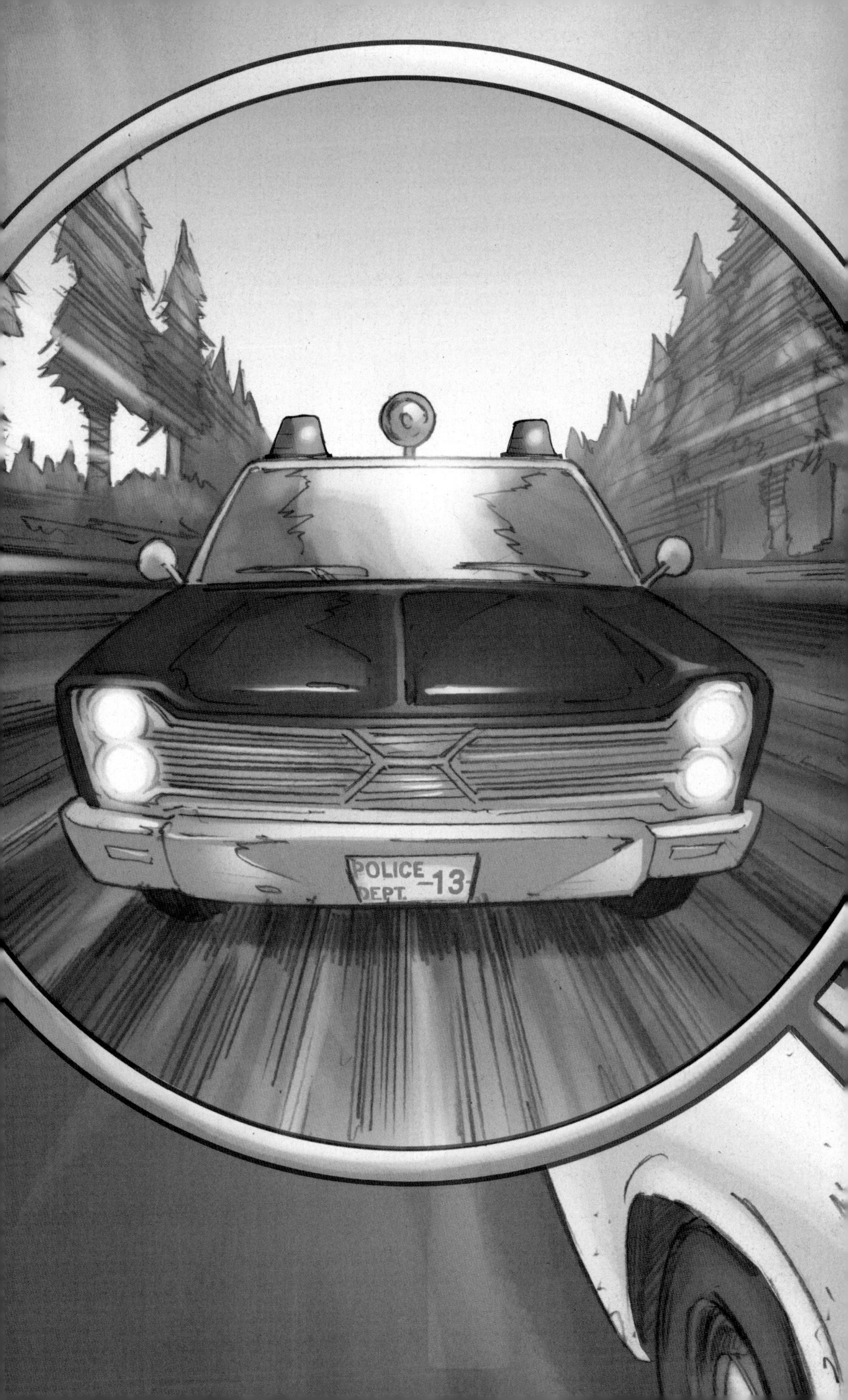
POLICE DEPT. -13-

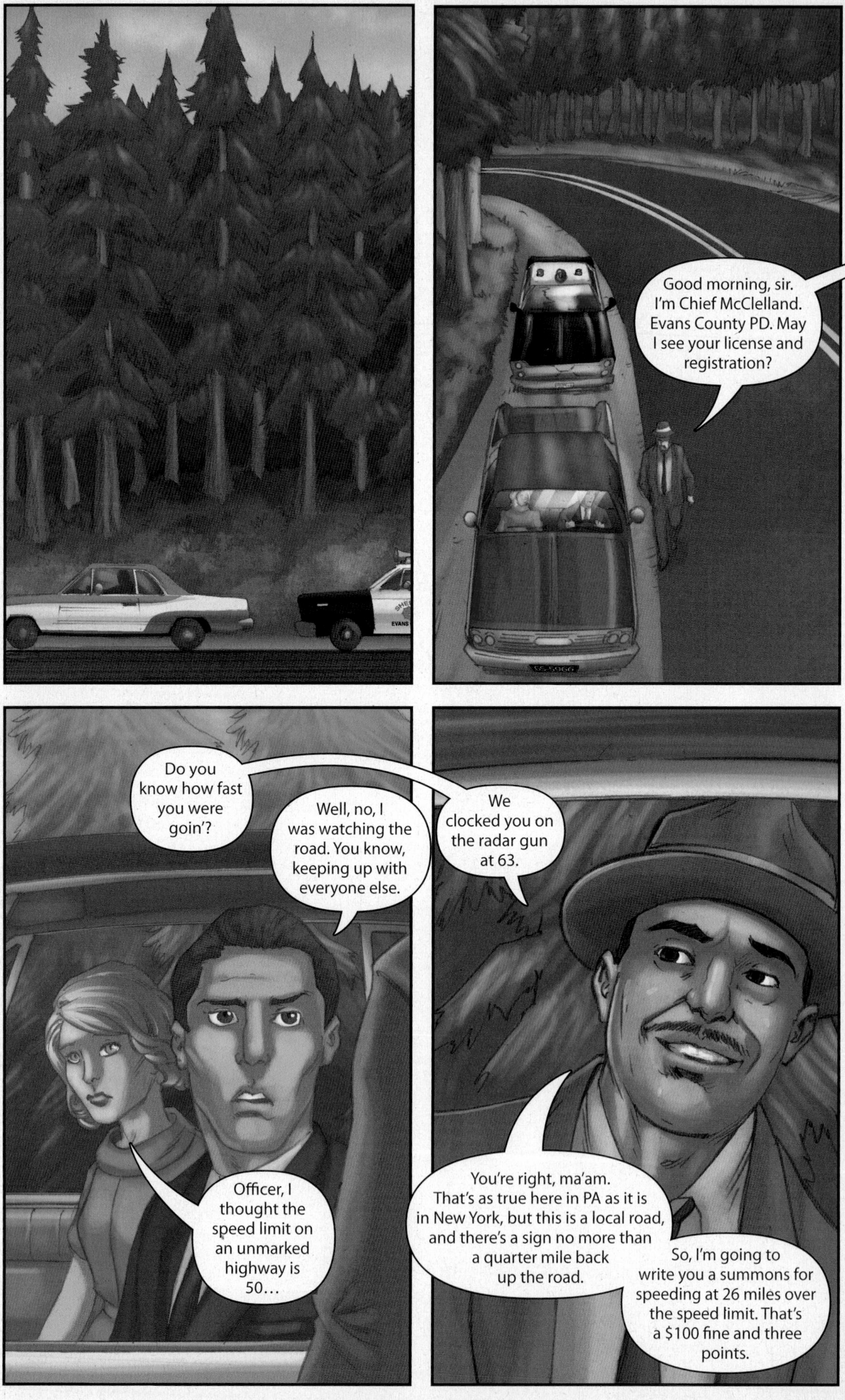
Good morning, sir. I'm Chief McClelland. Evans County PD. May I see your license and registration?
Do you know how fast you were goin'?
Well, no, I was watching the road. You know, keeping up with everyone else.
We clocked you on the radar gun at 63.
Officer, I thought the speed limit on an unmarked highway is 50…
You're right, ma'am. That's as true here in PA as it is in New York, but this is a local road, and there's a sign no more than a quarter mile back up the road.
So, I'm going to write you a summons for speeding at 26 miles over the speed limit. That's a $100 fine and three points.

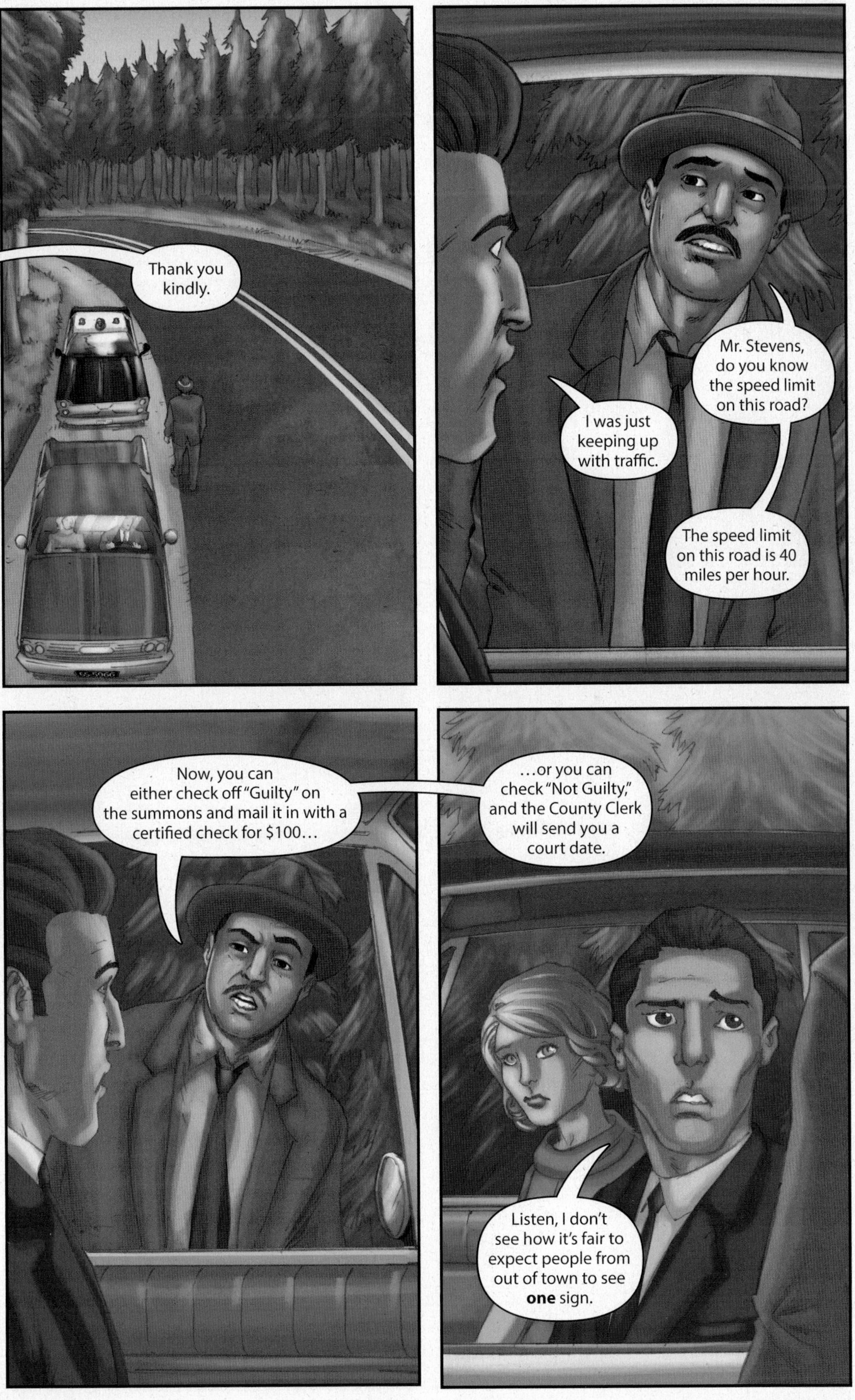

Thank you kindly.
Mr. Stevens, do you know the speed limit on this road?
I was just keeping up with traffic.
The speed limit on this road is 40 miles per hour.
Now, you can either check off "Guilty" on the summons and mail it in with a certified check for $100…
…or you can check "Not Guilty," and the County Clerk will send you a court date.
Listen, I don't see how it's fair to expect people from out of town to see **one** sign.

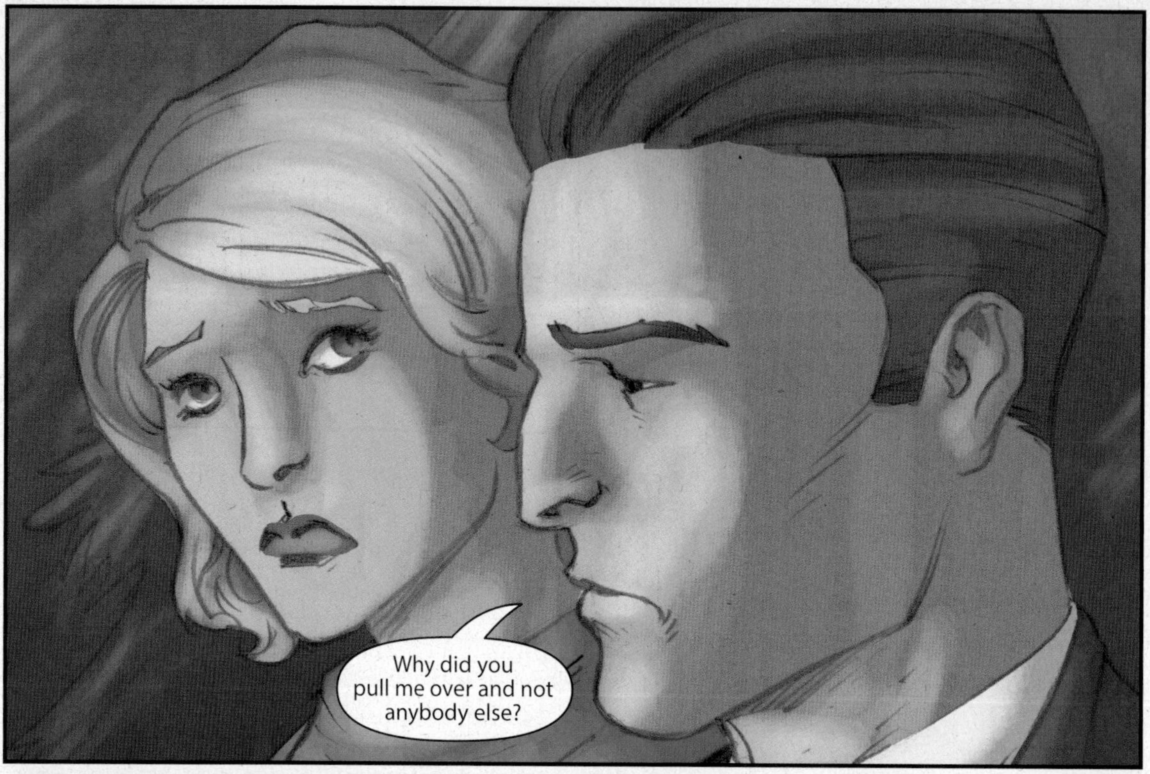
Why did you pull me over and not anybody else?

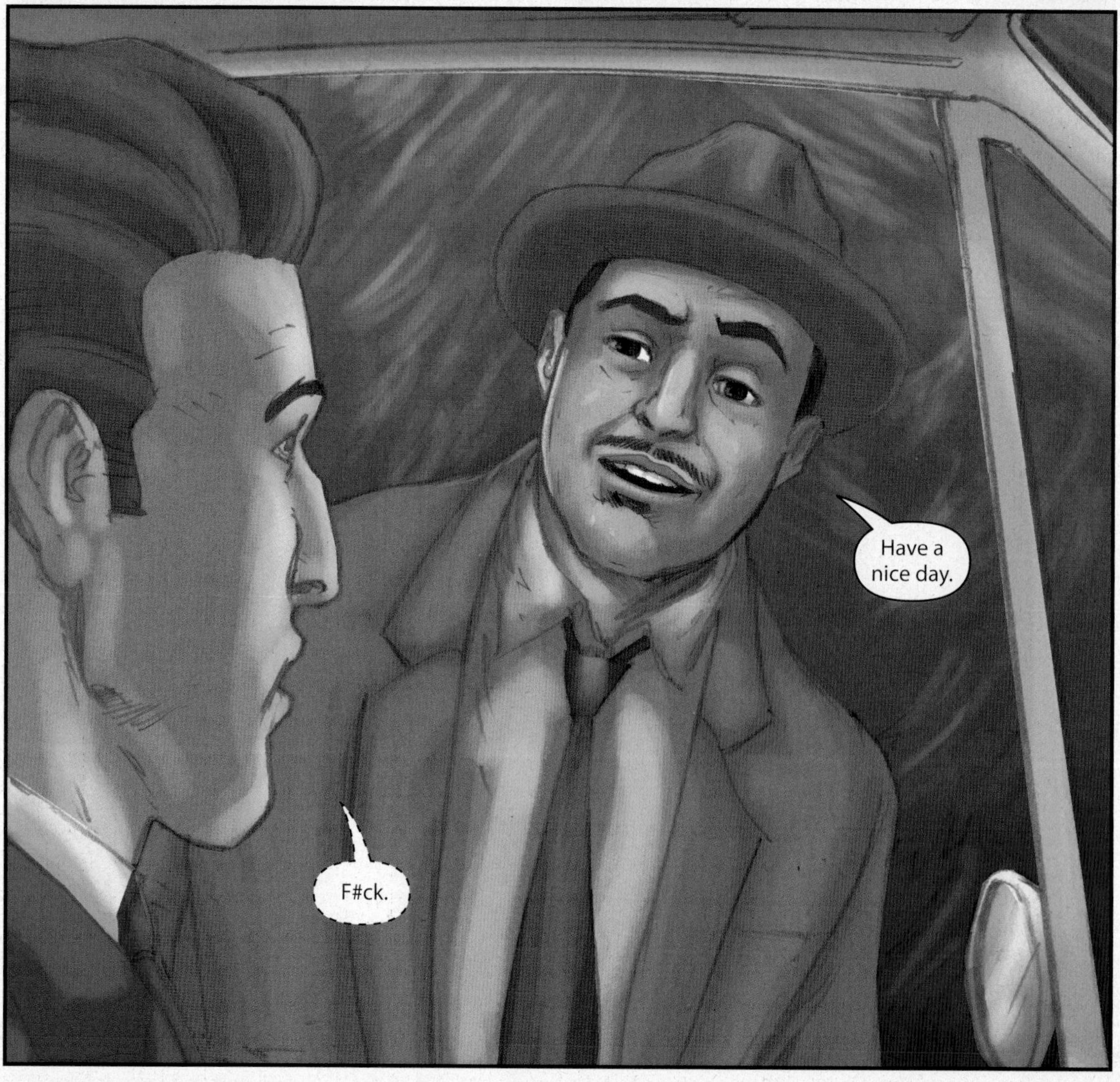
Have a nice day.
F#ck.

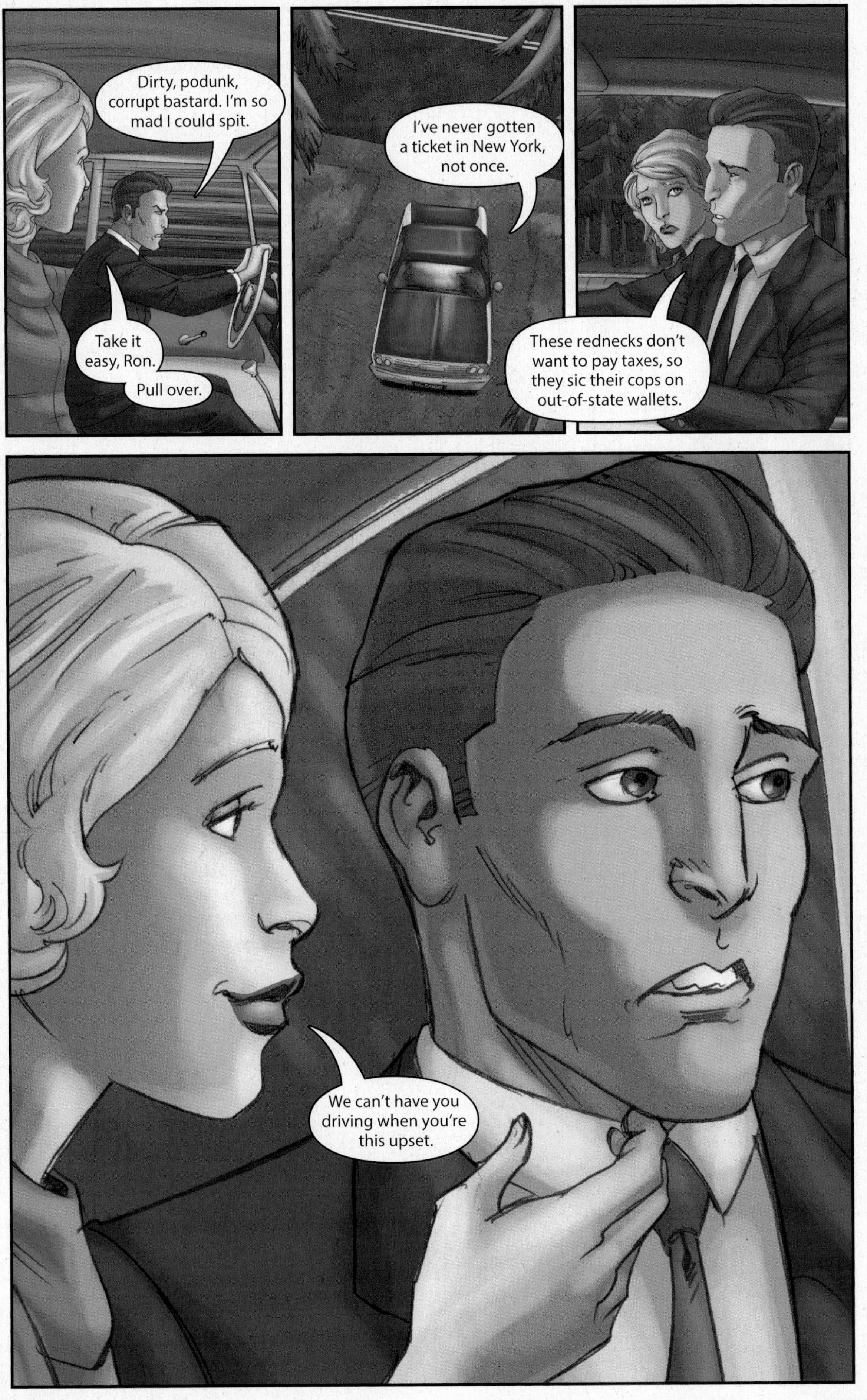

Dirty, podunk, corrupt bastard. I'm so mad I could spit.
Take it easy, Ron.
Pull over.
I've never gotten a ticket in New York, not once.
These rednecks don't want to pay taxes, so they sic their cops on out-of-state wallets.
We can't have you driving when you're this upset.

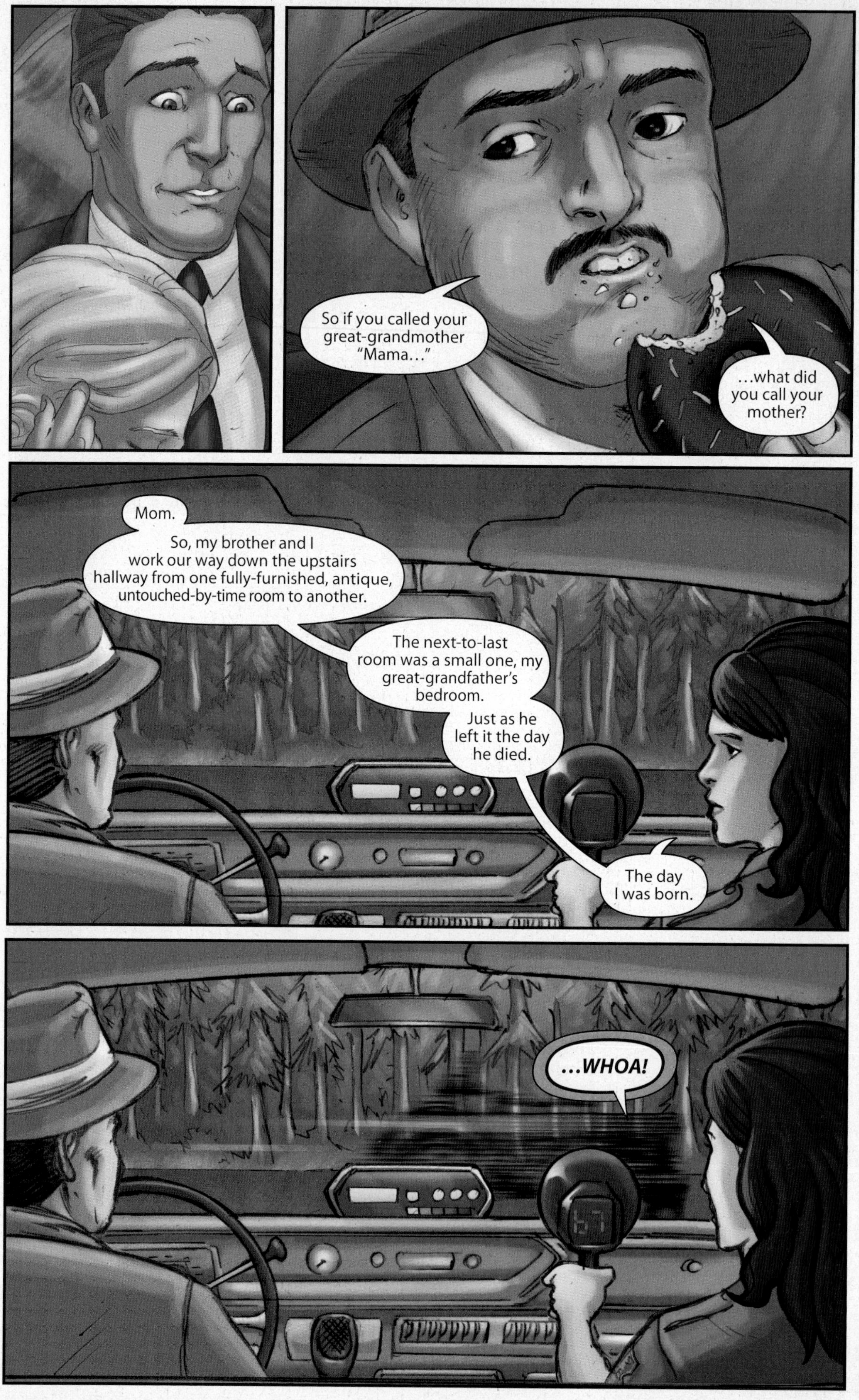
So if you called your great-grandmother "Mama…"
…what did you call your mother?
Mom.
So, my brother and I work our way down the upstairs hallway from one fully-furnished, antique, untouched-by-time room to another.
The next-to-last room was a small one, my great-grandfather's bedroom.
Just as he left it the day he died.
The day I was born.
…WHOA!

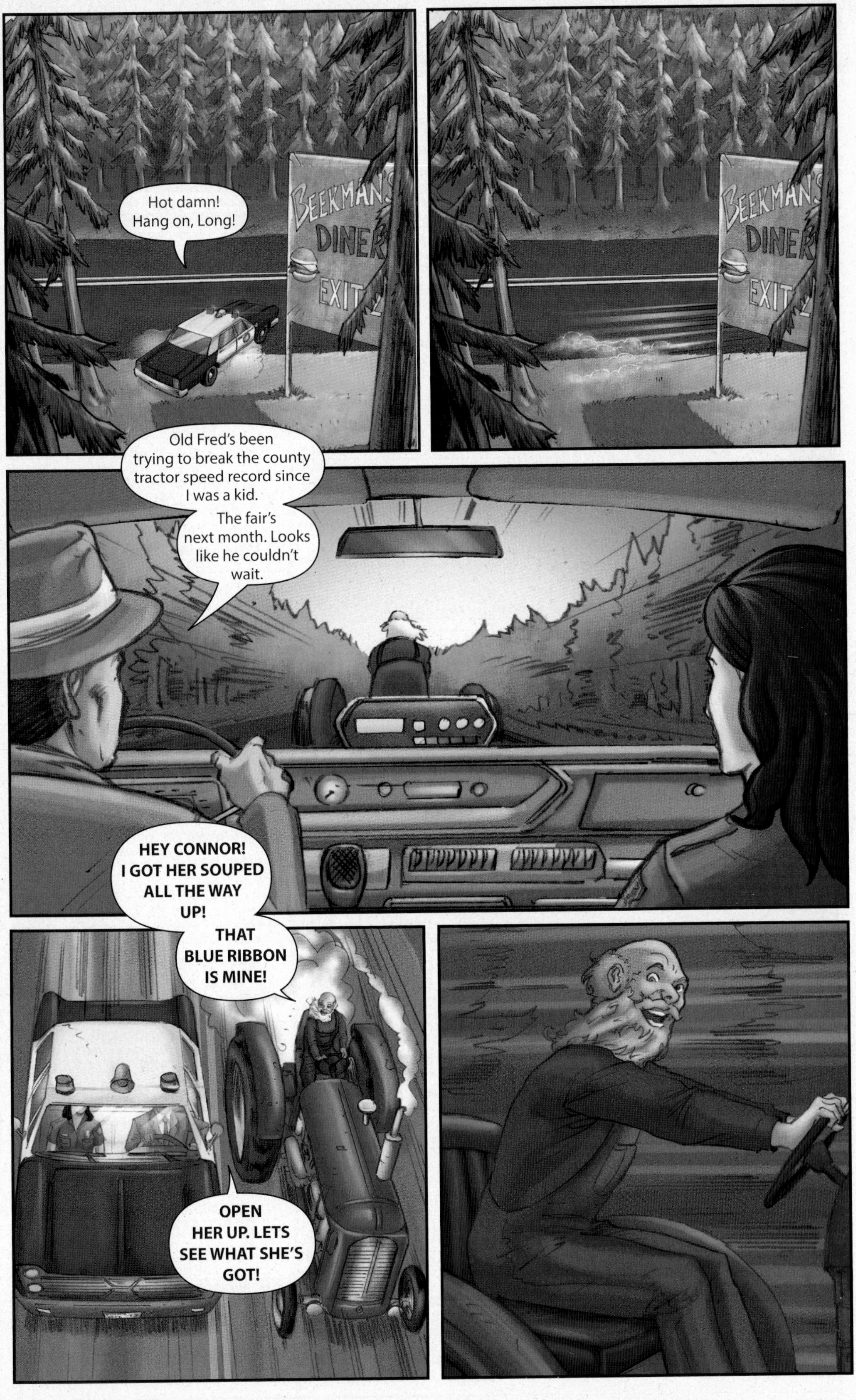
Hot damn! Hang on, Long!
BEEKMAN'S DINER EXIT
Old Fred's been trying to break the county tractor speed record since I was a kid.
The fair's next month. Looks like he couldn't wait.
HEY CONNOR! I GOT HER SOUPED ALL THE WAY UP!
THAT BLUE RIBBON IS MINE!
OPEN HER UP. LETS SEE WHAT SHE'S GOT!

1960s Job Classifieds

Help Wanted—Female

CLERK TYPIST EXPD
gen'l office duties internat'l co., mid-tn, $90-100. Mr. A. H. Olingy TN

CLERK, LITE STENO $95
Catholic Church Org. Hrs 9-4:30
Agency,   John St.,

CLERKS $80-85
Retail chain good at figures. Expd
Park Ave South

CLERK TYP/ASST BKPR $85
Charming import ofc ass't. Fee negot.
AGENCY, SPECIALISTS,

CLERKS, NO TYPING, $290
NO FIGURES—NO EXP NEC! HSG!
CO hires today! Boyle Agency

BOOKKEEPER-ASSISTANT
Accounts receivable, general, pleasant surroundings, good pay, benefits. Standard Food Products,

BOOKKEEPER—ASST.
HEAVY EXP   RETAIL CHAIN
35 HOURS   OPPORTUNITY
Apply   B'way, 12th Floor.

CLERKS
HOUSEWIVES
FEE PAID $70-85
DAYS, EVENINGS OR NITES
MAN Agency   Broadway
Cortldt or Fulton sta. 8-6 daily, 9-1 Sat.

GAL FRIDAY
Salary open. Some knl bkkpg., typing, filing, etc, 1 girl ofc. Brooklyn. 788-8060.

GAL FRI   FEE PD $95
Good typist. Figure Facility.
Unusually interesting organization.
AGENCY   E. 48th

GAL FRIDAY $70-80
Knowl typing & lite modeling. Excel oppty for brite gal. Mademoiselle Furs, 7th Ave, NYC. 3rd Floor.

GAL FRI, NO STEN, FEE PD, $90
"SWANK MEN'S CLUB"
                (3) AGENCIES
5 AVE   W 42   Bway

GAL FRIDAY
General office work, good typing, good with figures. Miss Garr, AL 5-4400.

COLLEGE GRADUATES

COLLEGE grad trainee for mkt research. Famous intl. co. seeks figure oriented gals to learn analyst work. Future. Top benefits. Fee refunded. To $95.
                    E 42 St. (Lex)

COLL GRAD   80-85
ENGLISH MAJOR
Train Publishing Asst Ed/Editor
Agency   5th Ave 41st St

COLLEGE GRADS, Any Major, $90-110
—TRAVEL AGENCY—
Intel+Sls exp or pslty—exciting career
Agency   5th Ave 41 St.

Coll Grad, Home Eco Maj
FEE PAID $475
Test kitchen of well known company
Position Secur Agency,   Maiden La.

COLL GRAD $5,200
THINKING NOT TYPING
Co trains business methods. Any Major
Agency   5th Ave. 41 St.

Coll Psych Secty $100 Fee Pd
Some coll, oppty assist consultant. Marketing dept. Managerial psy group. 9-5.
AGENCY, SPECIALISTS,   E 42.

Help Wanted—Male

ELECTRONICS
FIELD ENGINEERS TECHNICIANS AND WRITERS
Immediate openings overseas and stateside for the following categories. Minimum of 3 years experience required.

GROUND COMMUNICATIONS

GROUND NAVAIDS

DIGITAL COMPUTER

SHIPBOARD ELECTRONICS

HEAVY GROUND RADAR

GROUND TELEMETRY

PRECISION TEST EQUIPMENT

DIESEL-ELECTRIC POWER
(OVERSEAS ONLY)

DIGITAL WRITERS

ELECTRONIC SUPPLY

INSTALLATION CRAFTSMEN

MACHINISTS
EXPERIMENTAL MACHINISTS
Excellent Company-Paid Benefits
Good Working Conditions
Congenial Atmosphere

All around machinists for modern model shops at our Syosset facility. Must be capable of setting up and operating all lathes, millers, grinder and jig borers for close tolerance work. Knowledge of measuring instruments and equipment necessary.

AIRLINE NAVIGATORS
FAA LICENSED
Pacific flying, Oakland based. Write or call Saturn Airways Inc, PO Box 26, Oakland International Airport, Oakland, California. Telephone ( ) 562-2719.

AIRLINE $75-$100 TRAINEES
NO EXP. CO TRAINS. RESV
Agency   E 42 St
AGENCY   B'way
(NEAR WALL STREET)

AIRLINE   IMMEDIATE
EXCLUSIVE WITH OUR AGENCY
AGENTS
AIRLINE OPPORTUNITIES AGENCY
Hillside Ave Jamaica   3666

ACCOUNTANTS
SEMI-SENIORS
National CPA Firm has a number of openings for men with 2-4 years of good audit and tax experience. Permanent positions for qualified men. Please submit all essential information preliminary to an interview. Replies held in confidence. PO Box Bowling Green Station NY. NY. 1004.

AEROSPACE
Apollo/ Saturn V Openings New York Interviews, February 21 through 26

The   Space Division has immediate openings for engineers, management staff and technicians on the NASA Apollo/Saturn V program. Assignments are at Cape Kennedy, Huntsville, New Orleans and the Mississippi Test Facility at Bay St. Louis, Miss.

Senior Computer Operator
Immediate long term temporary positions available for work in a modern Data Processing Installation on I.B.M. 360. Should have 360 experience plus minimum 2-3 years heavy computer operational experience (1401 - 1410) with tape "on-line" background. Programming knowledge helpful.

COLLEGE GRADUATES

COLLEGE GRAD
$5200-$6000 + CO CAR
Fine old establ Co. offers immed career oppty ofc mgt trng prog for ambitious & sincere man. If you are recent college grad & draft deferred, this job is yours. Sal $5200-6000 start. Co car, fee paid by Co. Call Joe Martin. Snelling & Snelling Agency,   Court St, Bklyn. UL 5-5100

COLL GRADS FEE PD. $57-6500
MANAGEMENT
Train in all phases of admin., start methods planning dept, any major.
Agency,   5th Ave., 41 St.

COLL GRAD — STAFF MGR TRNG
WITH NATL CO IN AUTOMOTIVE FIELD. ROTATION TRNG LEADS TO HIGH LEVEL EXEC SPOT WITHIN 1 YR. $6.000. PART FEE REIMB.
AGENCY,   W. 44

COLL GRADS "NO EXP NEC" $6-8000
PROGRAMMING
Analytical mind? — Puzzle solver?
Free testing.   Agency   W 40

COLL GRADS Fee Refunded $5700-$6500
EXEC MANAGEMENT
Trnee spot all phases admin; work with Co Pres-any major-lead to $12M.
AGENCY   5 Av Rm

COLL GRAD $100
LIBERAL ARTS
Co. trains correspondent. No typing.
Agency   5th Ave 41st St

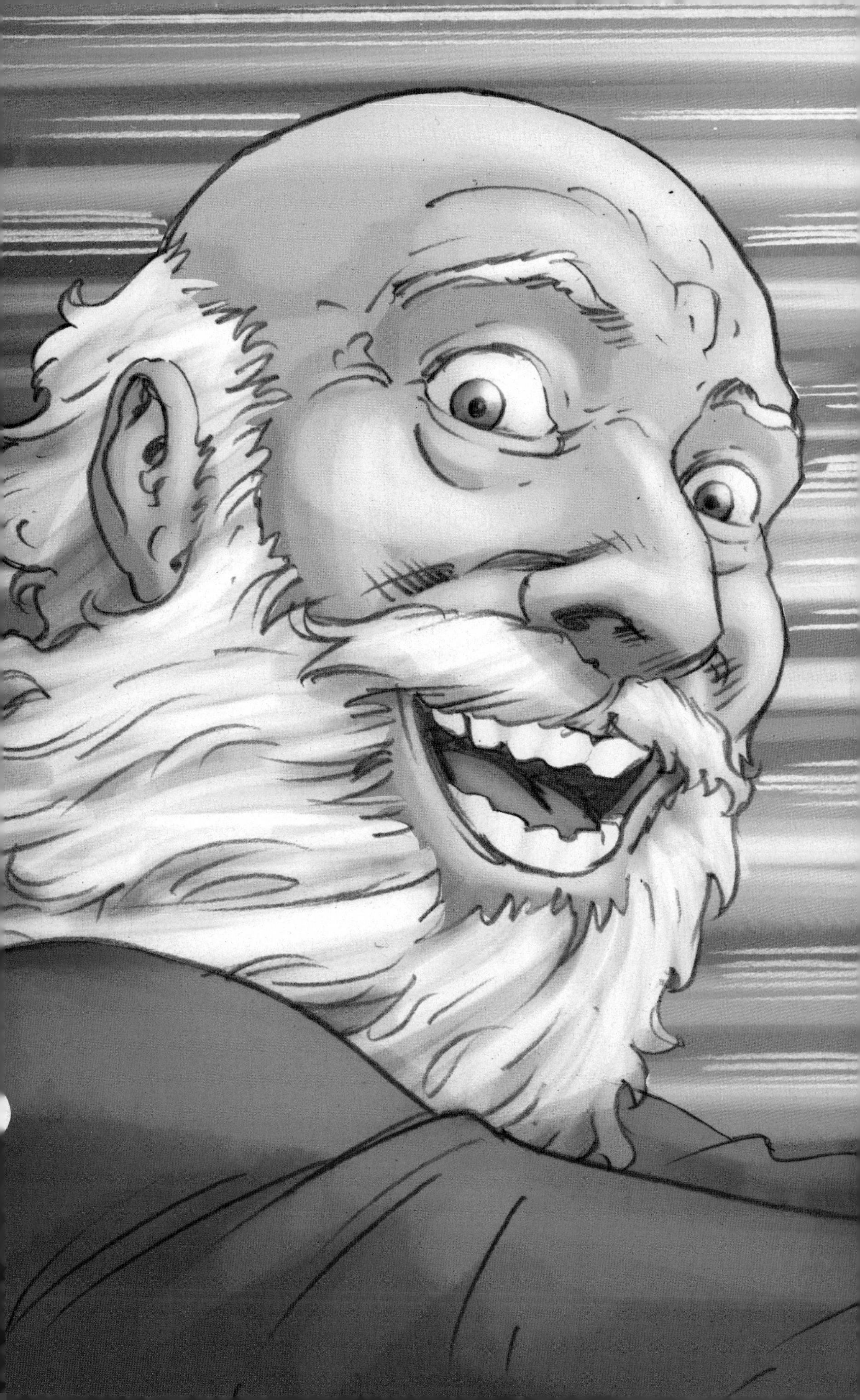

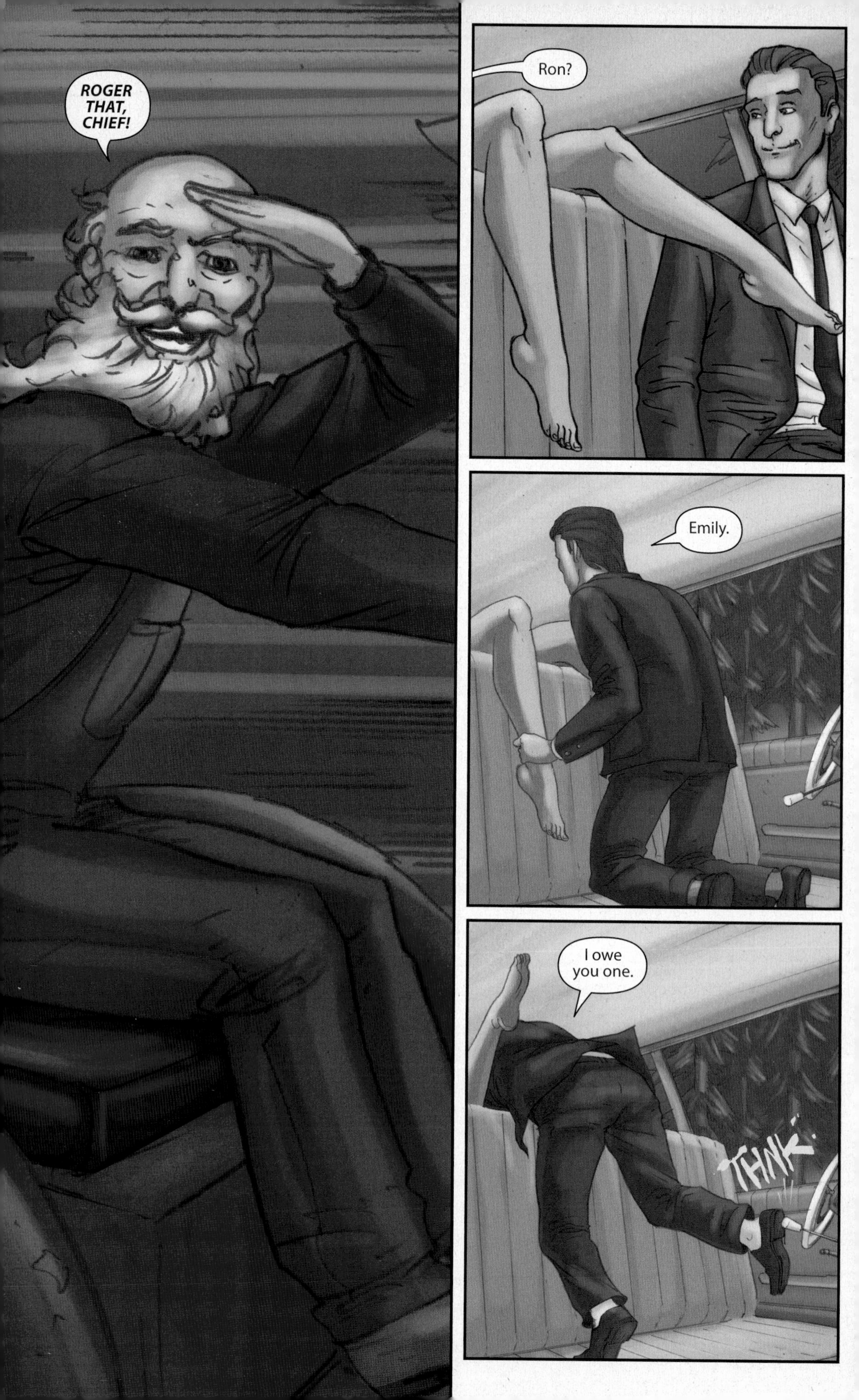
ROGER THAT, CHIEF!
Ron?
Emily.
I owe you one.
THNK!

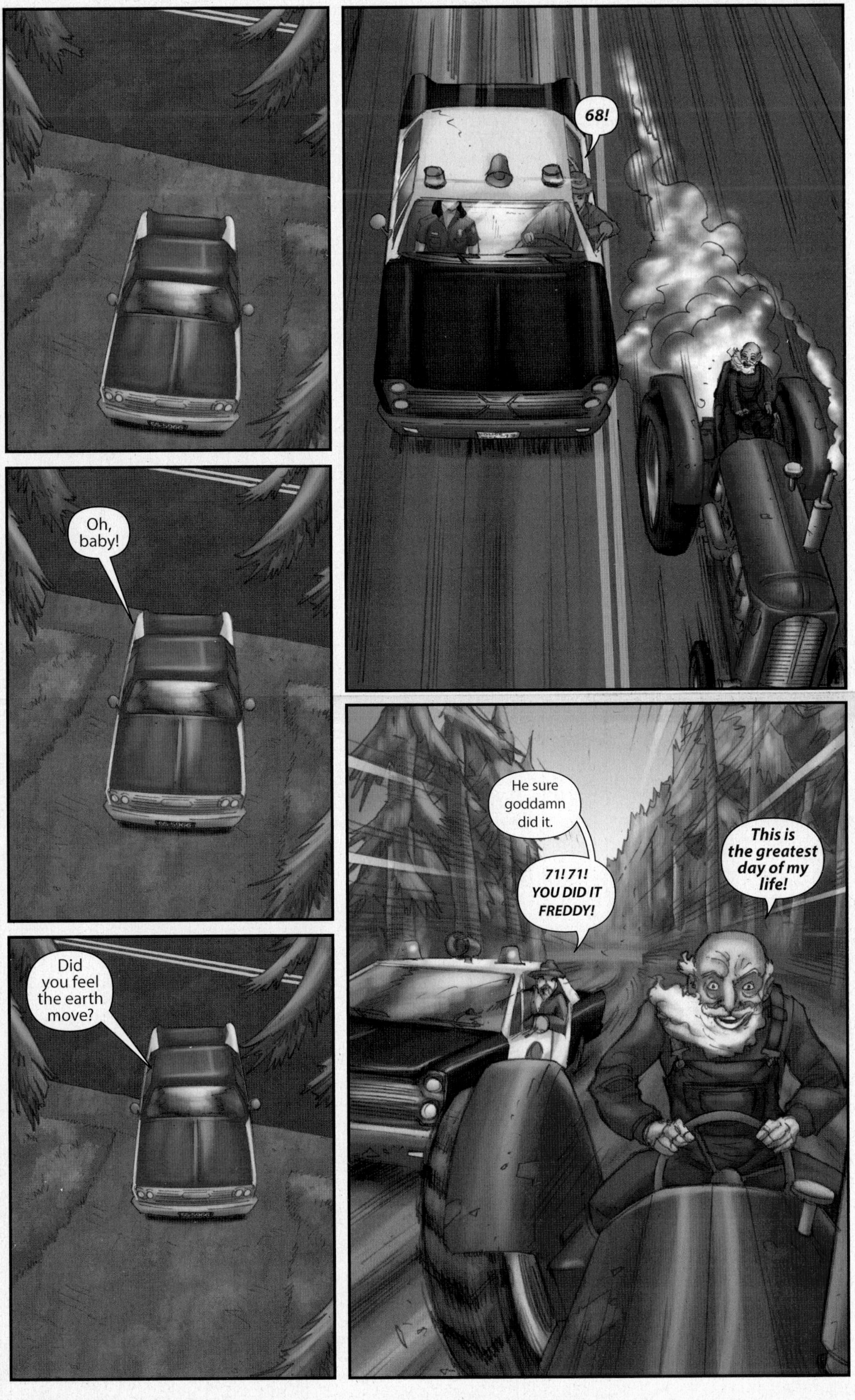
Oh, baby!
Did you feel the earth move?
68!
He sure goddamn did it.
71! 71! YOU DID IT FREDDY!
This is the greatest day of my life!

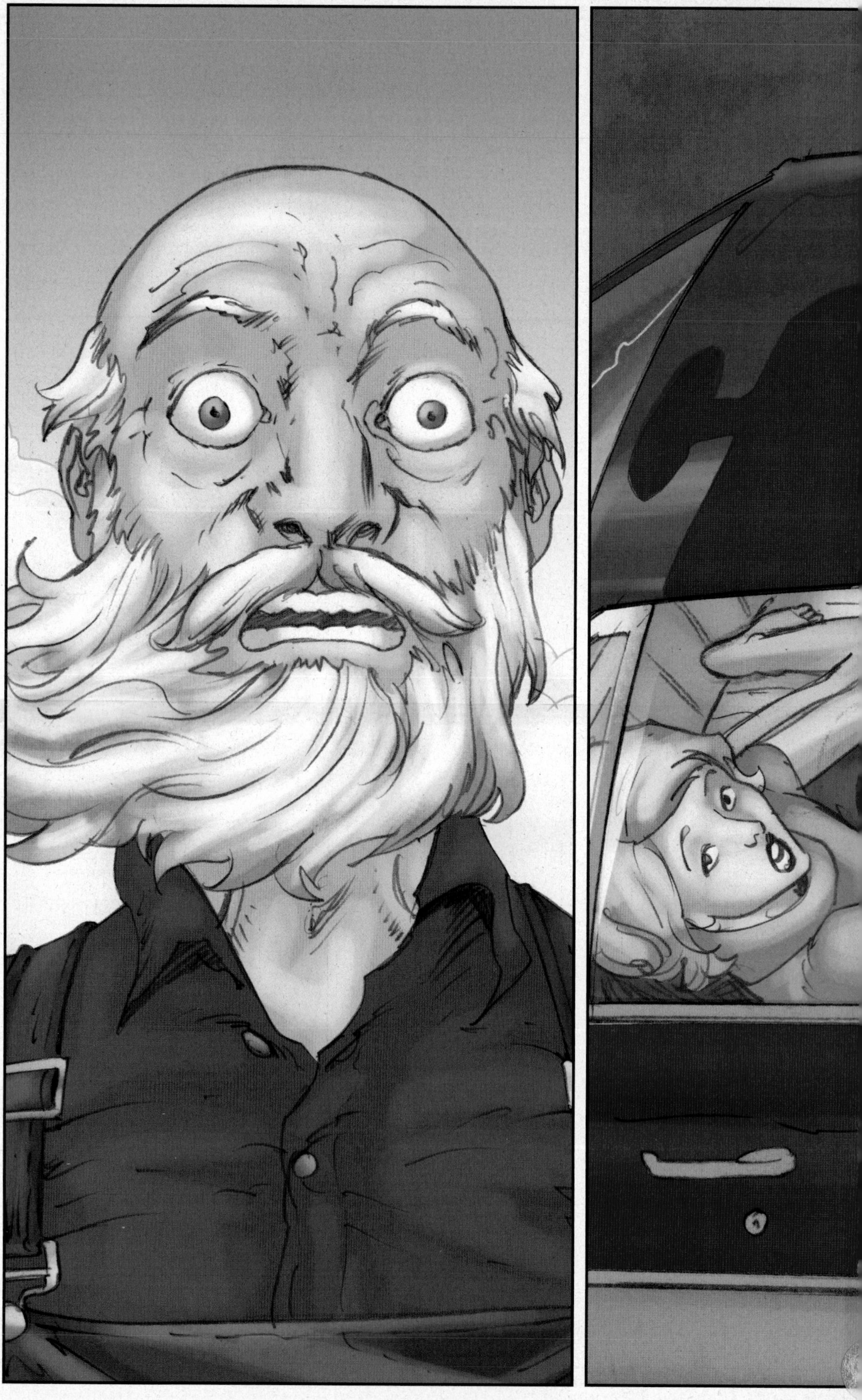

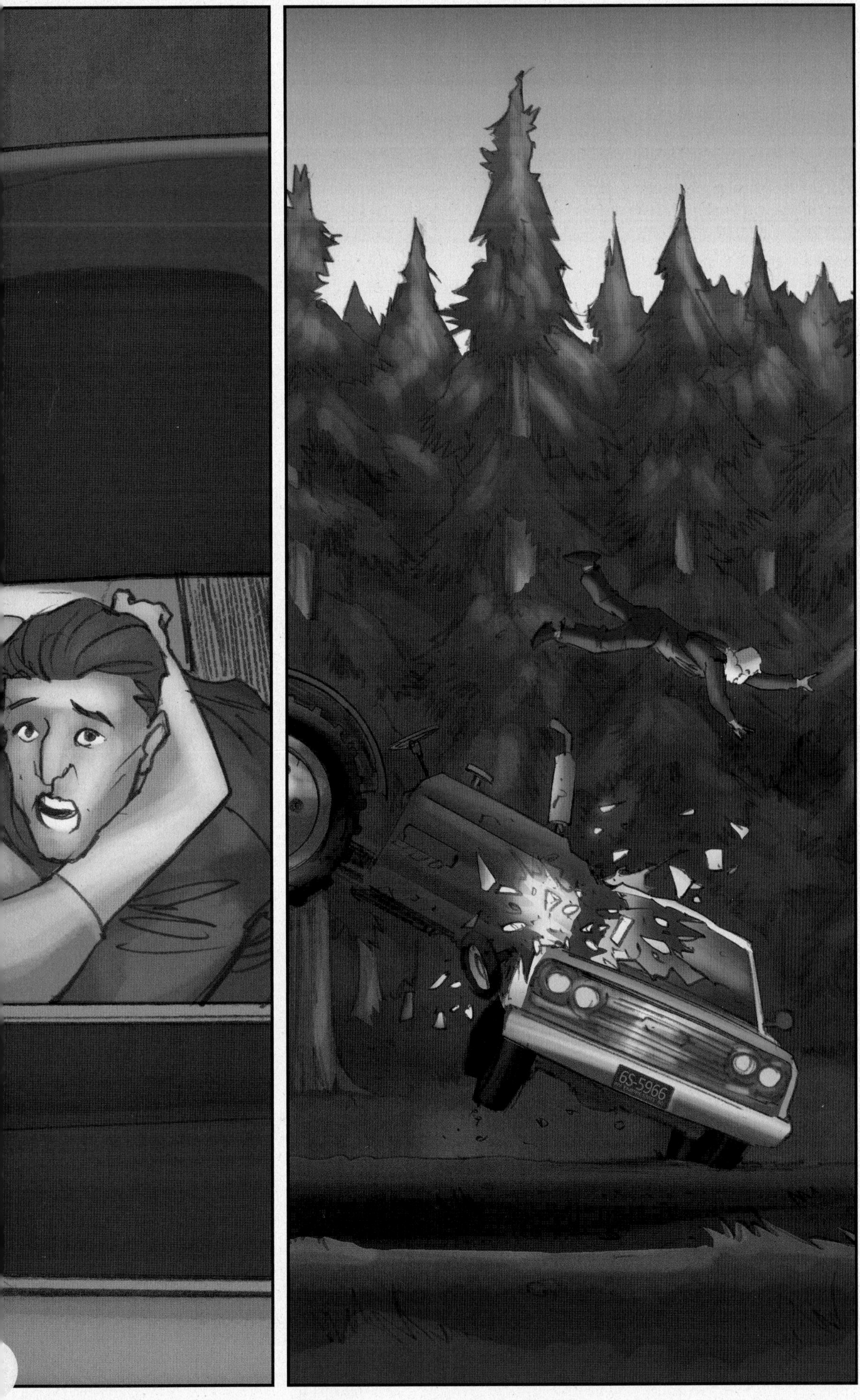

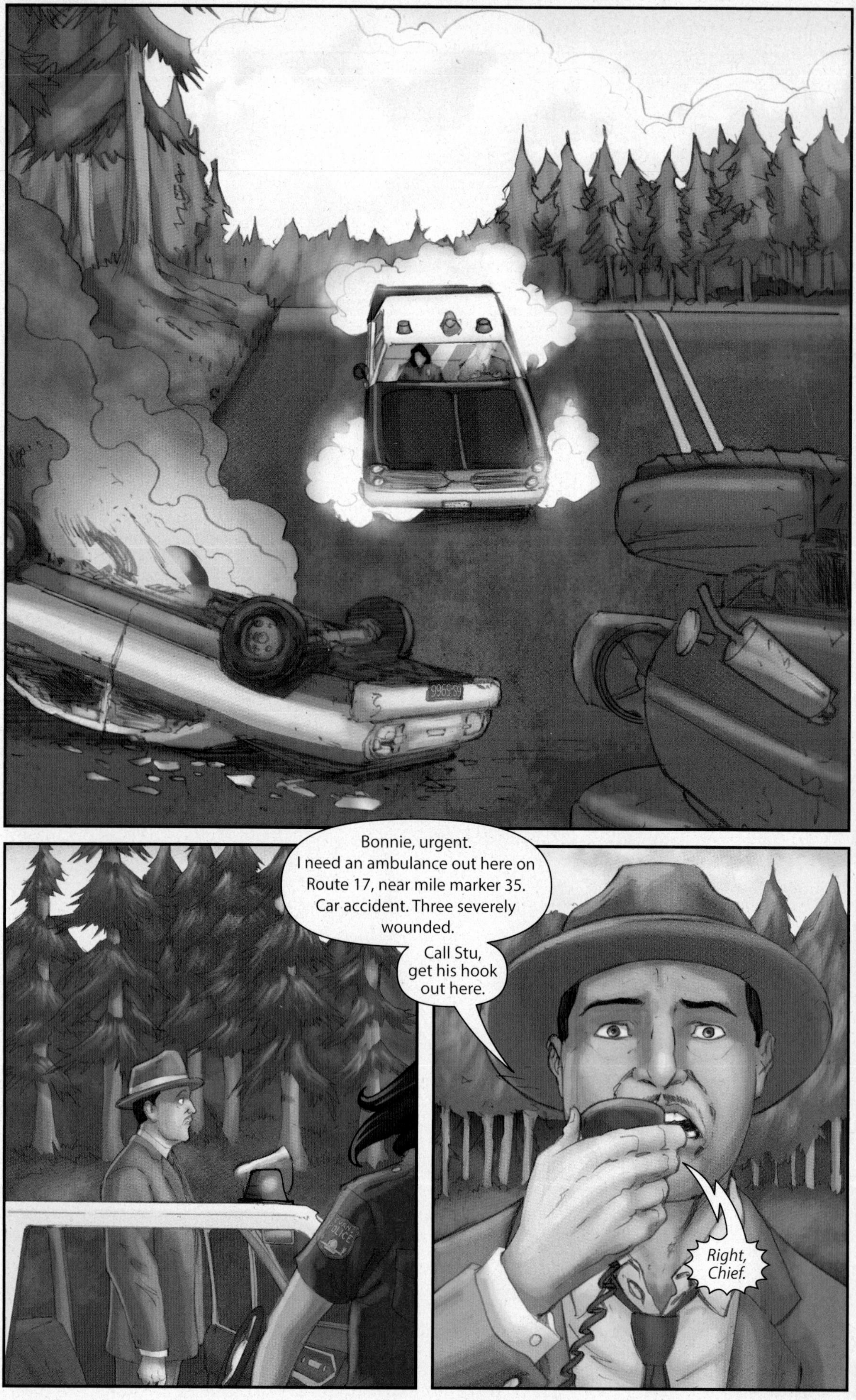
Bonnie, urgent.
I need an ambulance out here on Route 17, near mile marker 35. Car accident. Three severely wounded.
Call Stu, get his hook out here.
Right, Chief.

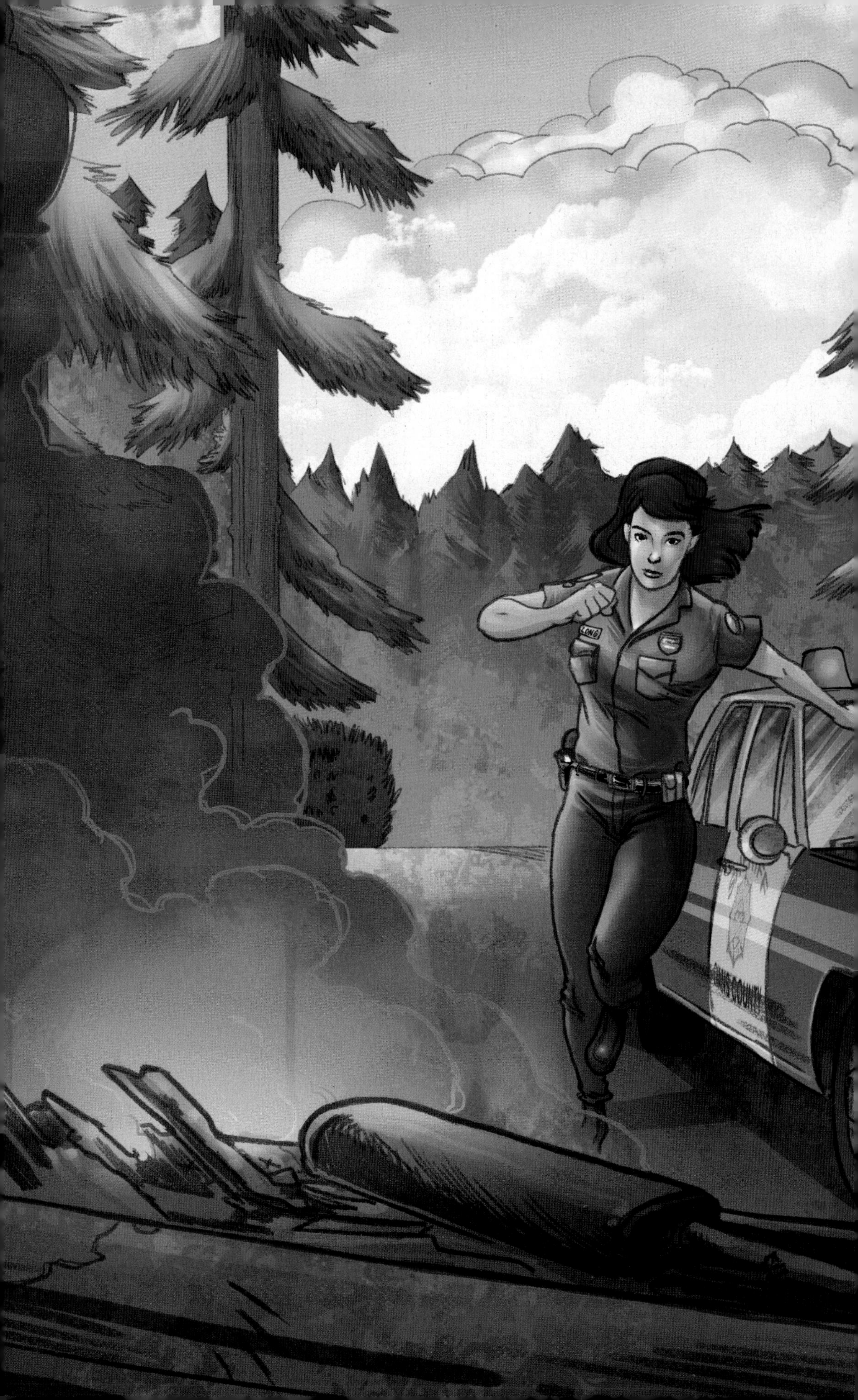
LONG

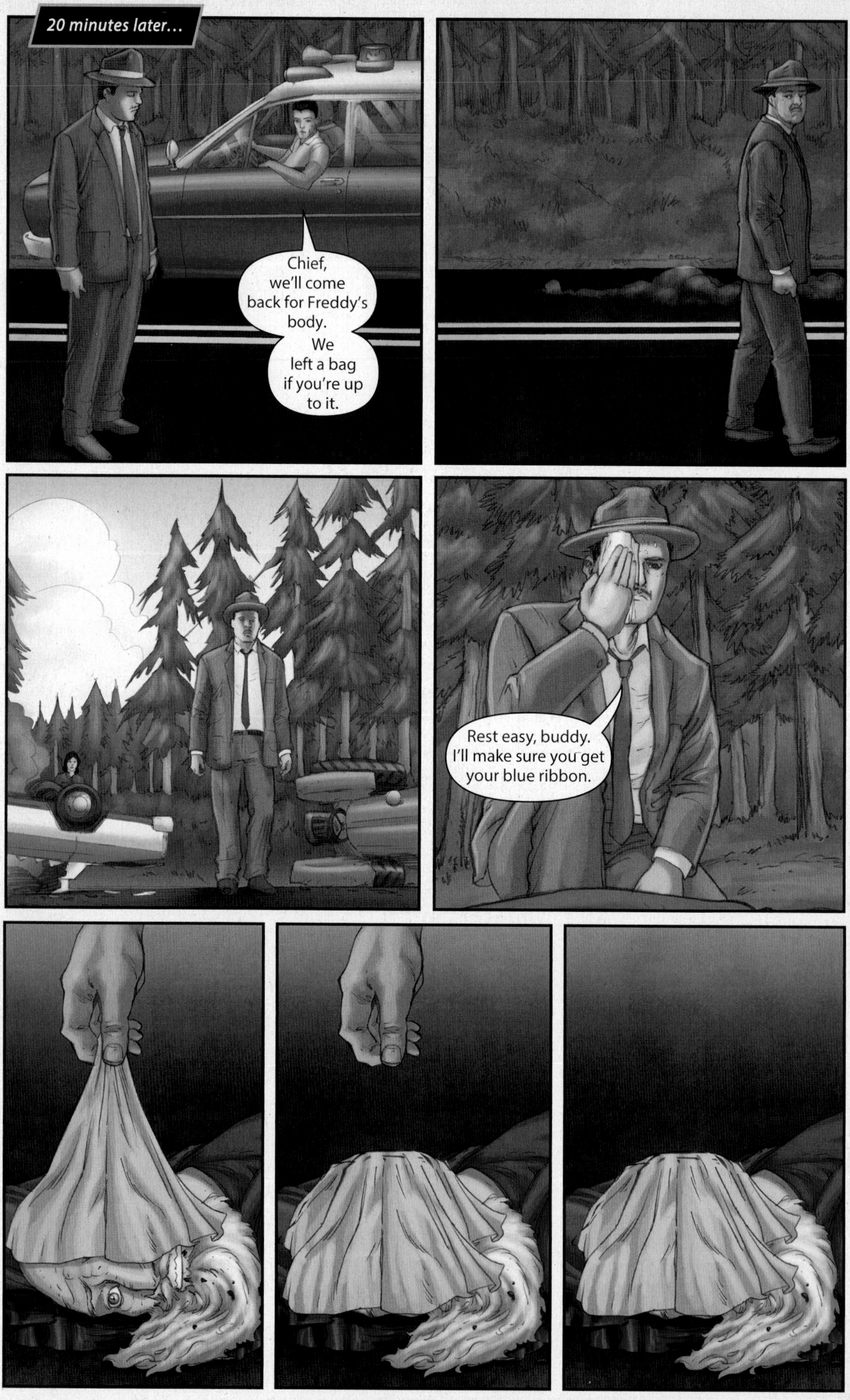
20 minutes later…
Chief, we'll come back for Freddy's body.
We left a bag if you're up to it.
Rest easy, buddy. I'll make sure you get your blue ribbon.

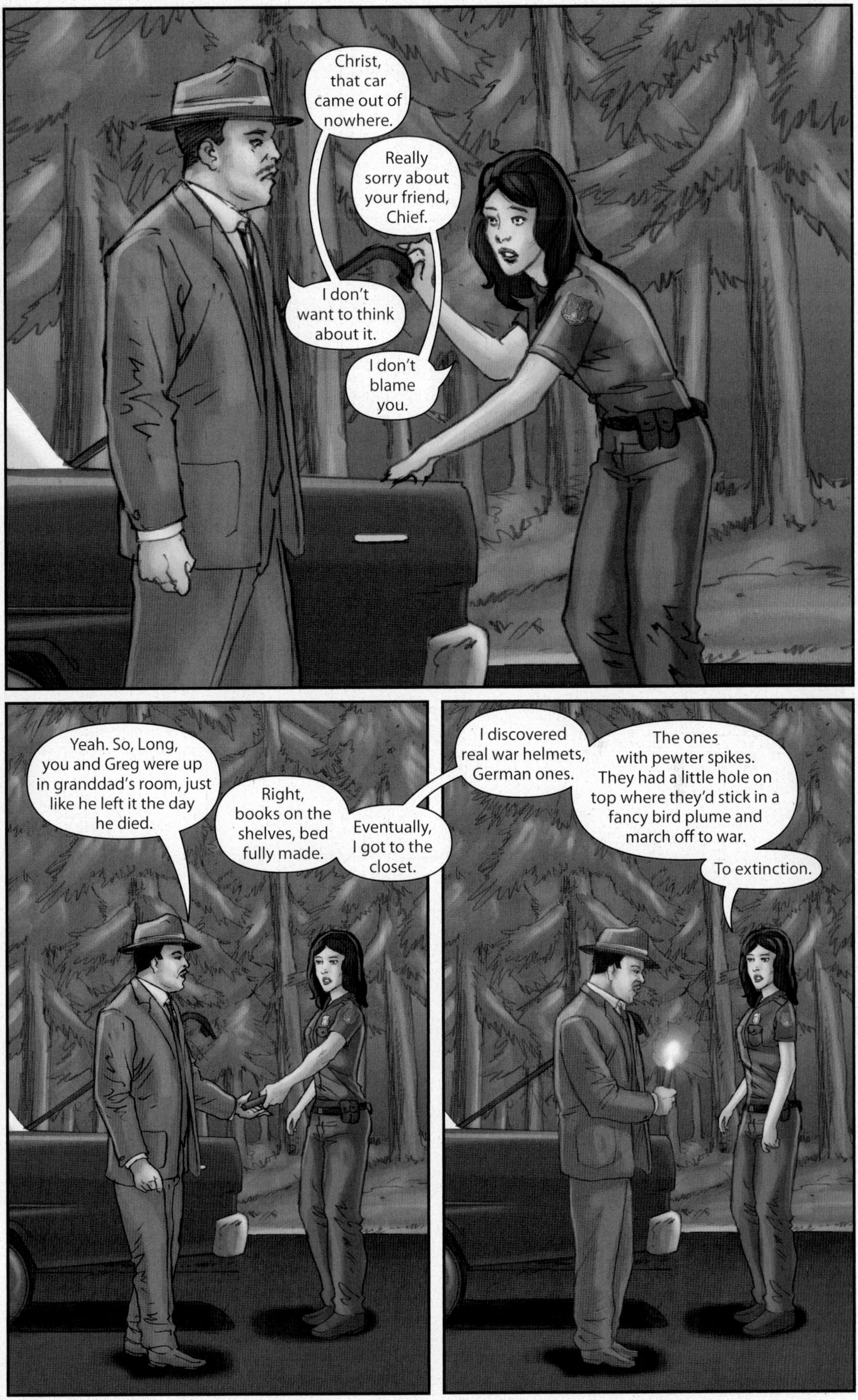
Christ, that car came out of nowhere.
Really sorry about your friend, Chief.
I don't want to think about it.
I don't blame you.
Yeah. So, Long, you and Greg were up in granddad's room, just like he left it the day he died.
Right, books on the shelves, bed fully made.
Eventually, I got to the closet.
I discovered real war helmets, German ones.
The ones with pewter spikes. They had a little hole on top where they'd stick in a fancy bird plume and march off to war.
To extinction.

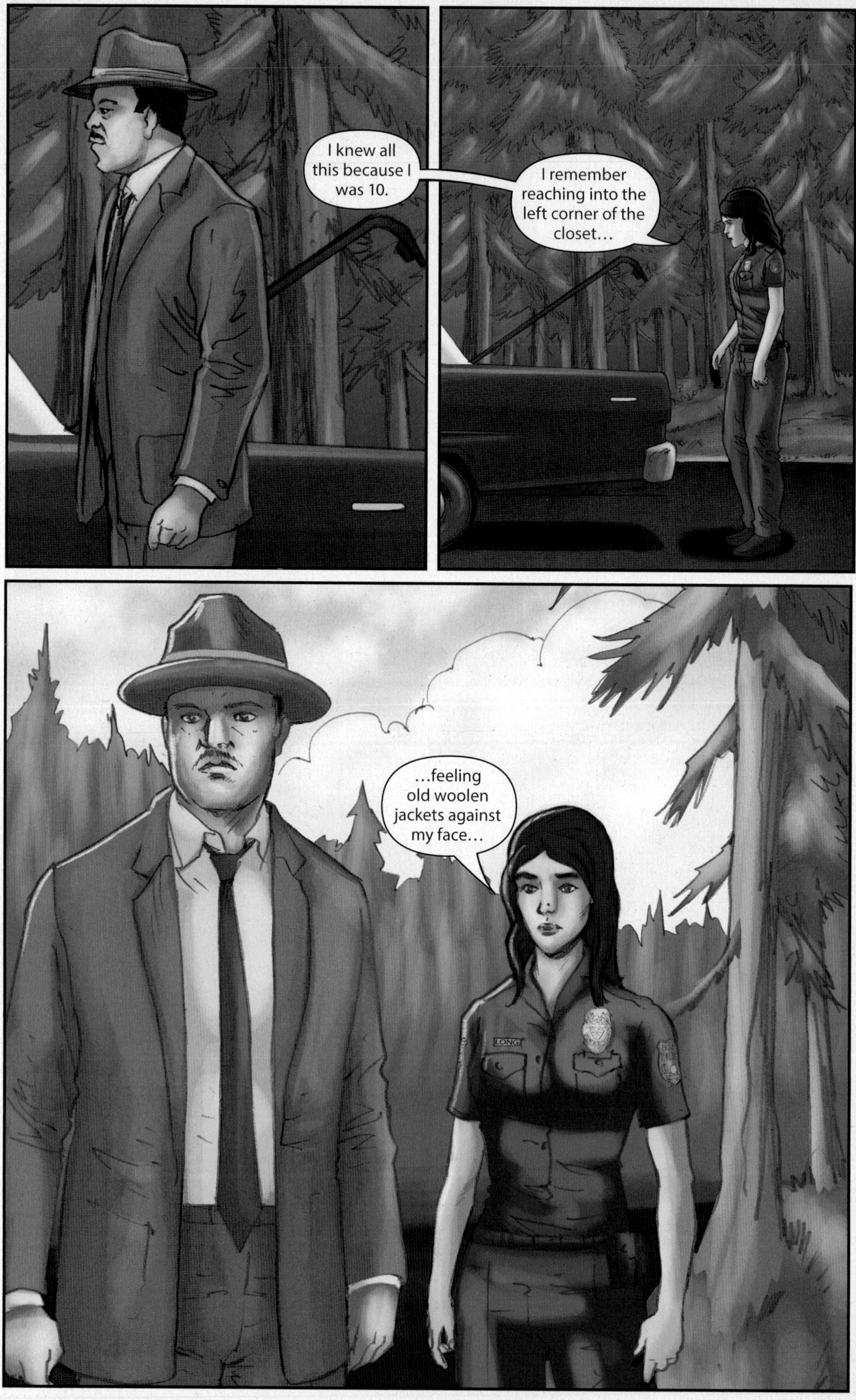
I knew all this because I was 10.
I remember reaching into the left corner of the closet…
…feeling old woolen jackets against my face…
LONG

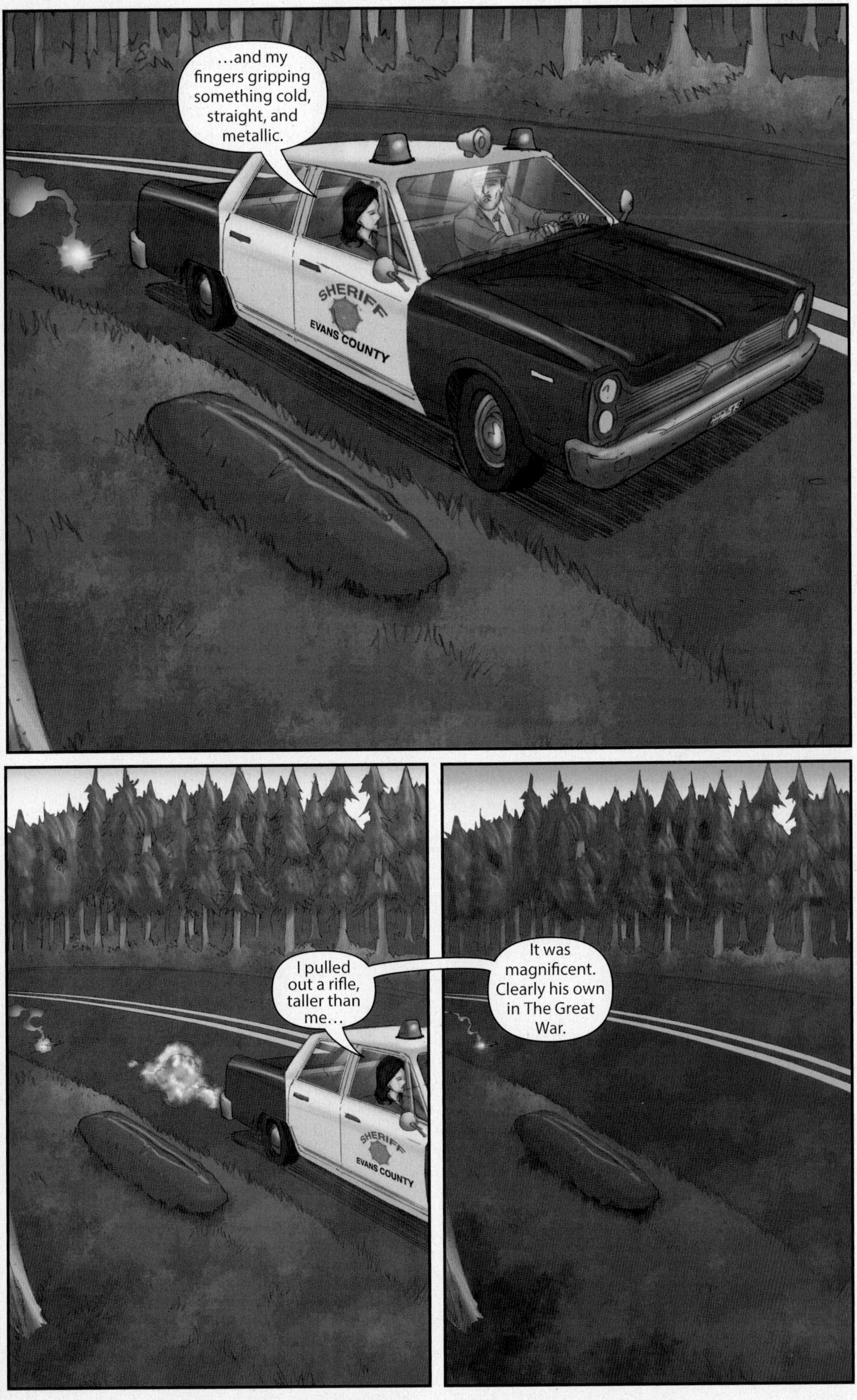
…and my fingers gripping something cold, straight, and metallic.
SHERIFF
EVANS COUNTY
I pulled out a rifle, taller than me…
SHERIFF
EVANS COUNTY
It was magnificent. Clearly his own in The Great War.

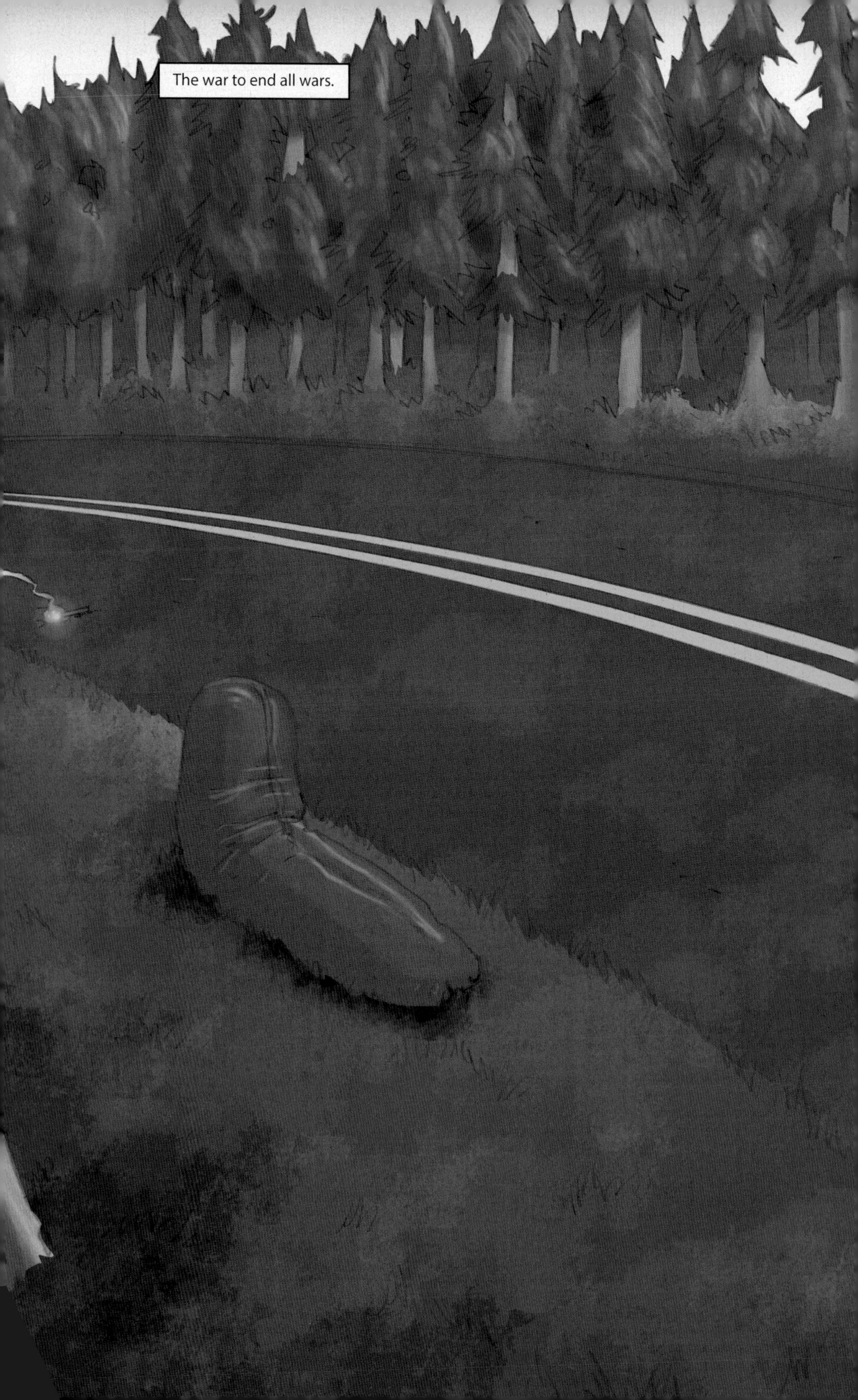
The war to end all wars.

2

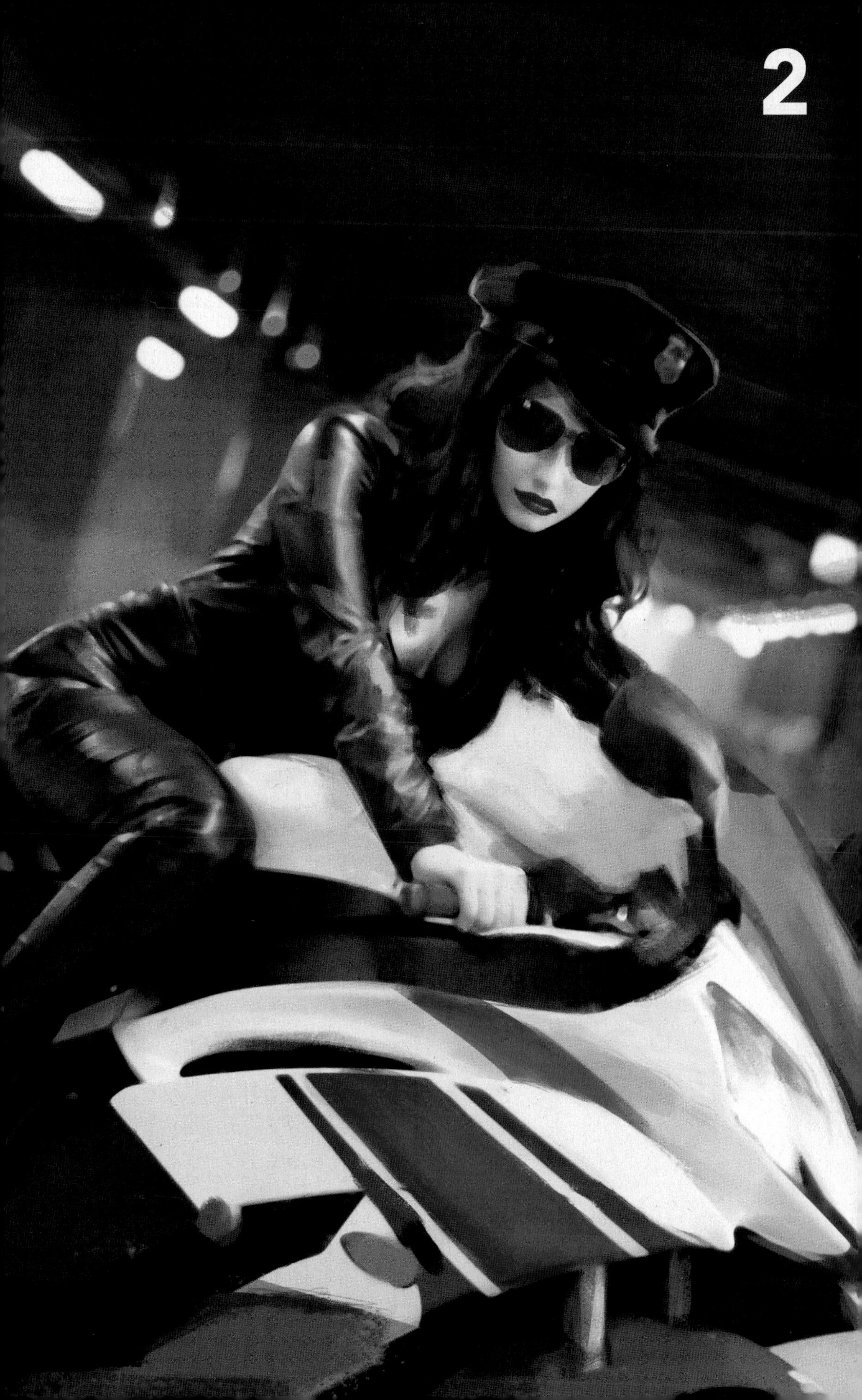

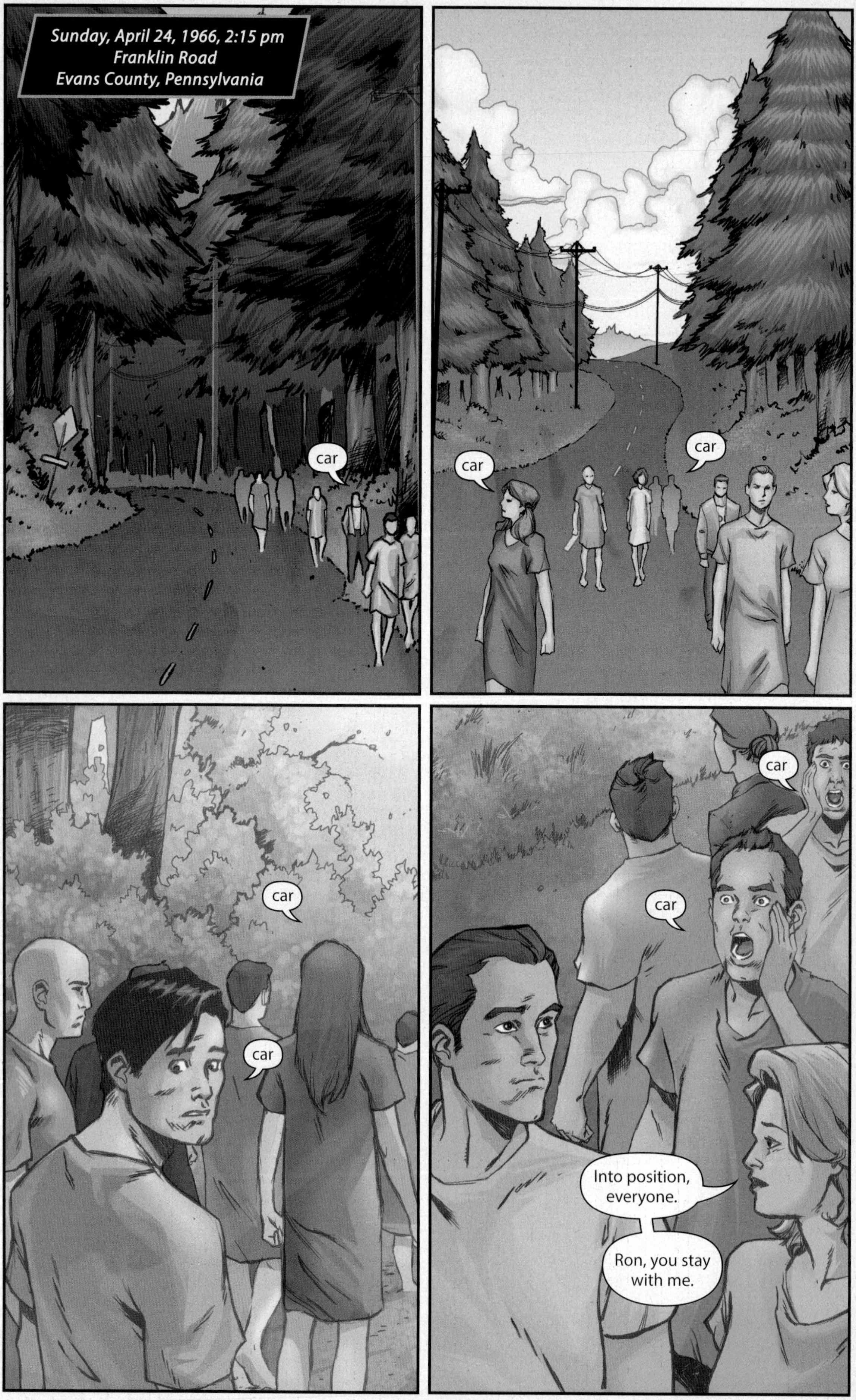
Sunday, April 24, 1966, 2:15 pm
Franklin Road
Evans County, Pennsylvania
car
car
car
car
car
car
car
Into position, everyone.
Ron, you stay with me.

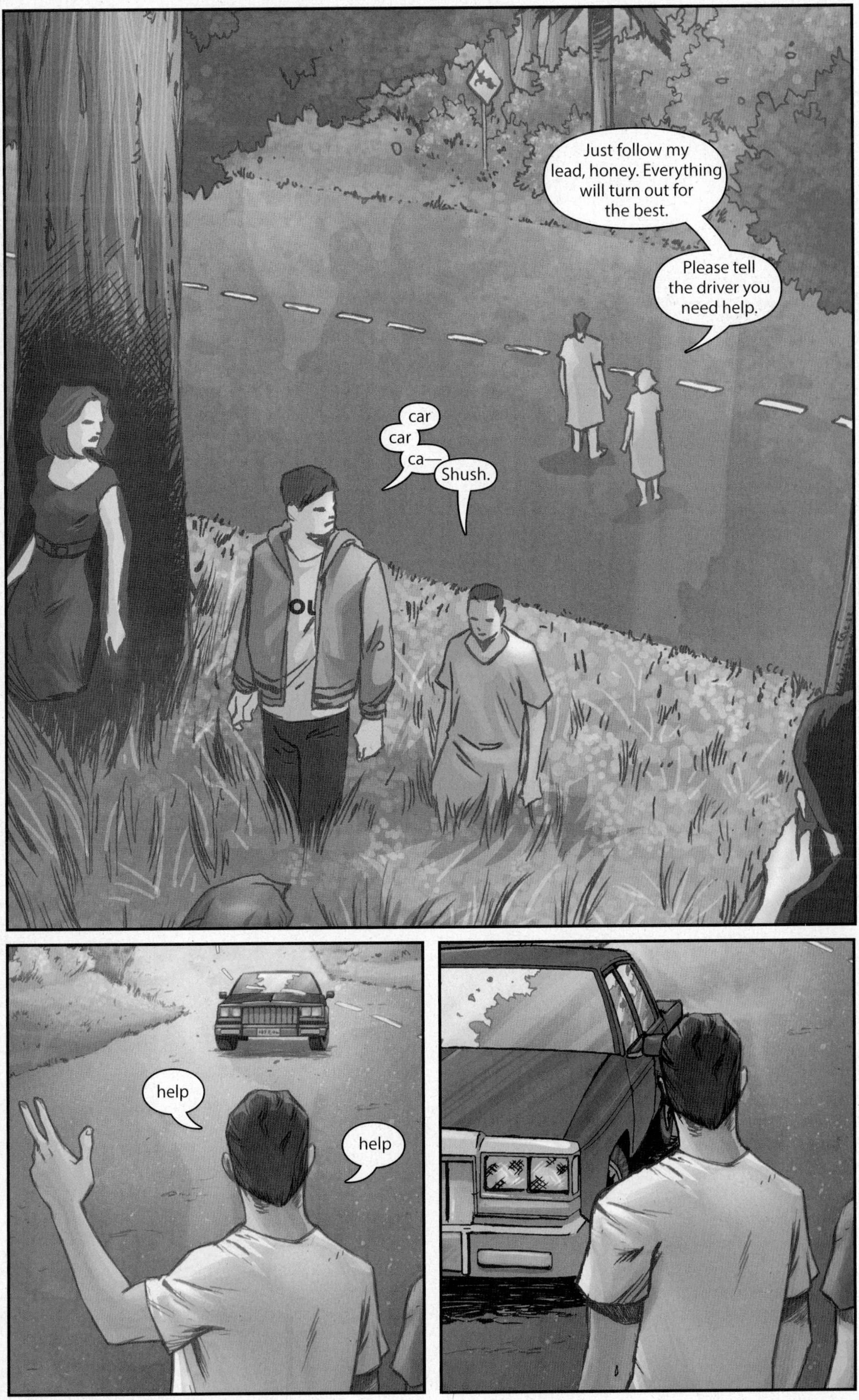
Just follow my lead, honey. Everything will turn out for the best.
Please tell the driver you need help.
car
car
ca—
Shush.
help
help

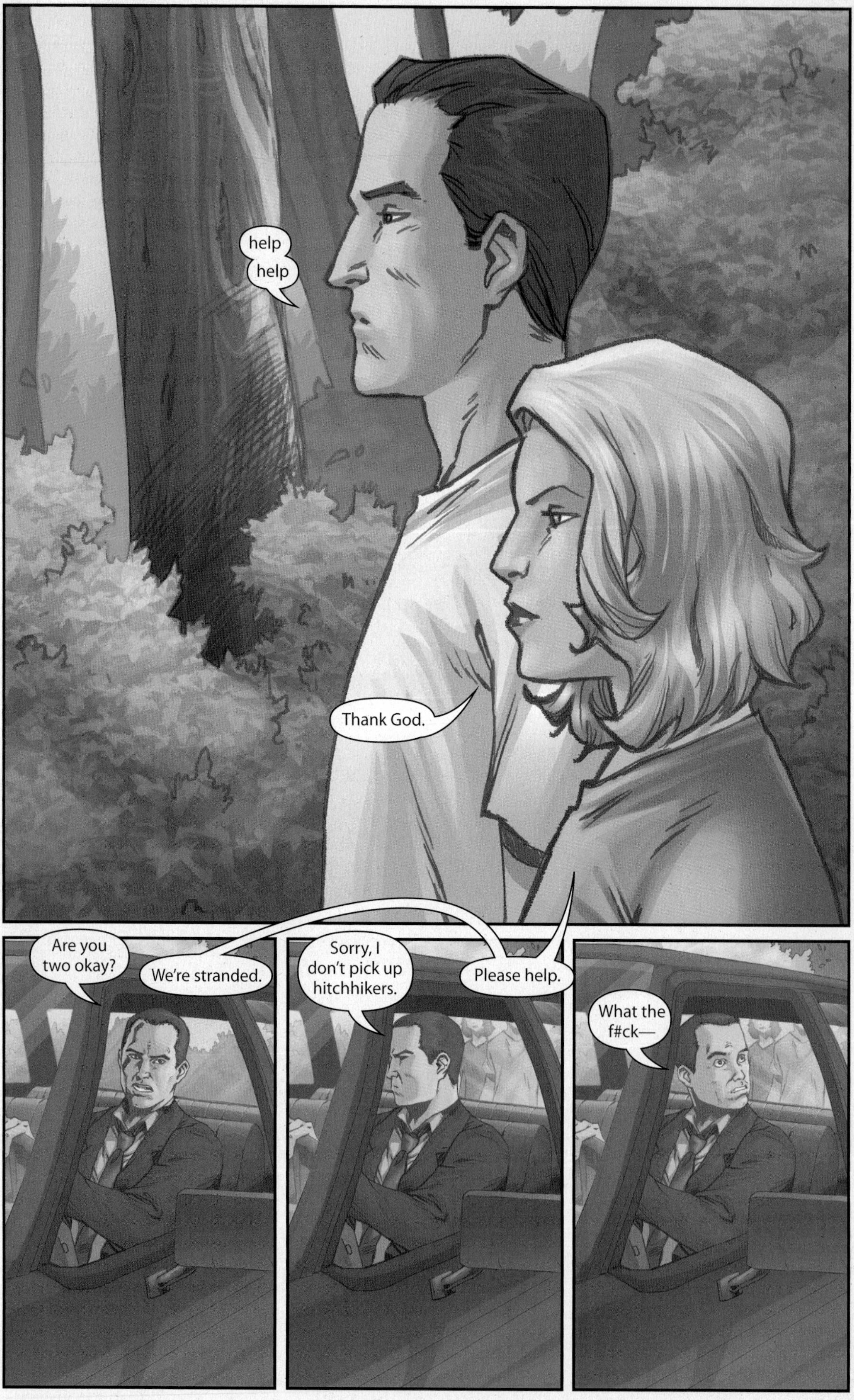
help
help
Thank God.
Are you two okay?
We're stranded.
Sorry, I don't pick up hitchhikers.
Please help.
What the f#ck—

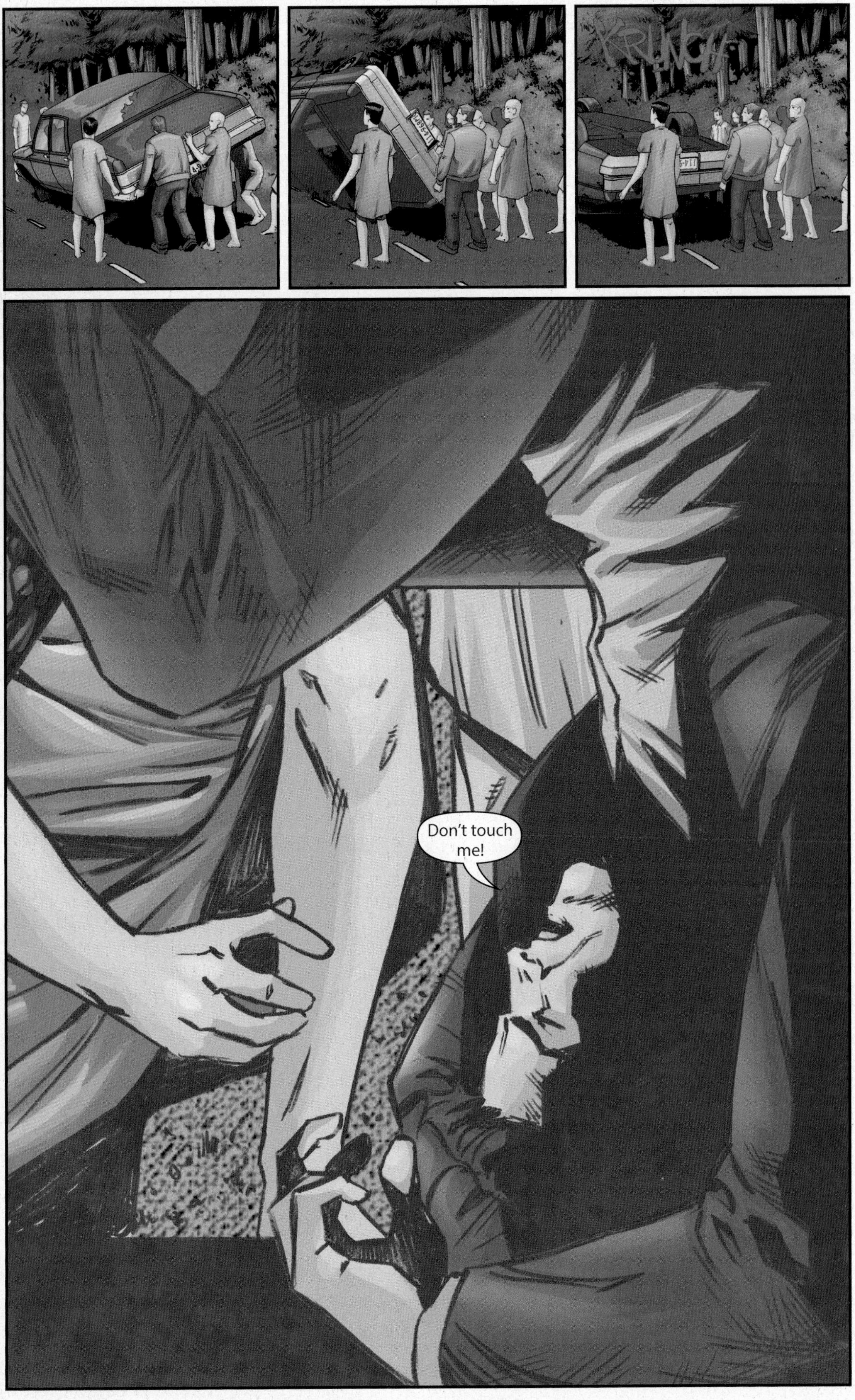
KRUNCH
Don't touch me!

THEN NOW

USA

Health & Nutrition	1960s	2010s	Increase
Average female adult	140.2lbs	166.3lbs	18.6%
Average male adult	166.3lbs	195.5lbs	17.6%
Adult obesity	10.7%	35.9%	235.5%
Childhood obesity	9.0%	39.9%	333.3%
US population with diabetes	2,770,000	29,100,000	950.5%
Estimated daily caloric intake	2,200	3,300	50.0%
Pounds per person per year			
All sugars	114.0	152.0	33.3%
Corn sweeteners	15.0	85.0	467.0%
High fructose corn syrup	0.2	43.7	2175.0%
Meat	161.7	252.7	56.3%
Cheese	9.5	33.2	249.0%
Added fats	47.8	83.9	75.5%
Grains	142.5	175.2	23.0%
Soft drinks	18.3	46.5	154.0%

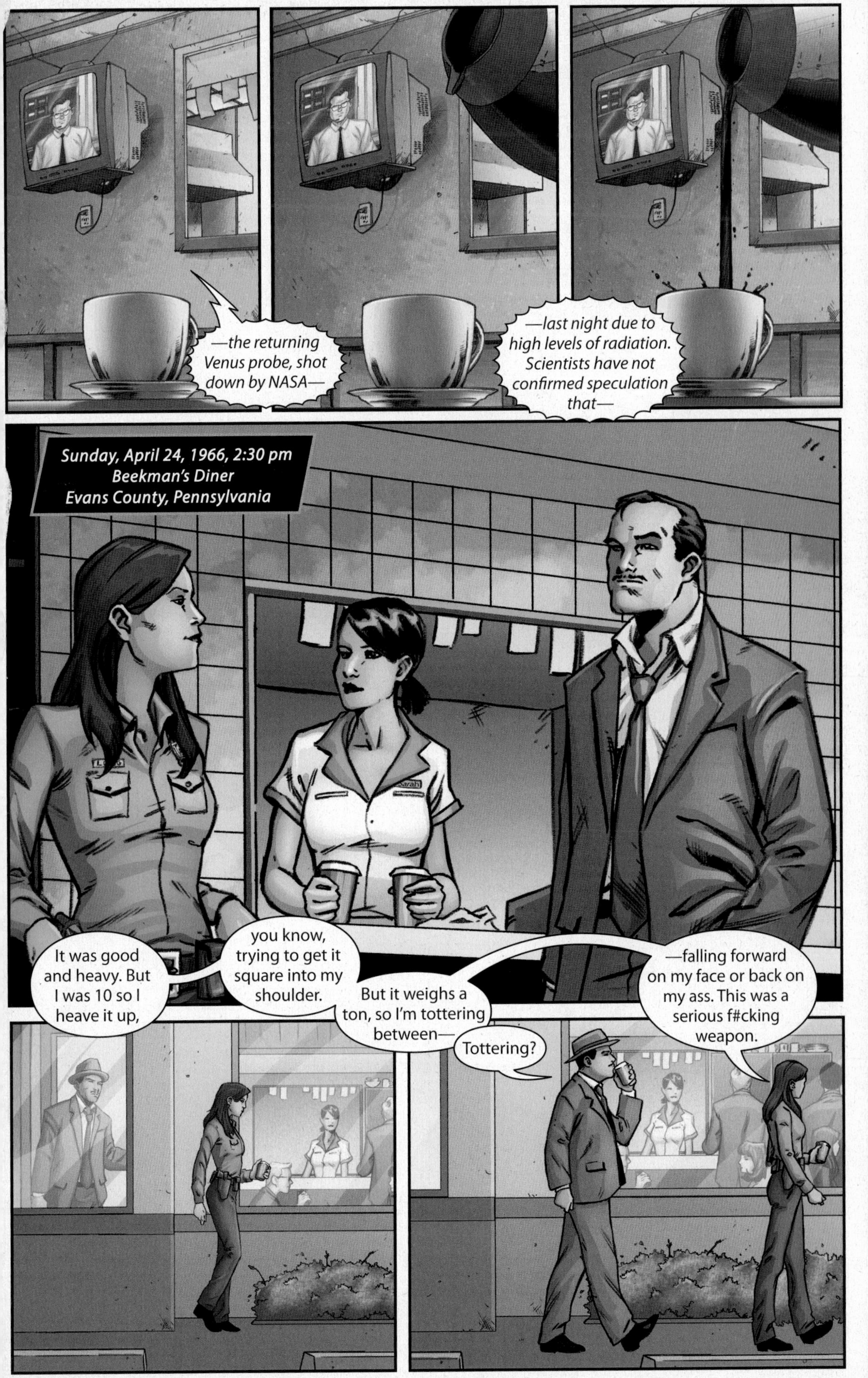
—the returning Venus probe, shot down by NASA—
—last night due to high levels of radiation. Scientists have not confirmed speculation that—
Sunday, April 24, 1966, 2:30 pm
Beekman's Diner
Evans County, Pennsylvania
It was good and heavy. But I was 10 so I heave it up,
you know, trying to get it square into my shoulder.
But it weighs a ton, so I'm tottering between—
Tottering?
—falling forward on my face or back on my ass. This was a serious f#cking weapon.

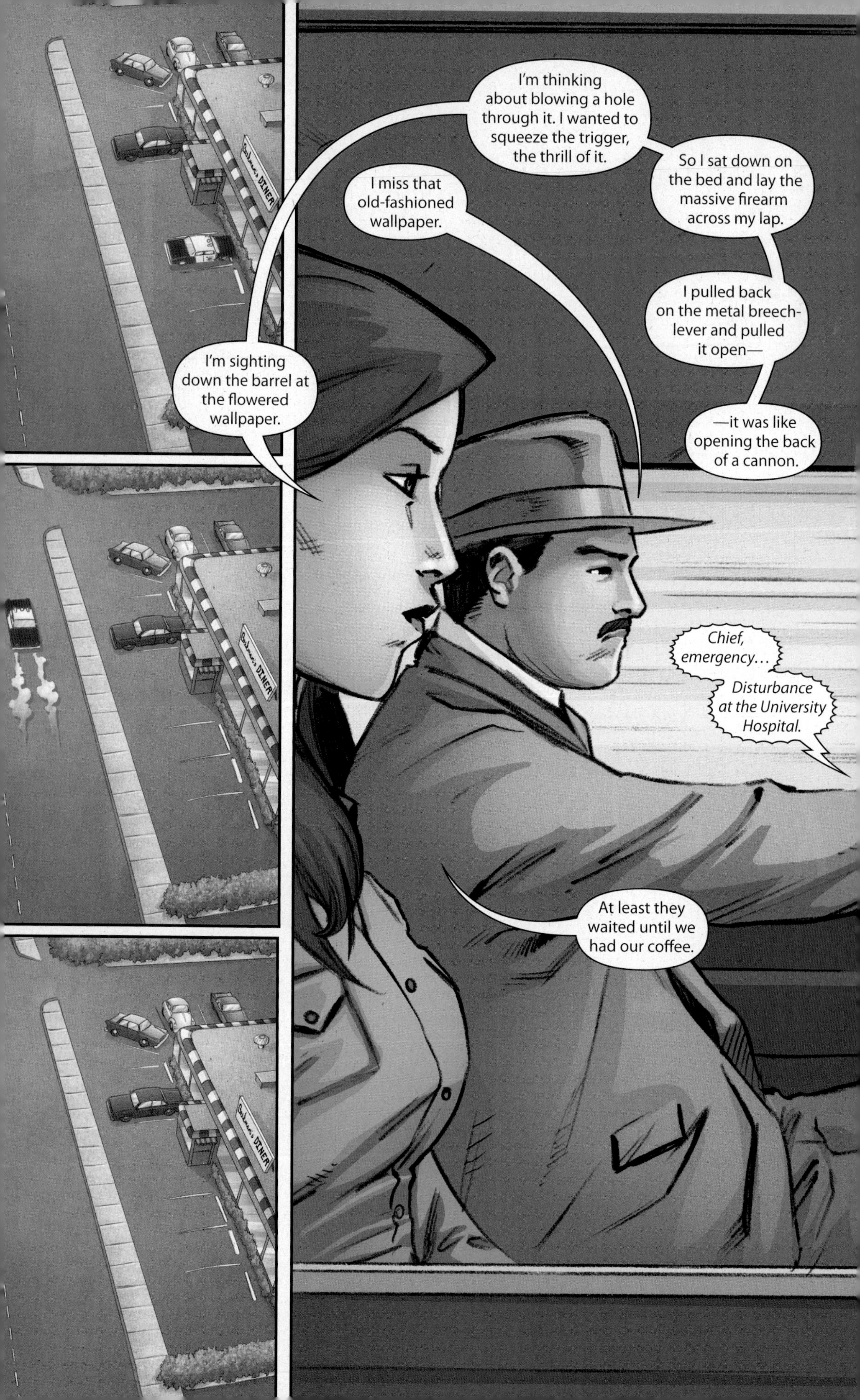

I'm sighting down the barrel at the flowered wallpaper.
I'm thinking about blowing a hole through it. I wanted to squeeze the trigger, the thrill of it.
I miss that old-fashioned wallpaper.
So I sat down on the bed and lay the massive firearm across my lap.
I pulled back on the metal breech-lever and pulled it open—
—it was like opening the back of a cannon.
Chief, emergency…
Disturbance at the University Hospital.
At least they waited until we had our coffee.
Bushman's DINER

ULTIMATE Cocktail Party

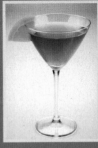

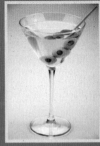

Sidecar
¾ ounce triple sec
¾ ounce lemon juice
1 ½ ounces cognac

Martini
2 ½ ounces dry gin
½ ounce dry vermouth
Green olive for garnish

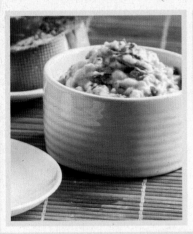

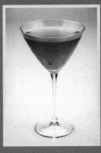

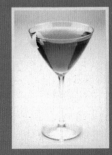

Manhattan
2 ounces bourbon whiskey
½ ounce sweet vermouth
½ ounce dry vermouth
2 dashes Angostura bitters
Maraschino cherry

Cosmo
2 ounces vodka
½ ounce triple sec
¾ ounce cranberry juice
¼ ounce fresh lime juice
1 2-inch orange peel/twist

Classic Onion Dip

Ingredients
1 ½ cups chopped onion
½ cup mayonnaise
3 tablespoons butter
1 teaspoon black pepper
¼ teaspoon salt
2 cups sour cream
1 tsp garlic powder

Directions:
- Heat butter in a saucepan. Add black pepper, salt, garlic powder, and onions. Sauté for 10 minutes.
- Mix mayonnaise, sour cream, and sautéed onions in large bowl. Serve at room temperature or chilled, if desired.

Swiss Fondue

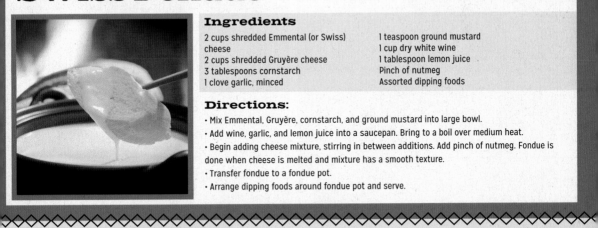

Ingredients
2 cups shredded Emmental (or Swiss) cheese
2 cups shredded Gruyère cheese
3 tablespoons cornstarch
1 clove garlic, minced
1 teaspoon ground mustard
1 cup dry white wine
1 tablespoon lemon juice
Pinch of nutmeg
Assorted dipping foods

Directions:
- Mix Emmental, Gruyère, cornstarch, and ground mustard into large bowl.
- Add wine, garlic, and lemon juice into a saucepan. Bring to a boil over medium heat.
- Begin adding cheese mixture, stirring in between additions. Add pinch of nutmeg. Fondue is done when cheese is melted and mixture has a smooth texture.
- Transfer fondue to a fondue pot.
- Arrange dipping foods around fondue pot and serve.

Deviled Eggs

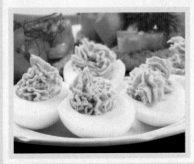

Ingredients
6 eggs
2 tablespoons mayonnaise
1 teaspoon of yellow mustard
Salt and black pepper to taste
Paprika

Directions:
- Hard boil eggs and slice into halves.
- Separate yolks from egg whites and place yolks in a bowl.
- Mash yolks using a fork. Add mayonnaise, mustard, salt, and pepper and stir.
- Spoon mixture into egg whites using a teaspoon. Sprinkle paprika to garnish.
- Chill eggs for 1 hour and serve.

Fondue image by naito8/Shutterstock | Onion dip image by Adriana Nikolova/Shutterstock | Deviled eggs image by Igot Dutina/Shutterstock

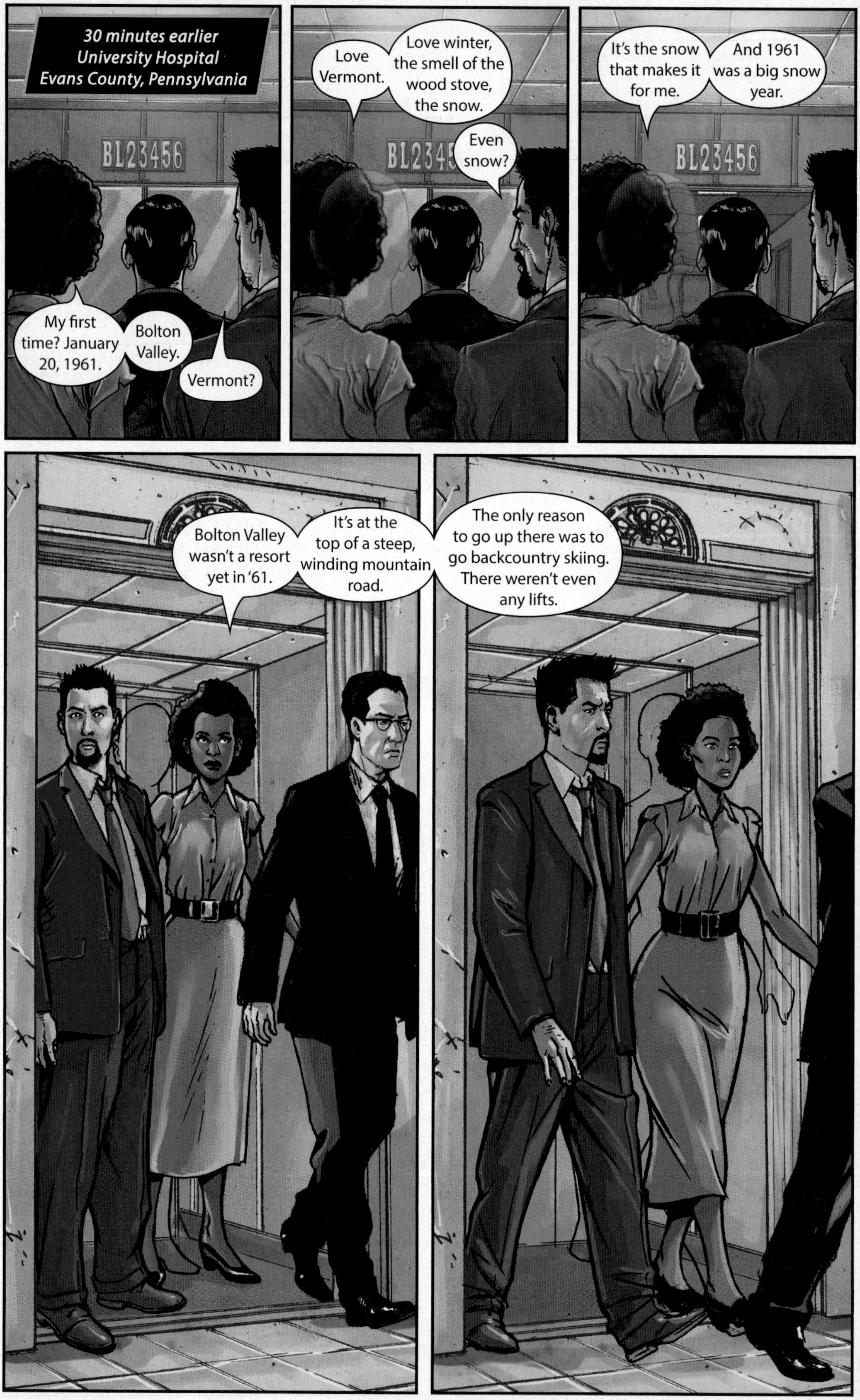
30 minutes earlier
University Hospital
Evans County, Pennsylvania
BL23456
My first time? January 20, 1961.
Bolton Valley.
Vermont?
Love Vermont.
Love winter, the smell of the wood stove, the snow.
Even snow?
It's the snow that makes it for me.
And 1961 was a big snow year.
Bolton Valley wasn't a resort yet in '61.
It's at the top of a steep, winding mountain road.
The only reason to go up there was to go backcountry skiing. There weren't even any lifts.

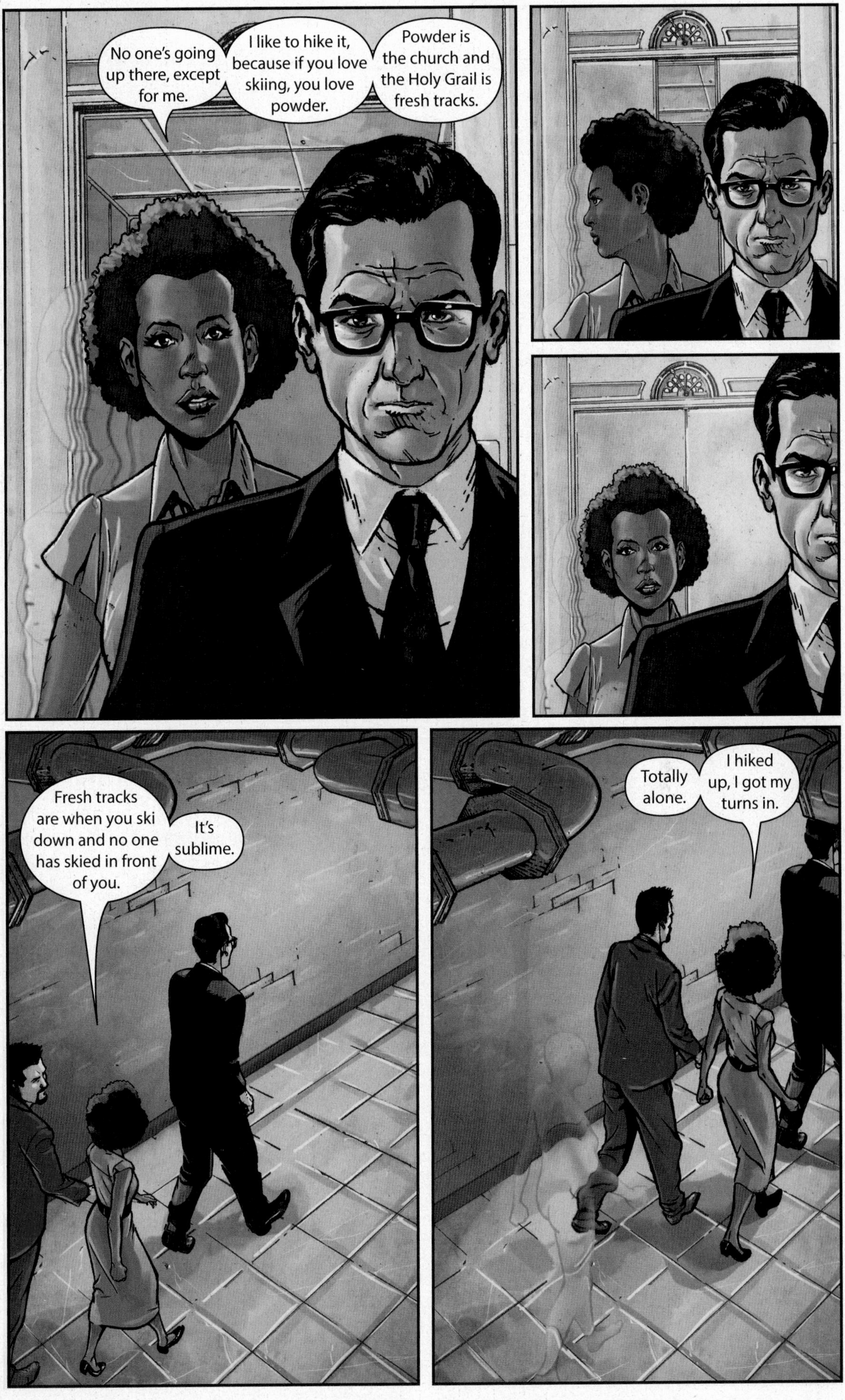
No one's going up there, except for me.
I like to hike it, because if you love skiing, you love powder.
Powder is the church and the Holy Grail is fresh tracks.
Fresh tracks are when you ski down and no one has skied in front of you.
It's sublime.
Totally alone.
I hiked up, I got my turns in.

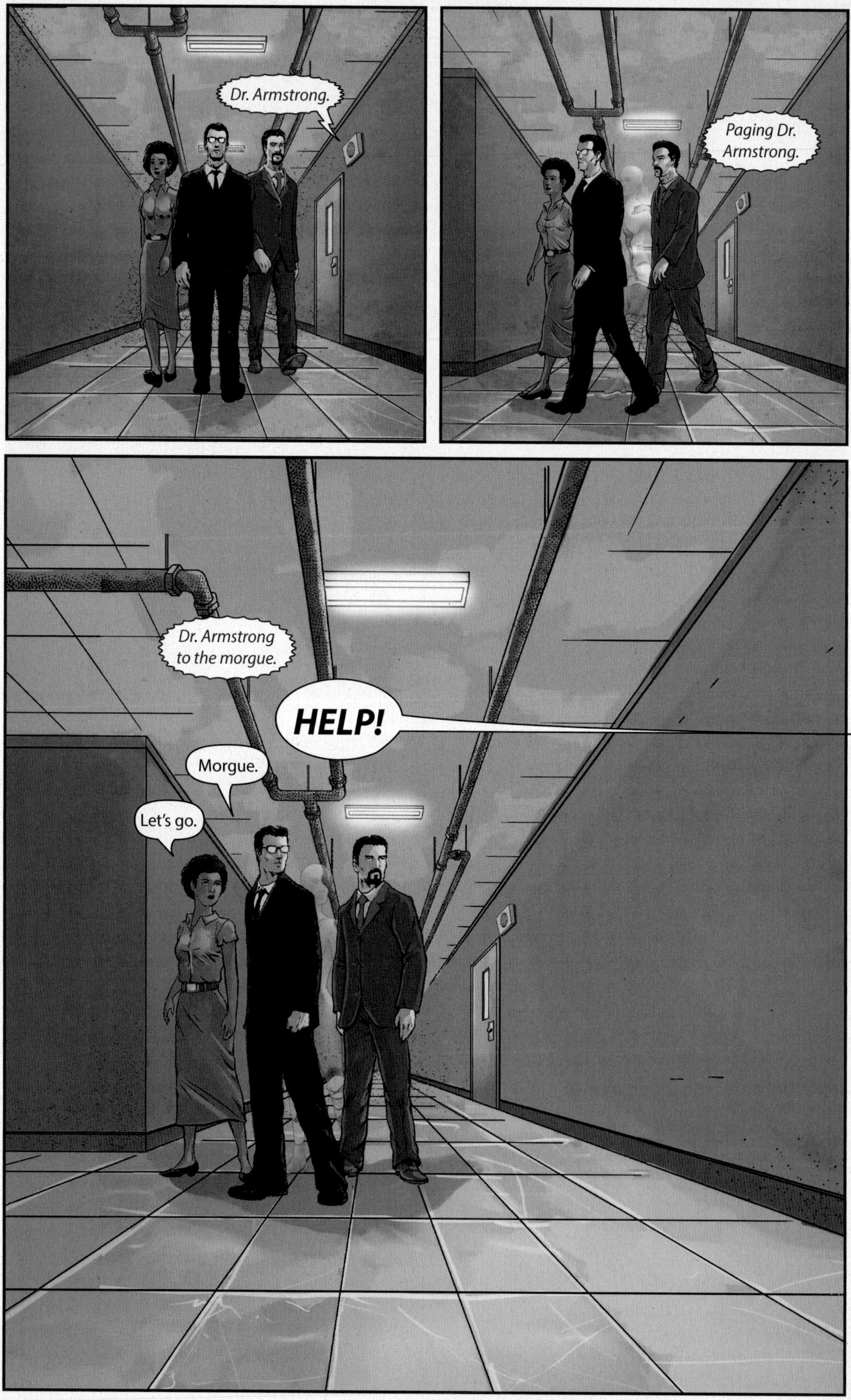

Dr. Armstrong.
Paging Dr. Armstrong.
Dr. Armstrong to the morgue.
HELP!
Morgue.
Let's go.

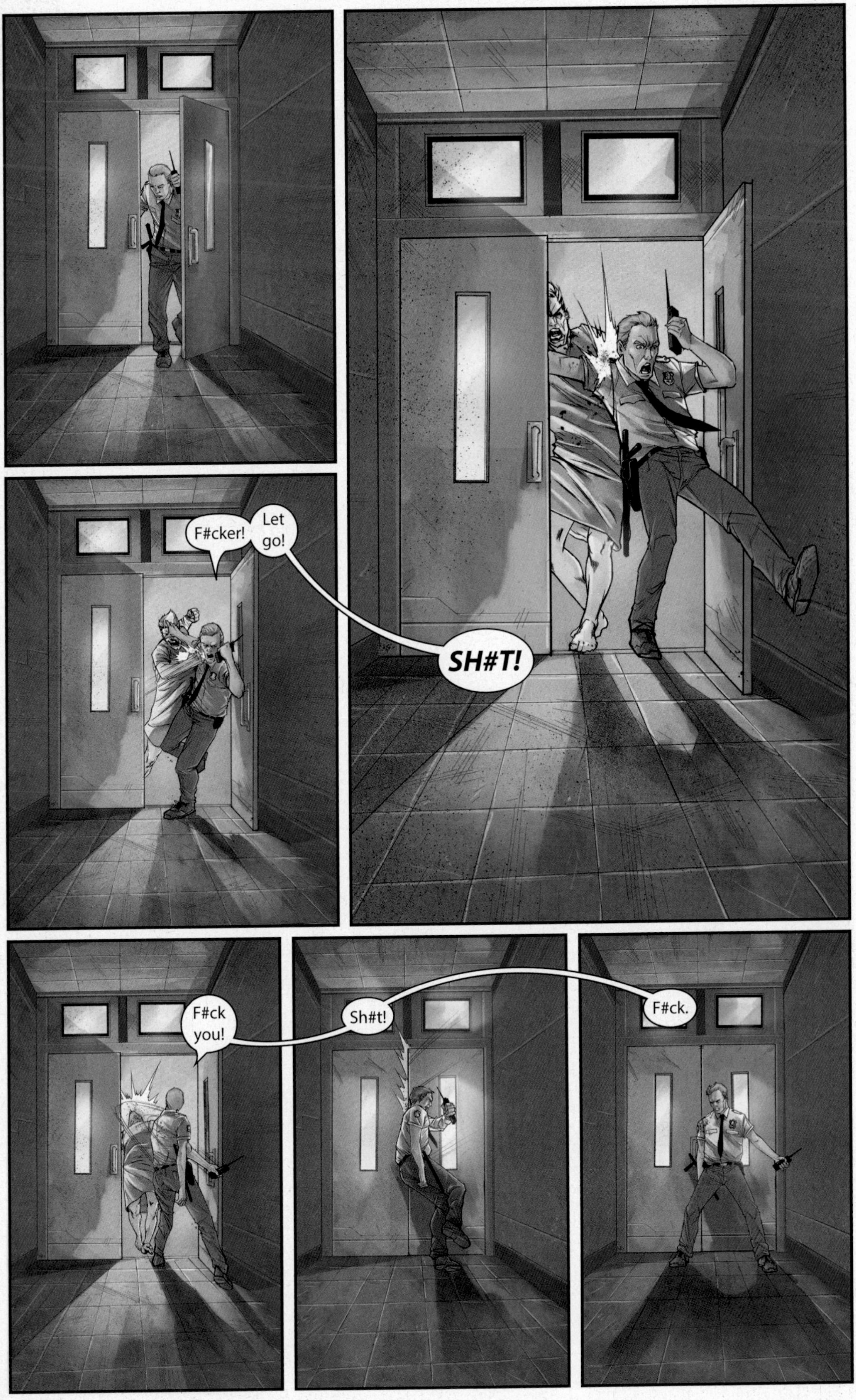
F#cker!
Let go!
SH#T!
F#ck you!
Sh#t!
F#ck.

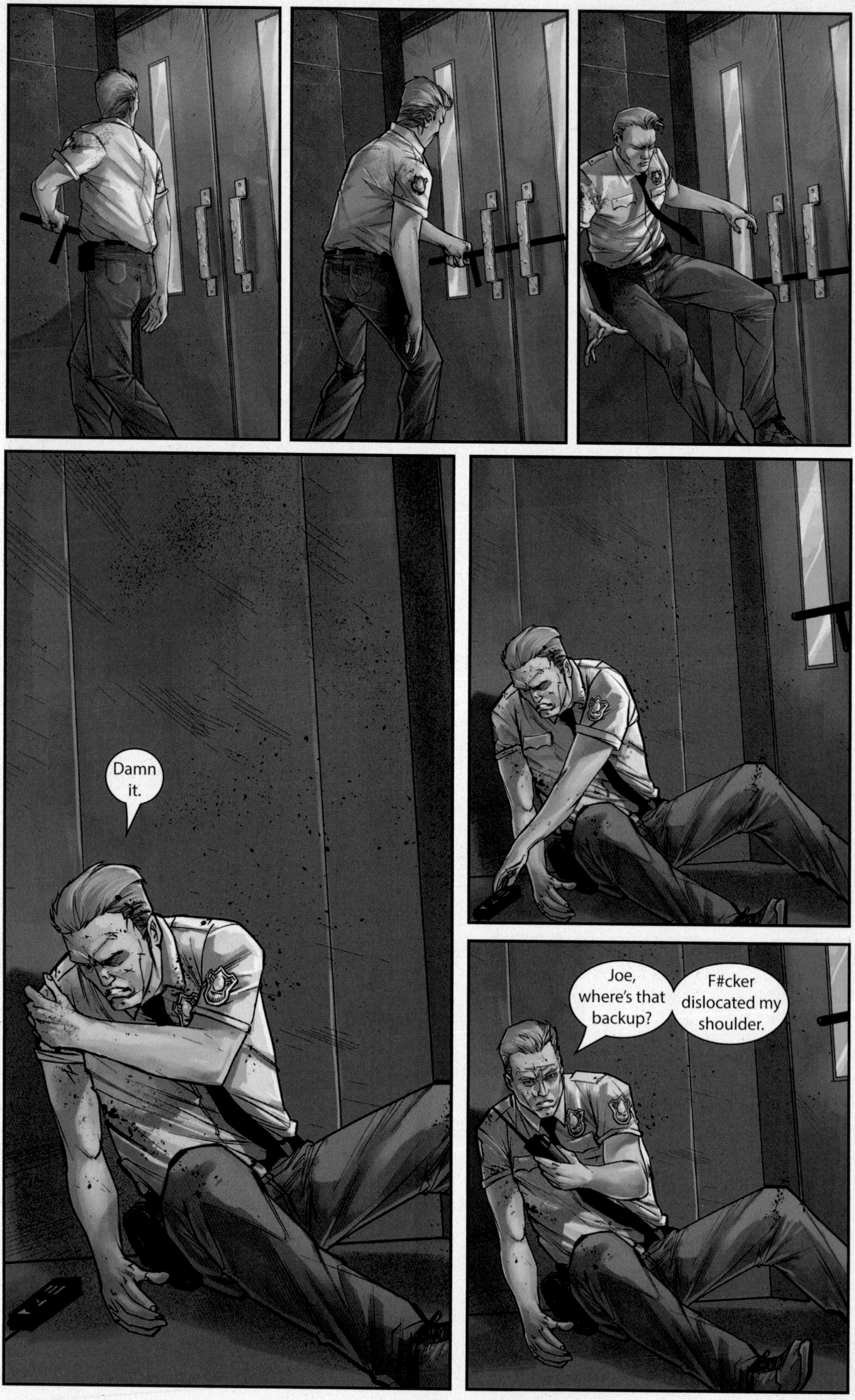
Damn it.
Joe, where's that backup?
F#cker dislocated my shoulder.

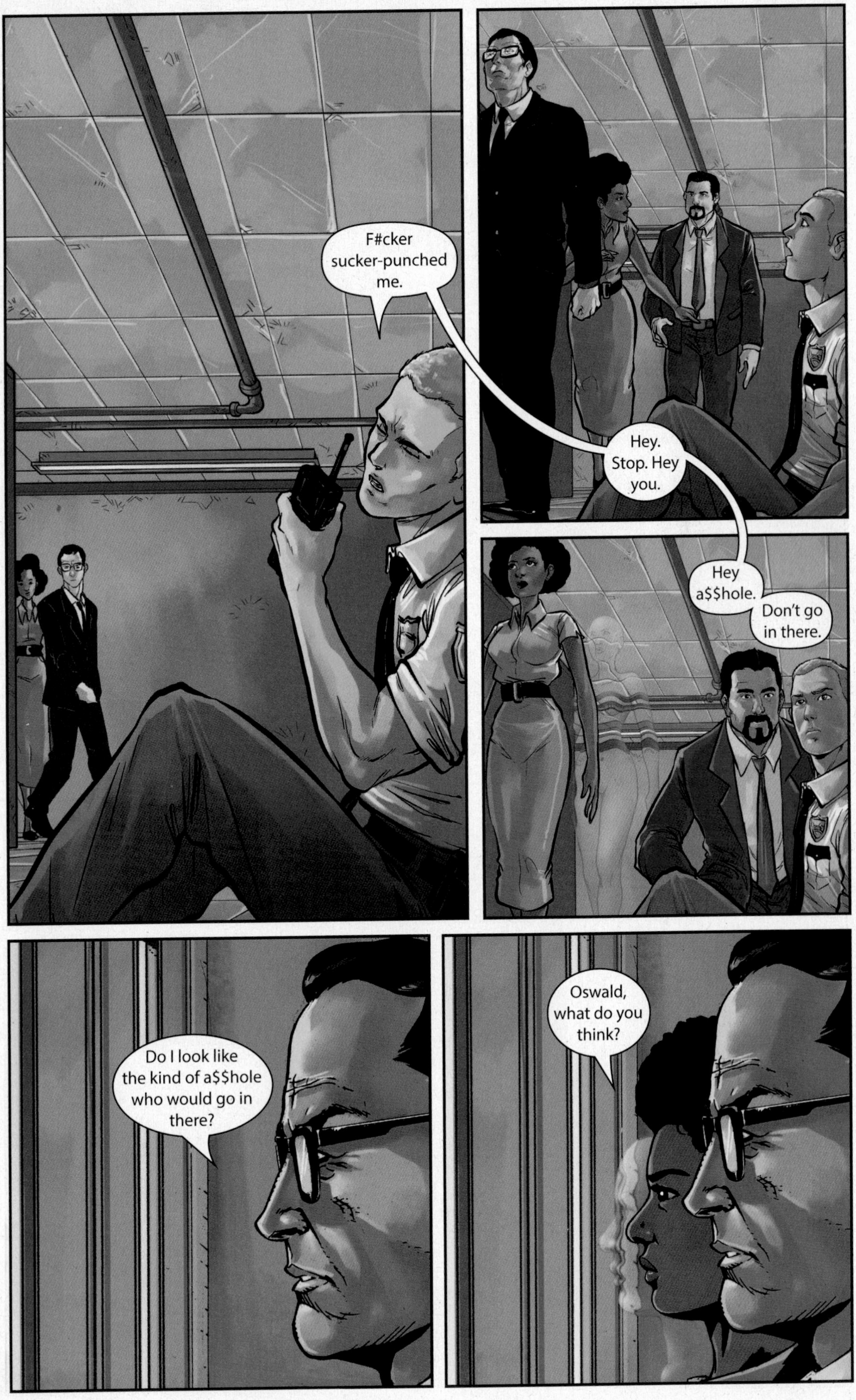
F#cker sucker-punched me.
Hey. Stop. Hey you.
Hey a$$hole.
Don't go in there.
Do I look like the kind of a$$hole who would go in there?
Oswald, what do you think?

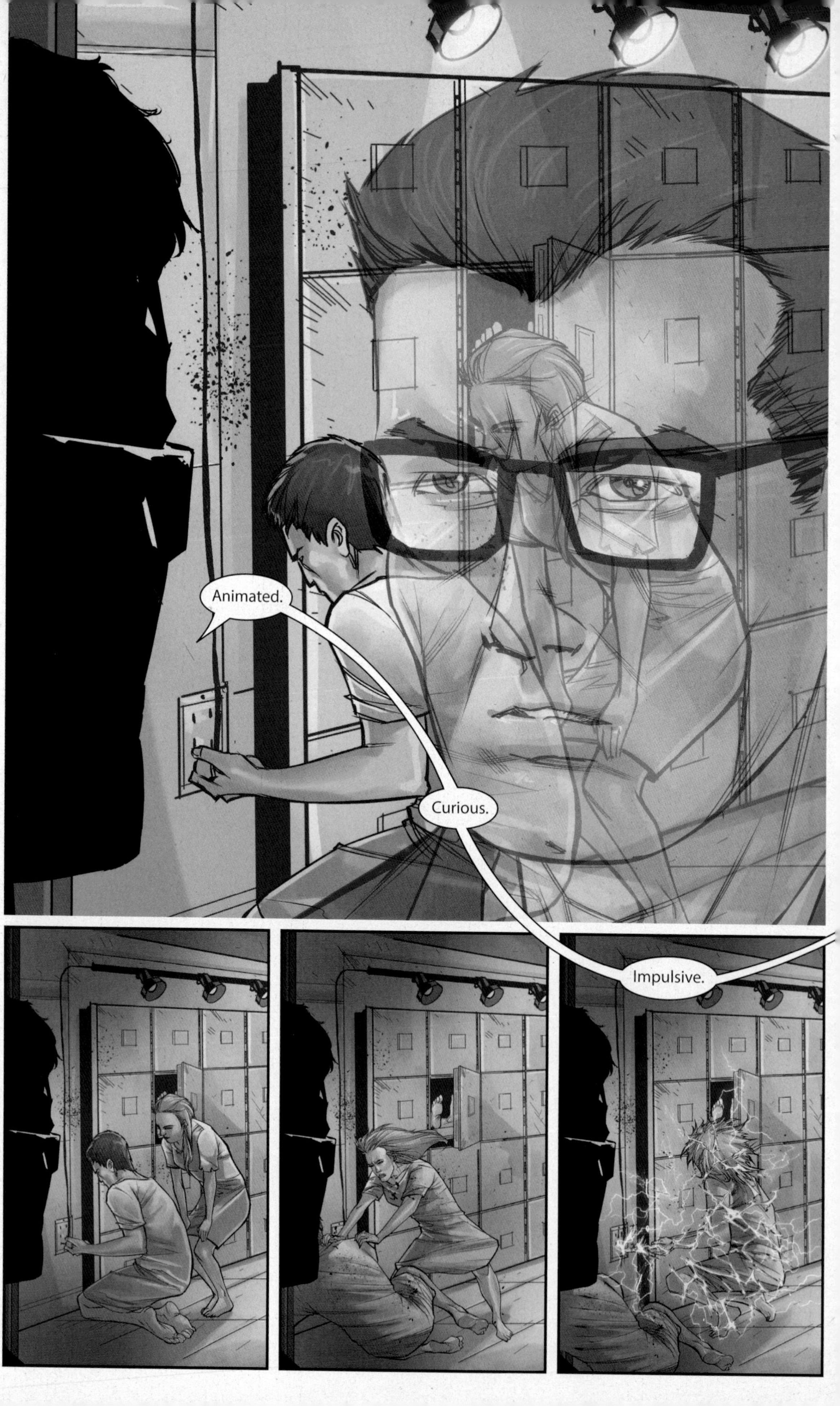
Animated.
Curious.
Impulsive.

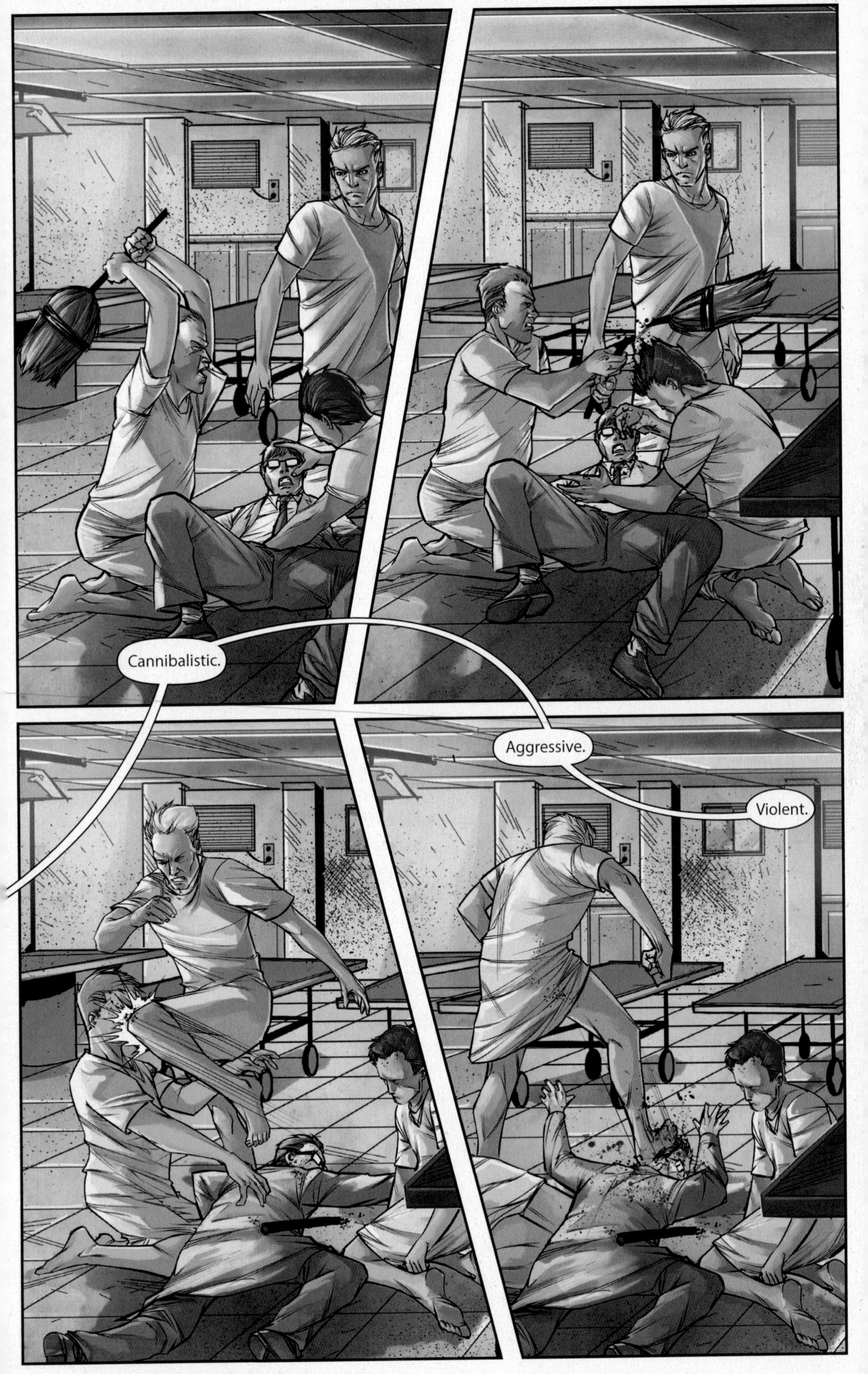
Cannibalistic.
Aggressive.
Violent.

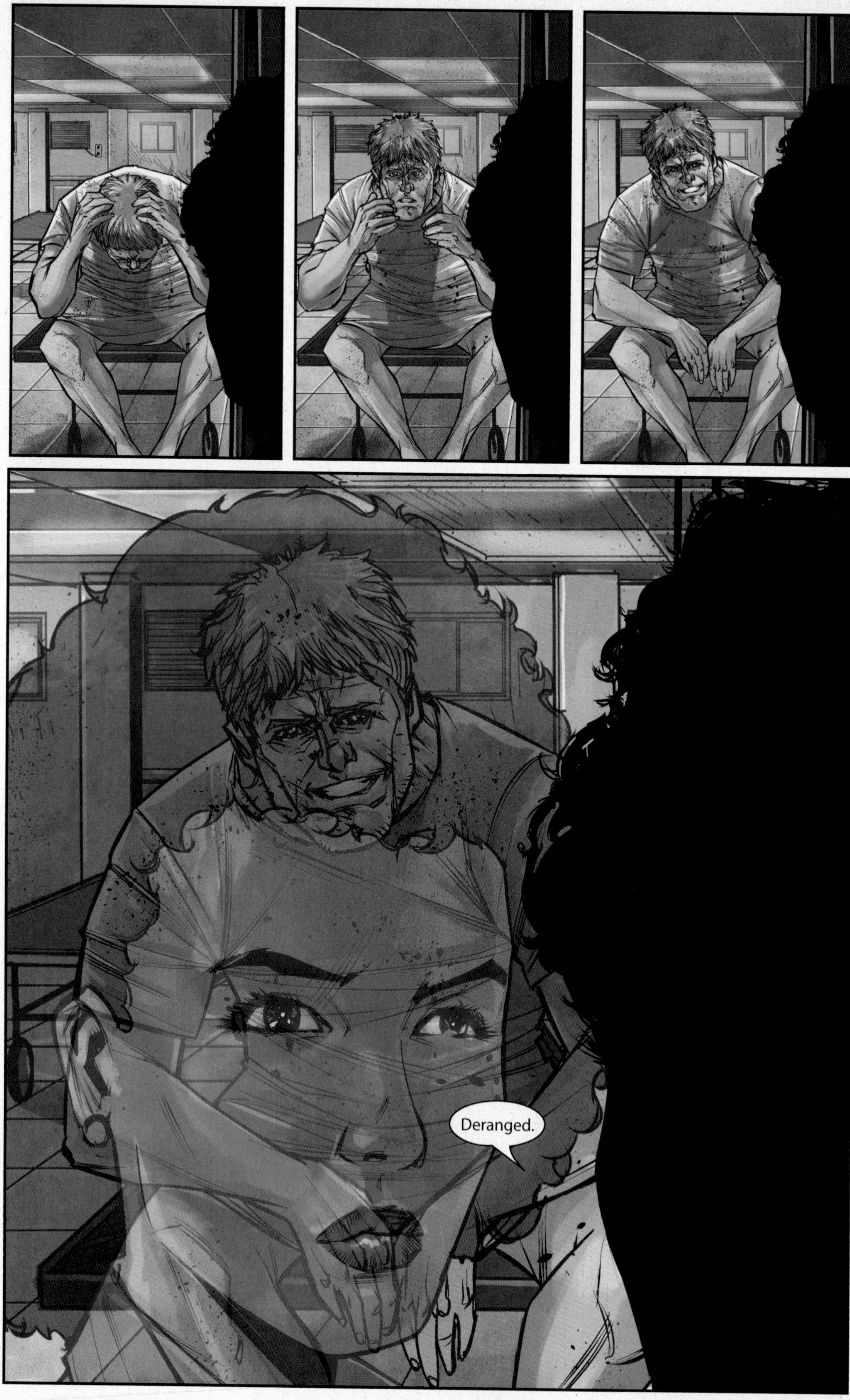
Deranged.

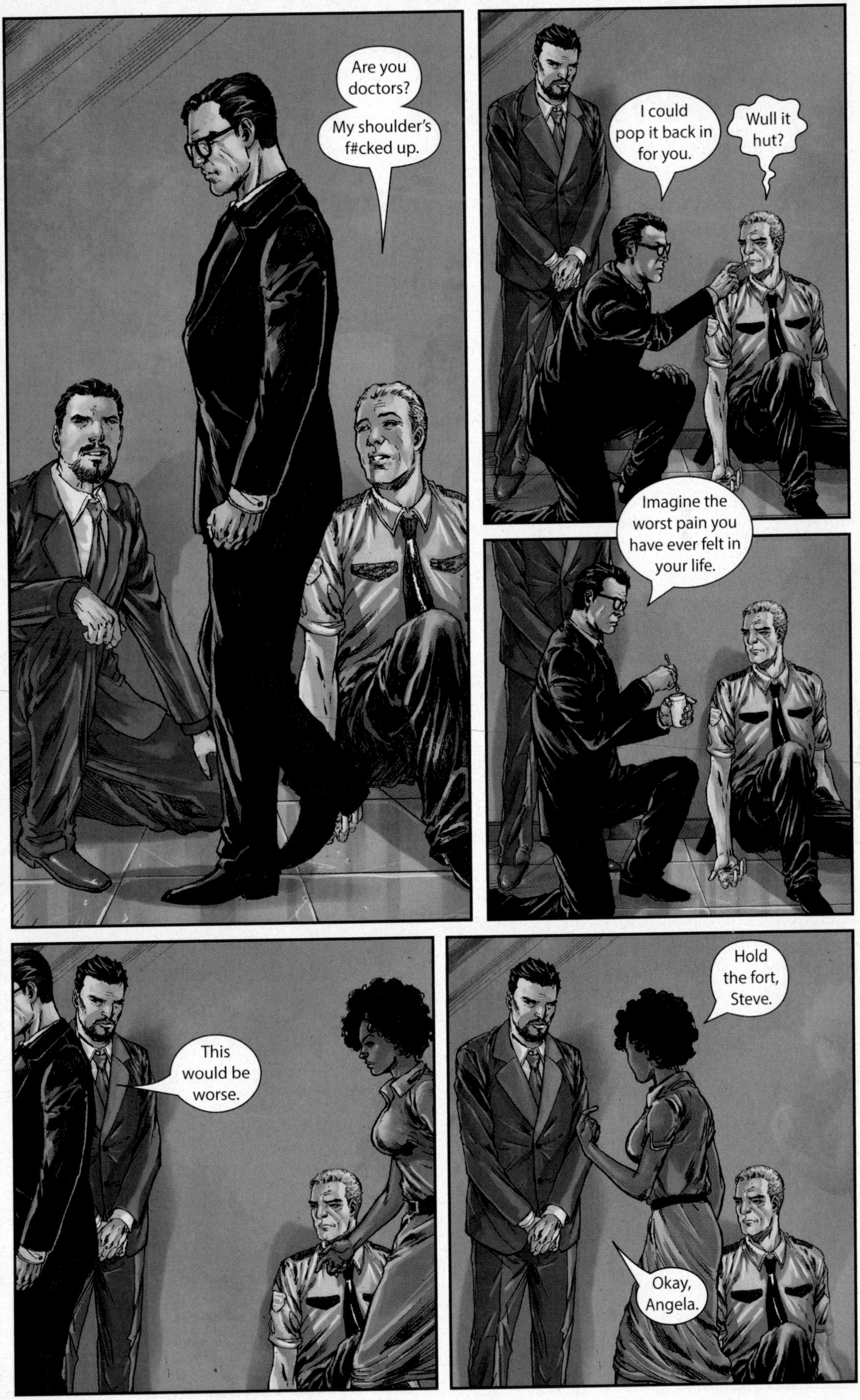
Are you doctors?
My shoulder's f#cked up.
I could pop it back in for you.
Wull it hut?
Imagine the worst pain you have ever felt in your life.
This would be worse.
Hold the fort, Steve.
Okay, Angela.

THE NATIONAL AIR AND SPACE ADMINISTRATION

October 4, 1957 – The Soviet Union launched *Sputnik*, the world's first man-made satellite, into space.

November 3, 1957 – The Soviet Union followed with *Sputnik 2*, which carried Laika, a canine. Laika survived the trip into space but died when the oxygen supply ran out.

January 31, 1958 – The United States launched its first satellite, *Explorer 1*.

August 19, 1960 – The Soviet Union launched *Sputnik 5* with a grey rabbit, 42 mice, two rats, flies, several plants, fungi, and two canines, Belka and Strelka; all passengers survived the trip to and from space.

April 12, 1961 – Soviet cosmonaut Yuri Gagarin became the first human in space.

May 5, 1961 – Alan Shepard became the first American in space.

May 25, 1961 – President John F. Kennedy rallied Congress and the nation to support the first manned mission to the moon, which became the Apollo program.

February 3, 1966 – The Soviet Union landed the first spacecraft on the moon; the United States followed with *Surveyor I* on June 2.

July 2, 1969 – American astronauts Neil Armstrong and "Buzz" Aldrin became the first men on the moon.

September 1976 – American probe *Viking 2* discovered water frost on Mars.

August and September 1977 – *Voyagers 1* and *2* were launched; each would transmit images of the outer planets over the decades while on their (still ongoing) journeys.

April 12, 1981 – The United States launched the first space shuttle *Columbia*.

August 6, 2012 – NASA's *Curiosity* rover landed on Mars.

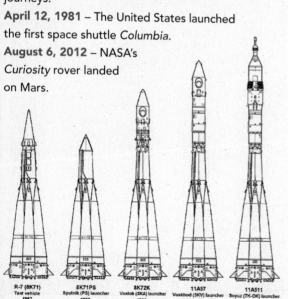

| R-7 (8K71) Test vehicle 1957 | 8K71PS Sputnik (PS) launcher 1957 | 8K72K Vostok (3KA) launcher 1960 | 11A57 Voskhod (3KV) launcher 1963 | 11A511 Soyuz (7K-OK) launcher 1966 |

SINCE *SPUTNIK'S* LAUNCH IN 1957

SATELLITES SENT INTO ORBIT	2,271
ACTIVE SATELLITES	1,381
UNITED STATES	568
RUSSIA	133
CHINA	177
ALL OTHER COUNTRIES	503
ACTIVE MILITARY SATELLITES	295
UNITED STATES	129
RUSSIA	75
CHINA	35
ALL OTHER COUNTRIES	56

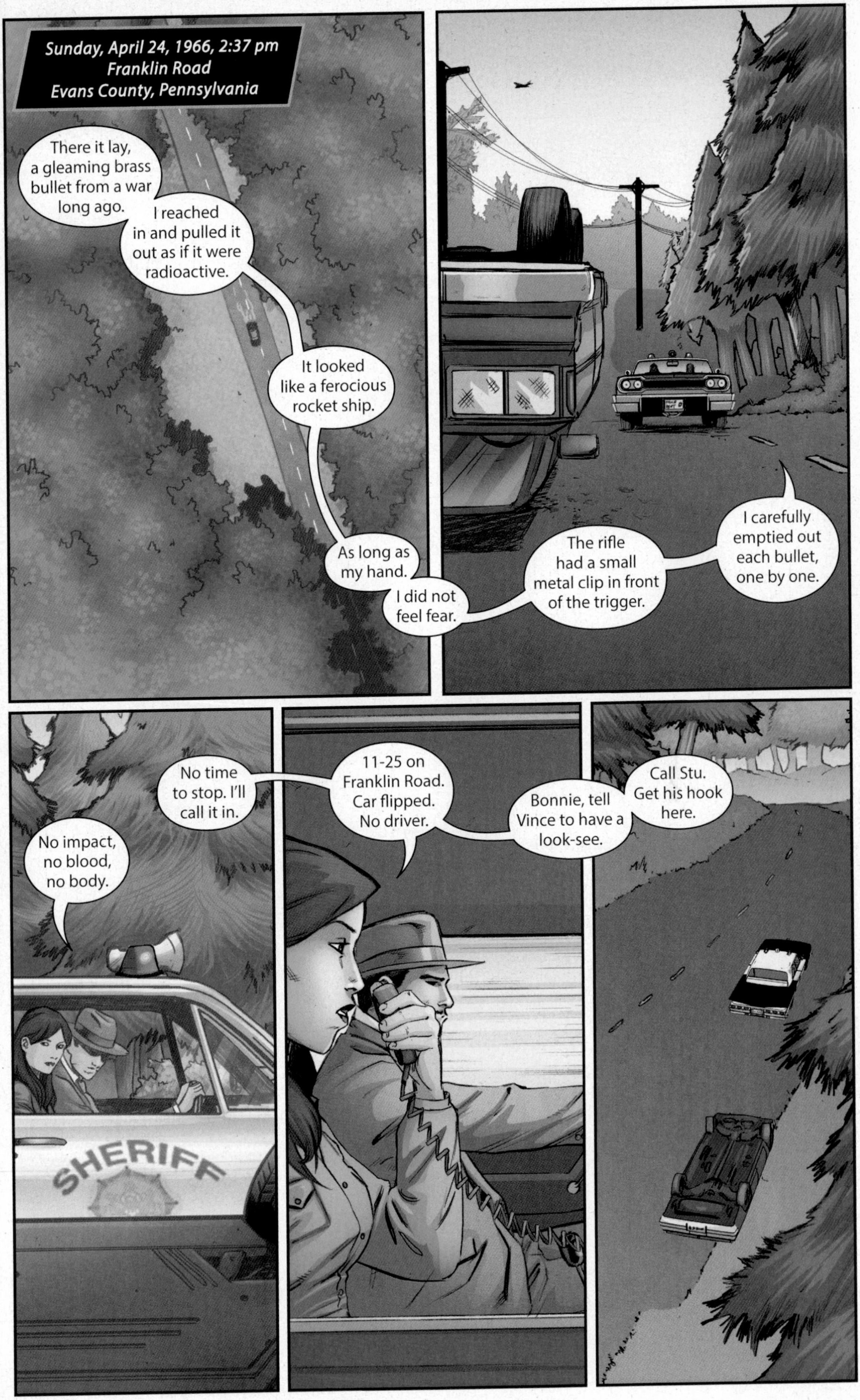
Sunday, April 24, 1966, 2:37 pm
Franklin Road
Evans County, Pennsylvania
There it lay, a gleaming brass bullet from a war long ago.
I reached in and pulled it out as if it were radioactive.
It looked like a ferocious rocket ship.
As long as my hand.
I did not feel fear.
The rifle had a small metal clip in front of the trigger.
I carefully emptied out each bullet, one by one.
No impact, no blood, no body.
No time to stop. I'll call it in.
11-25 on Franklin Road. Car flipped. No driver.
Bonnie, tell Vince to have a look-see.
Call Stu. Get his hook here.
SHERIFF

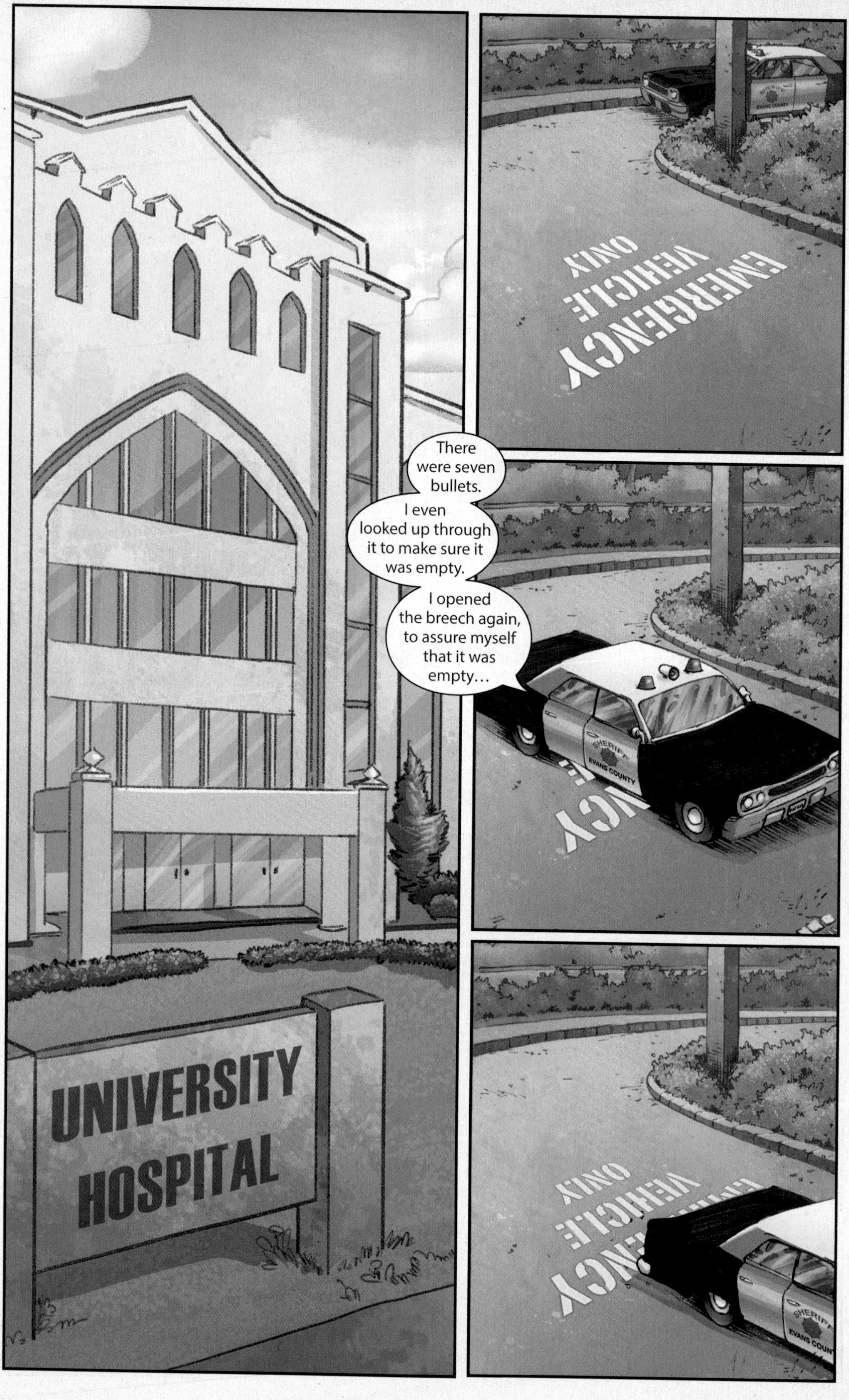
UNIVERSITY HOSPITAL
EMERGENCY VEHICLE ONLY
SHERIFF
EVANS COUNTY
There were seven bullets.
I even looked up through it to make sure it was empty.
I opened the breech again, to assure myself that it was empty…

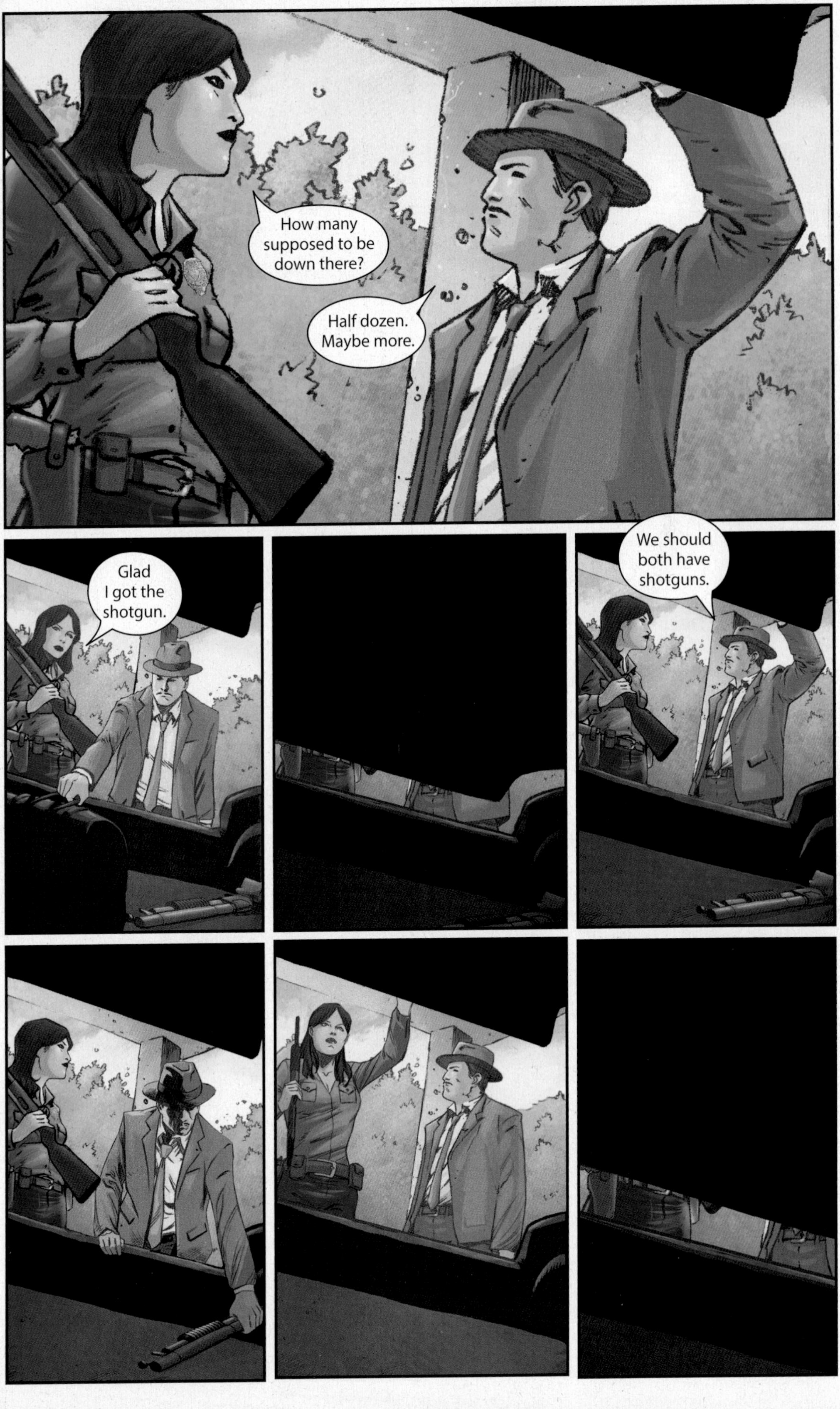
How many supposed to be down there?
Half dozen. Maybe more.
Glad I got the shotgun.
We should both have shotguns.

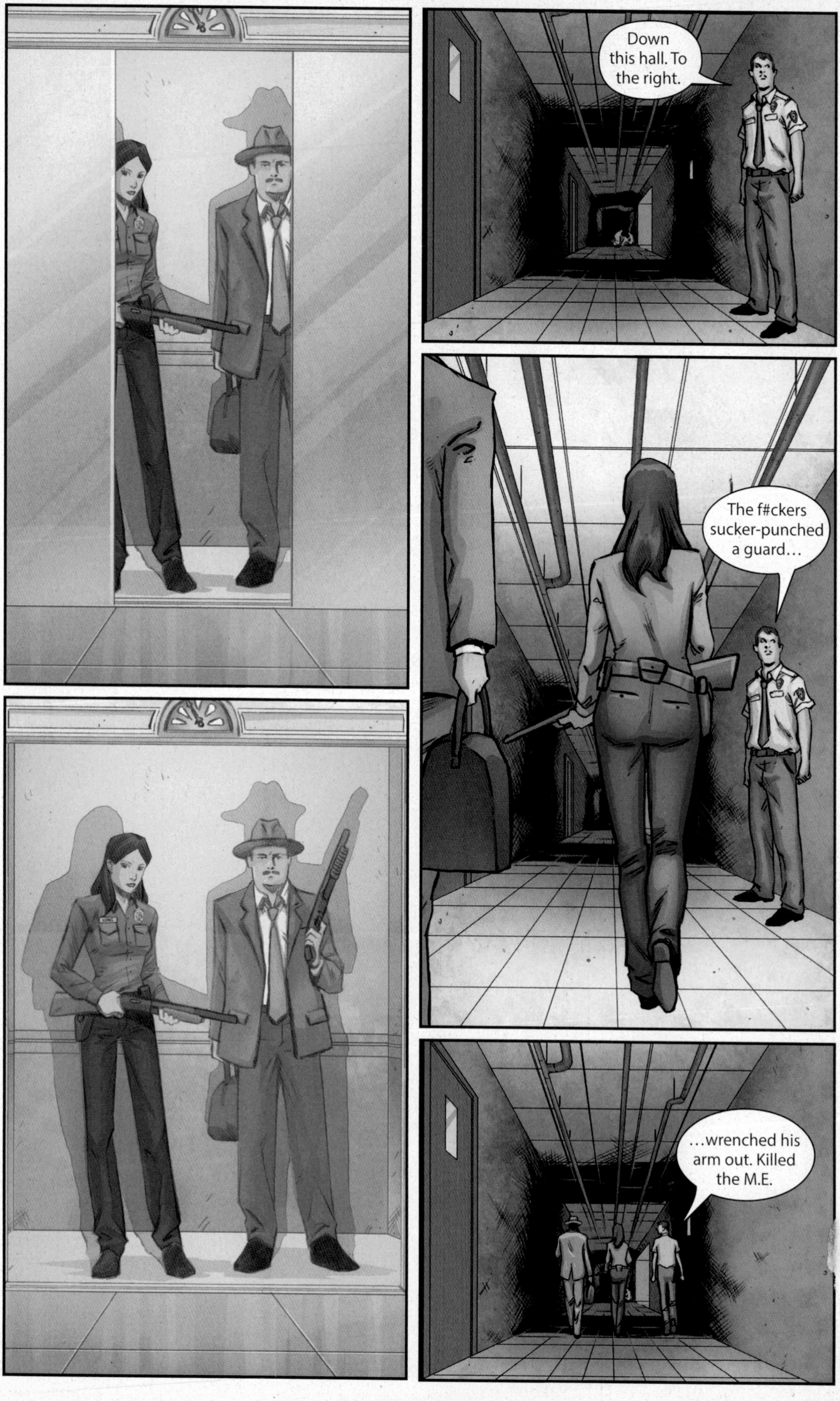
Down this hall. To the right.
The f#ckers sucker-punched a guard…
…wrenched his arm out. Killed the M.E.

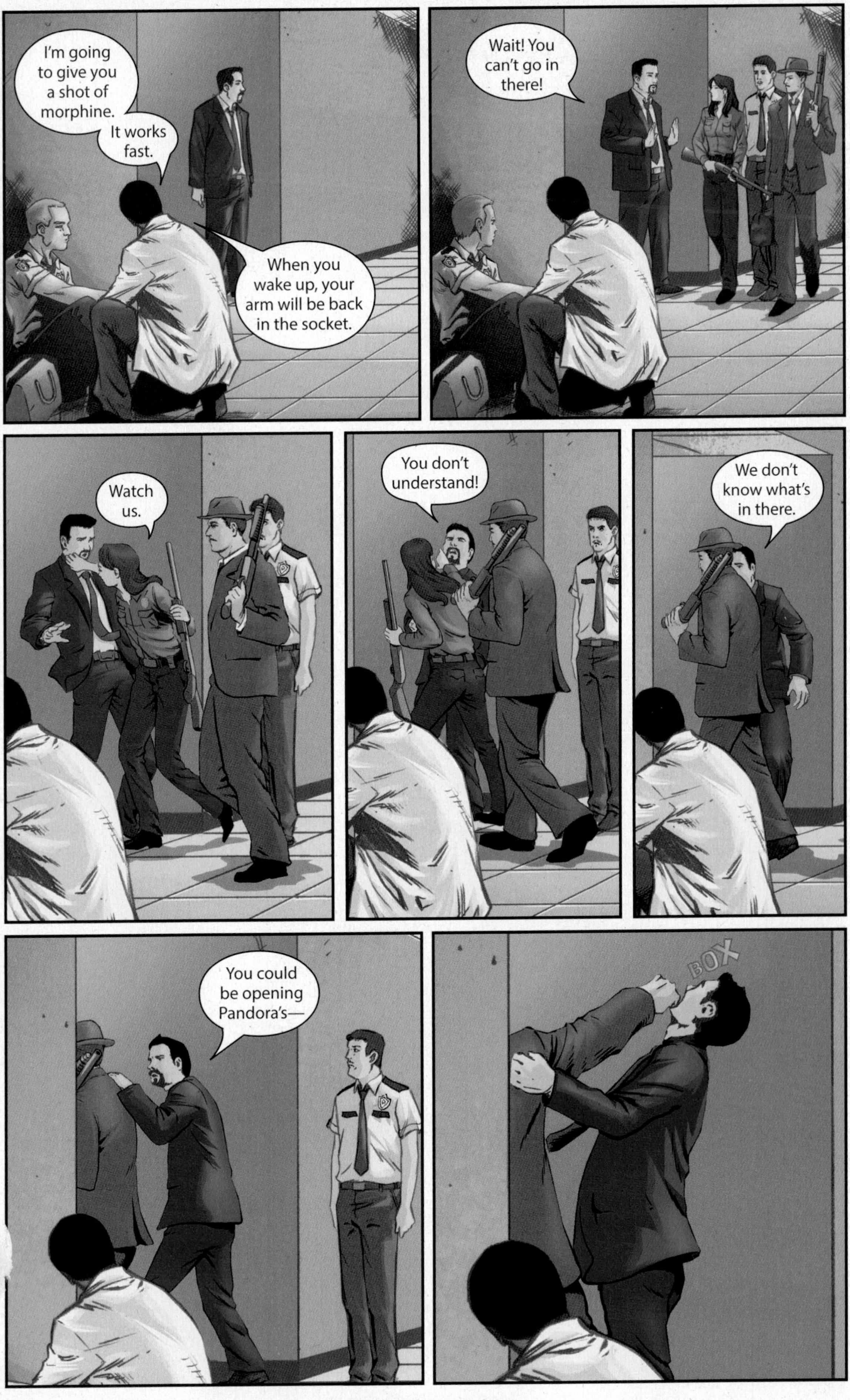

I'm going to give you a shot of morphine.
It works fast.
When you wake up, your arm will be back in the socket.
Wait! You can't go in there!
Watch us.
You don't understand!
We don't know what's in there.
You could be opening Pandora's—
BOX

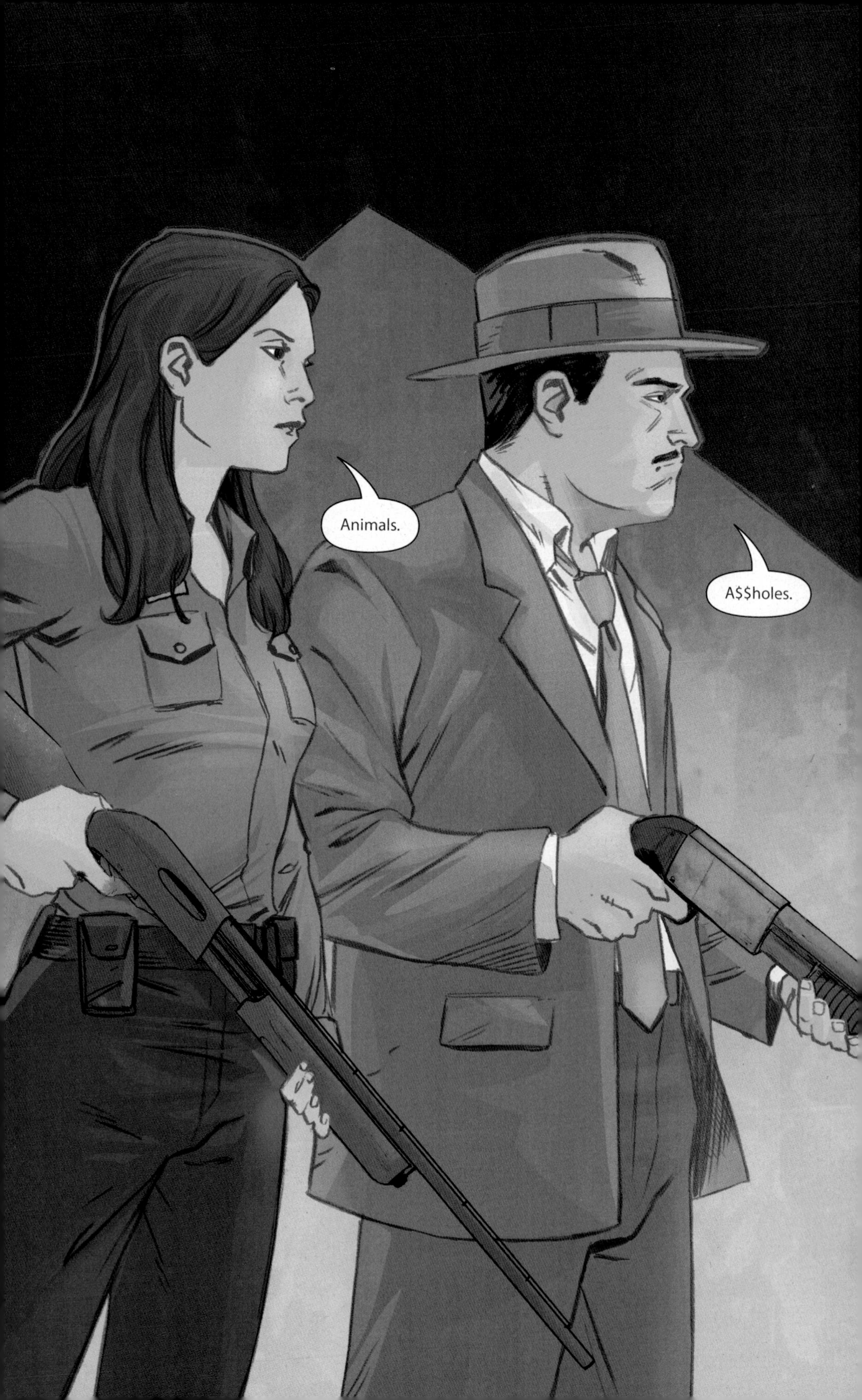
Animals.
A$$holes.

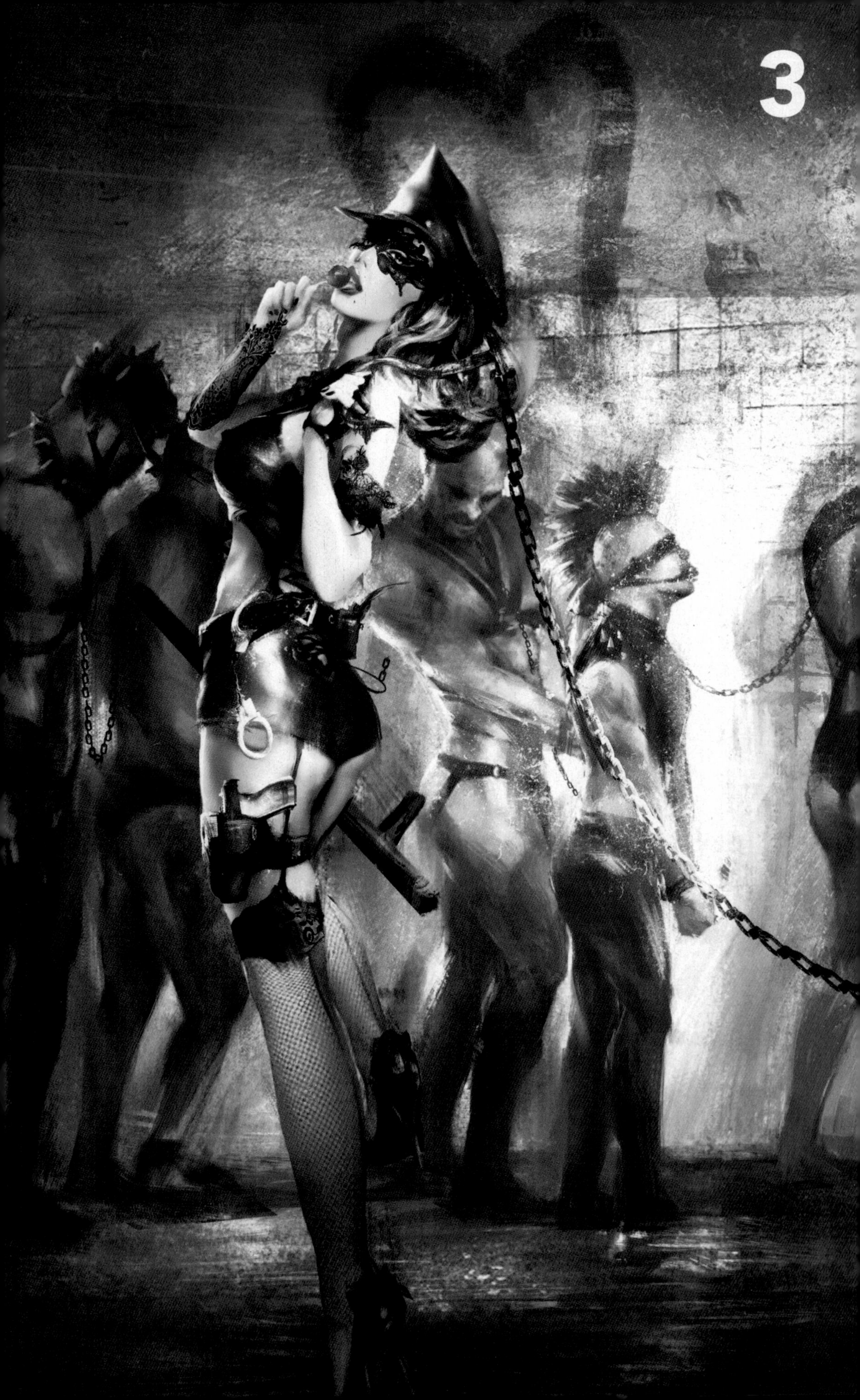
3

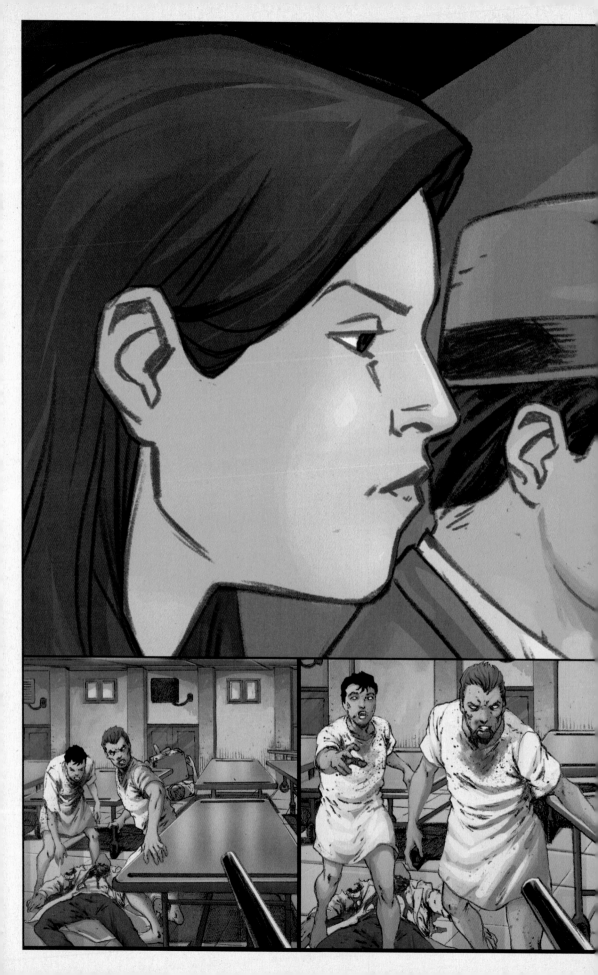

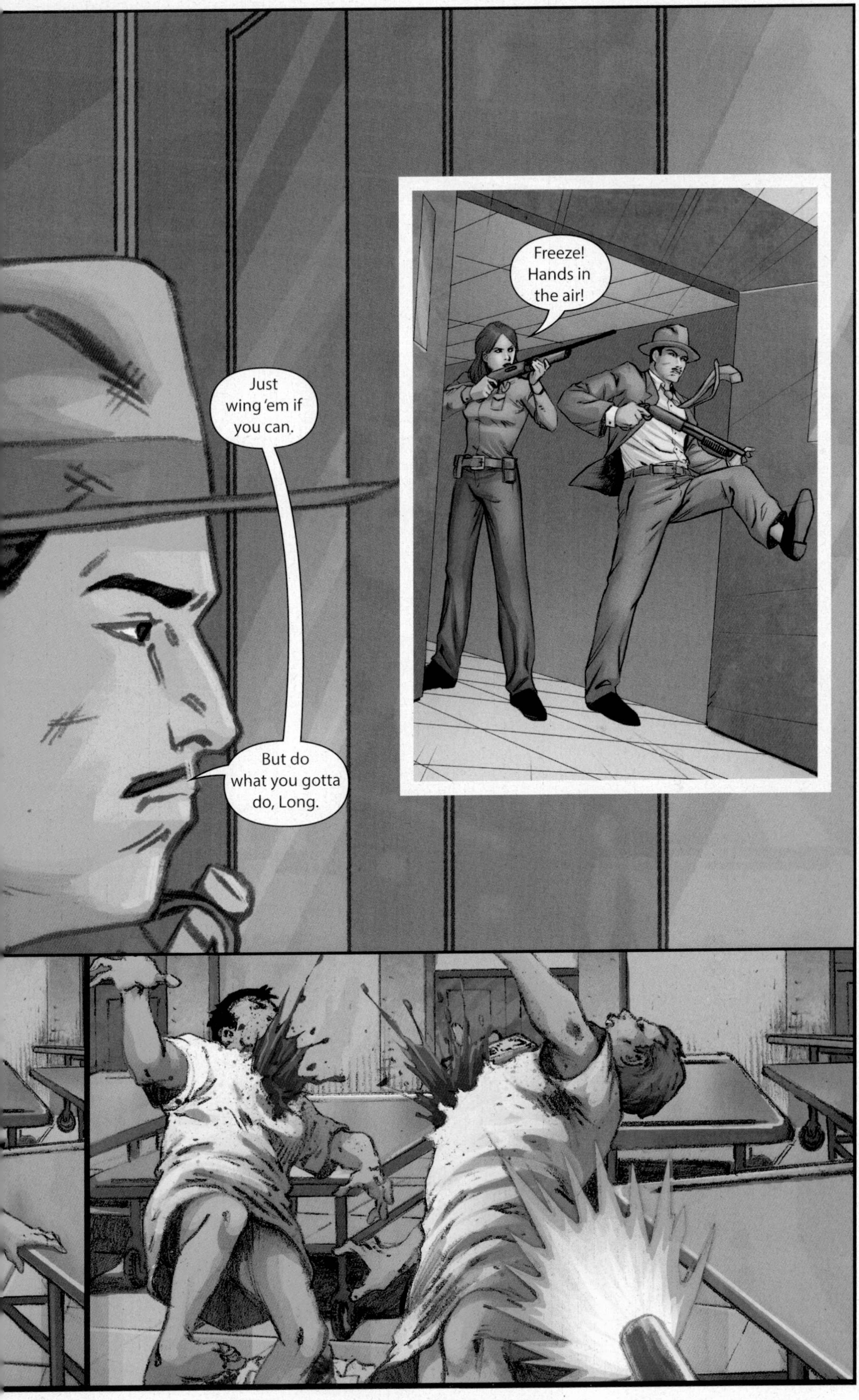
Just wing 'em if you can.
But do what you gotta do, Long.
Freeze! Hands in the air!

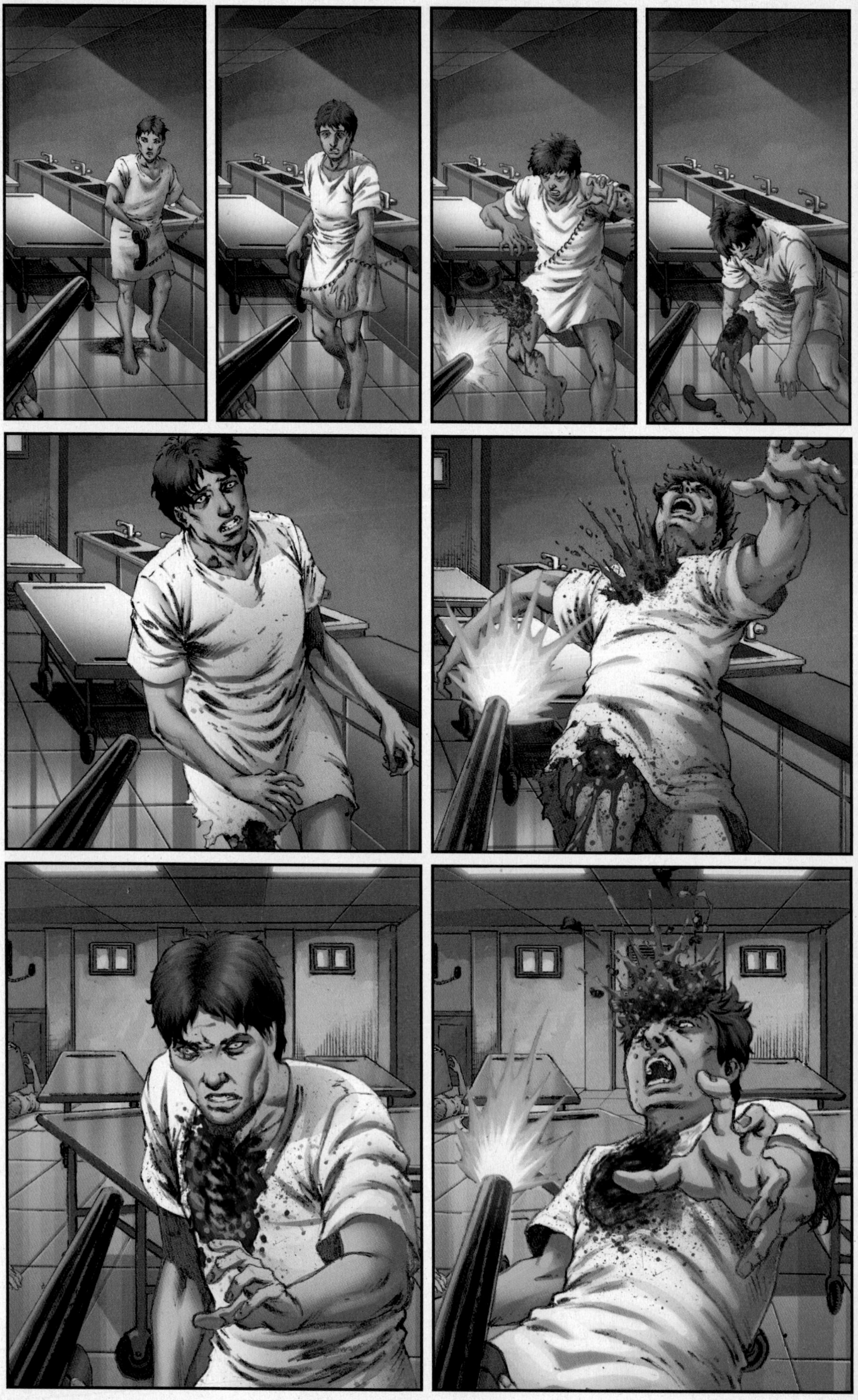

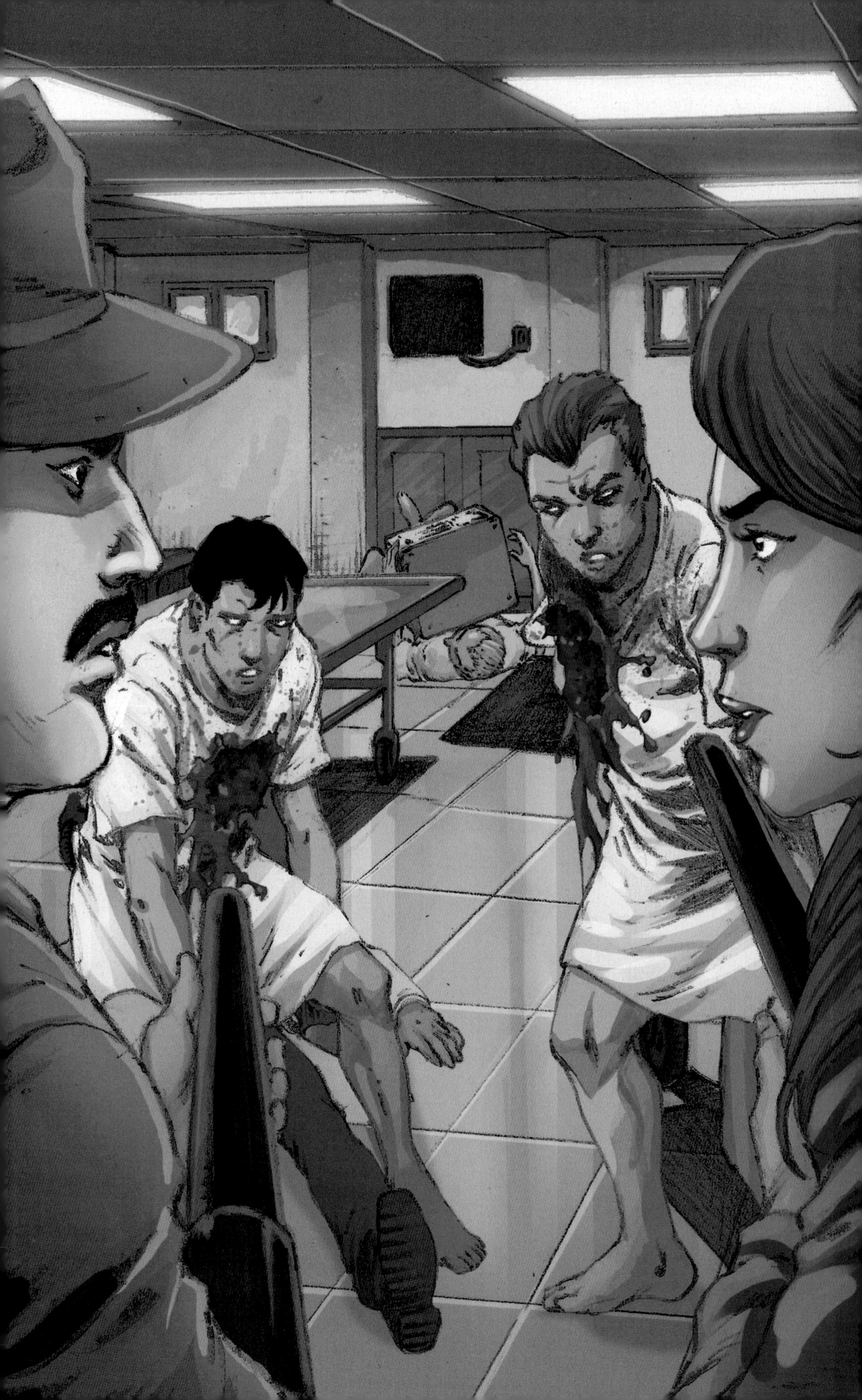

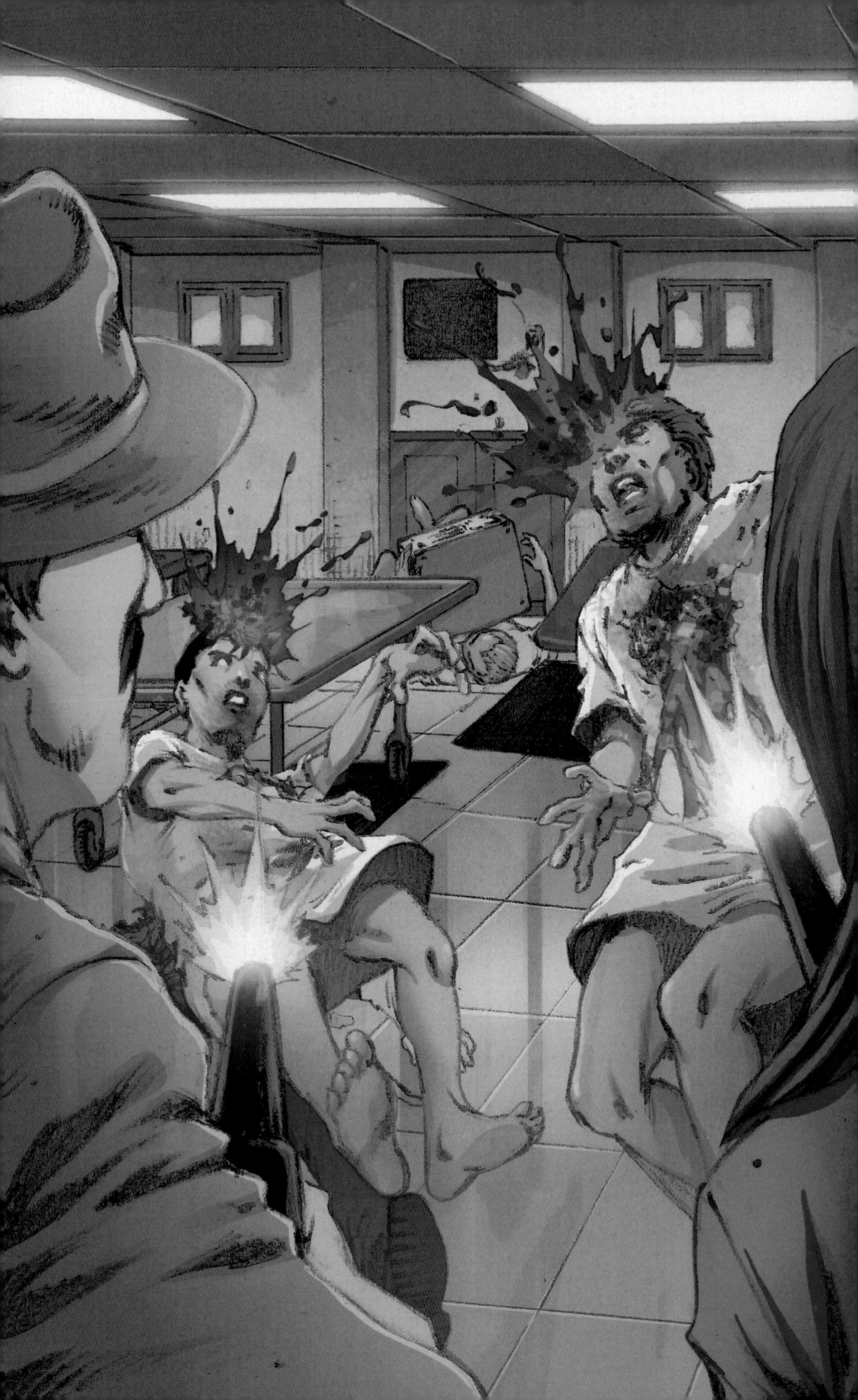

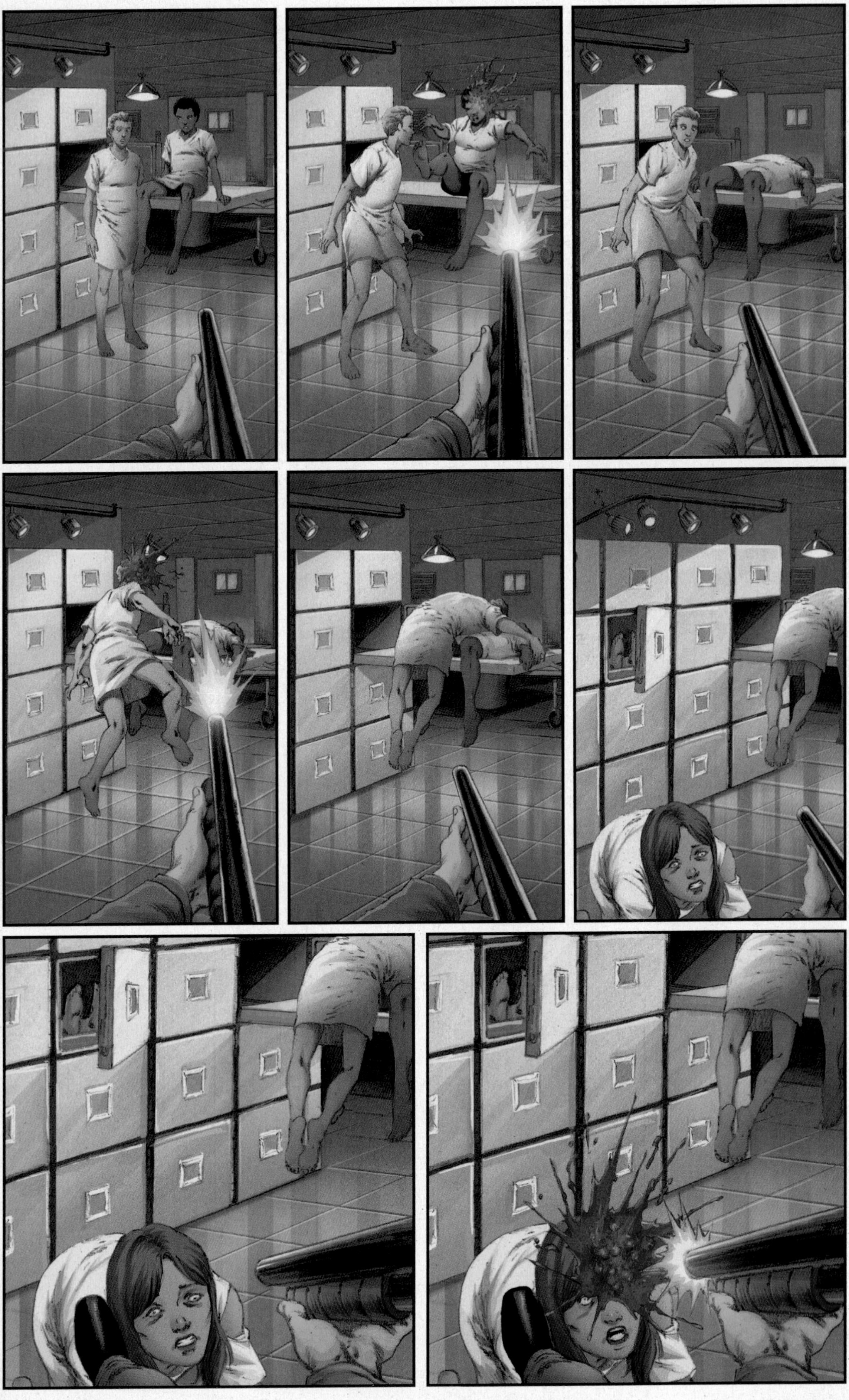

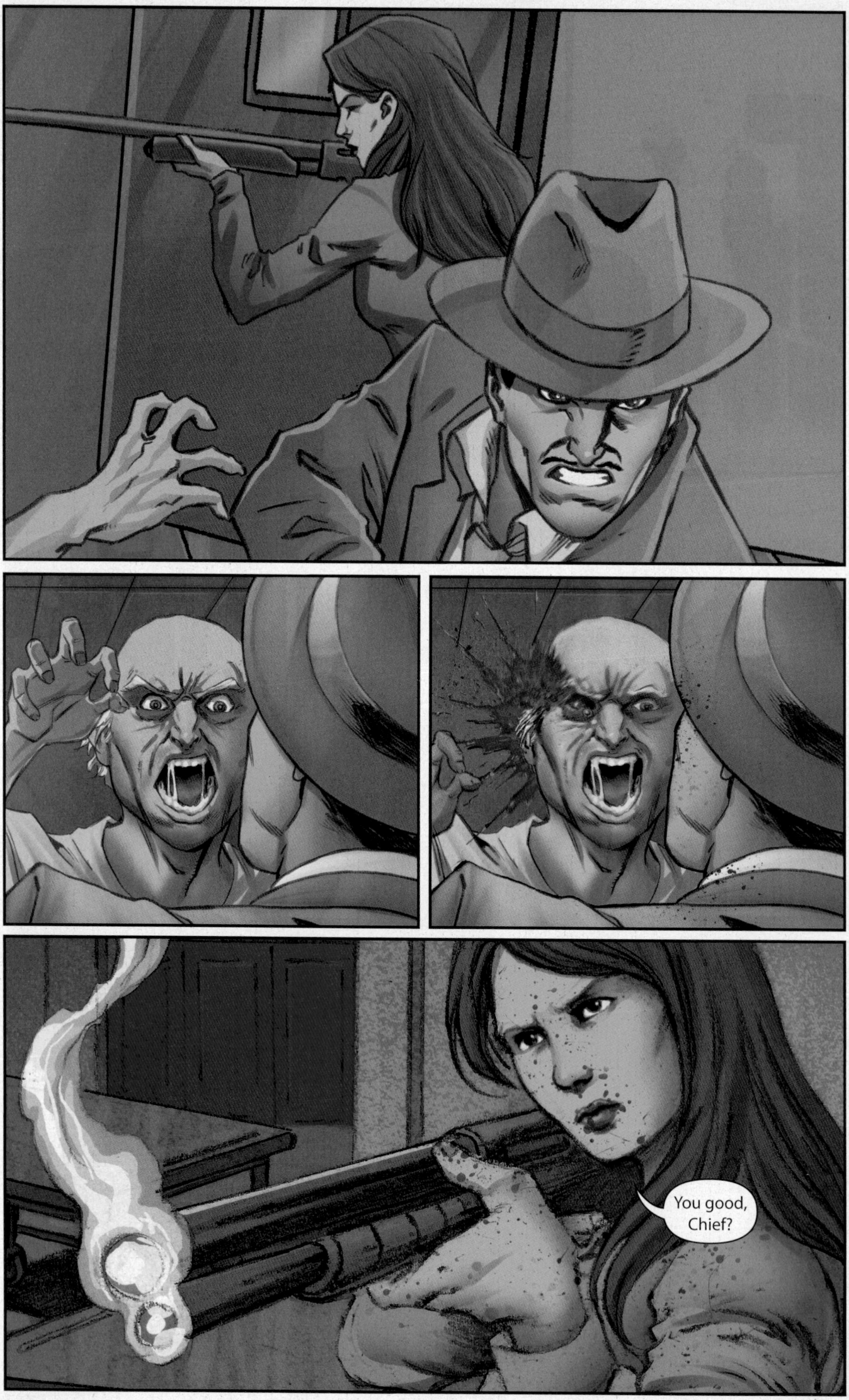
You good, Chief?

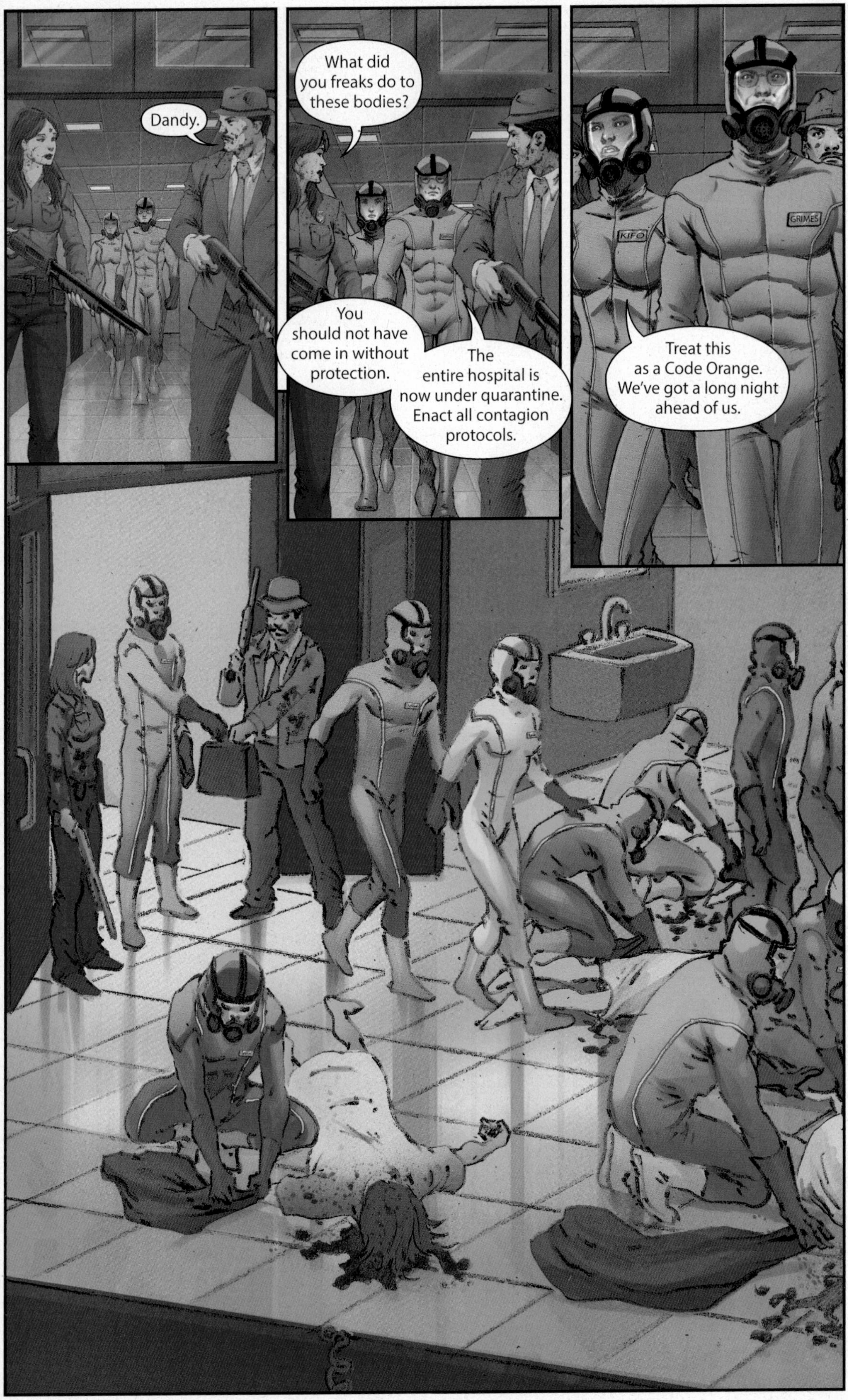
Dandy.
What did you freaks do to these bodies?
You should not have come in without protection.
The entire hospital is now under quarantine. Enact all contagion protocols.
KIFO
GRIMES
Treat this as a Code Orange. We've got a long night ahead of us.

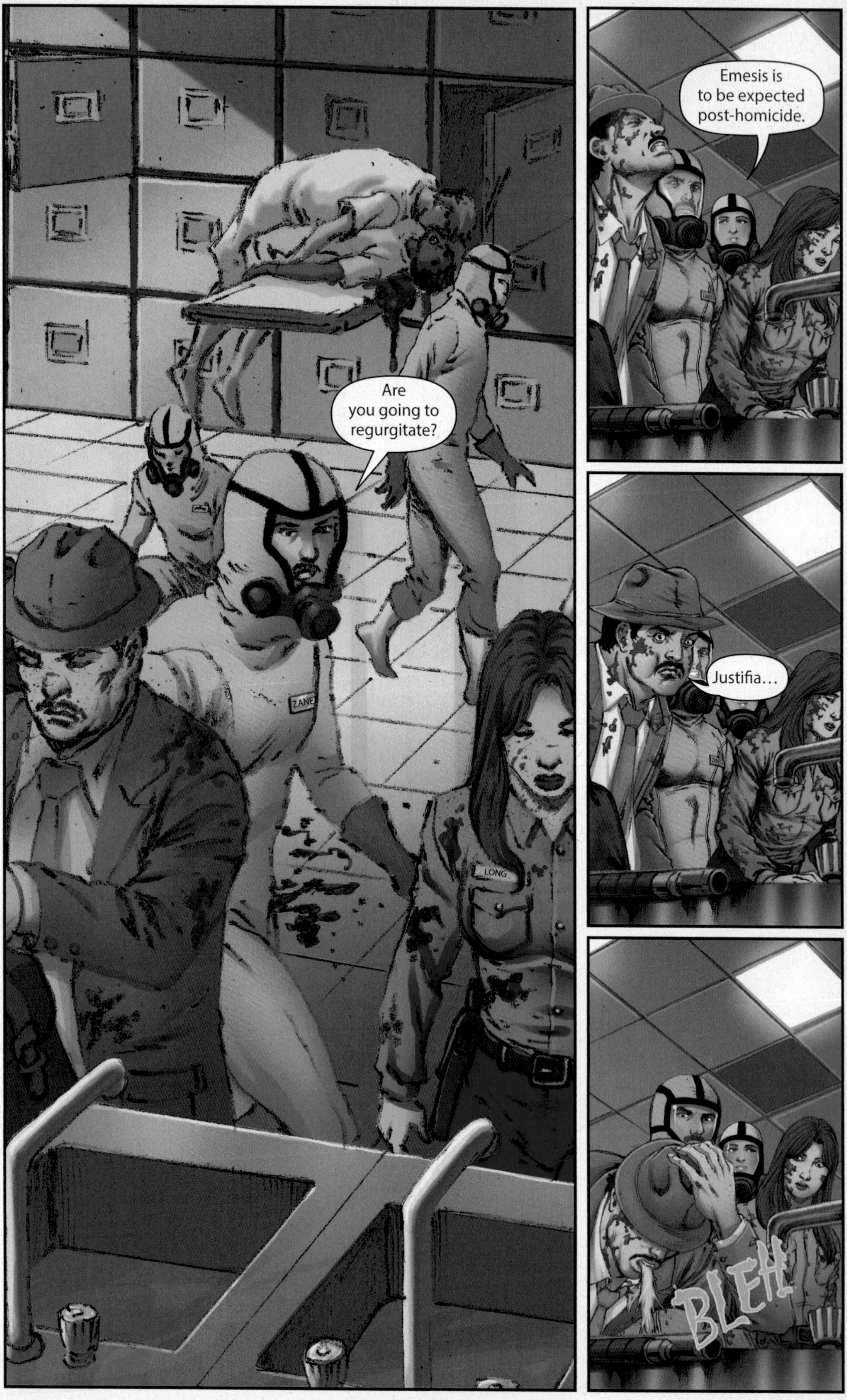
Are you going to regurgitate?
Emesis is to be expected post-homicide.
Justifia…
BLEH
ZANE
LONG

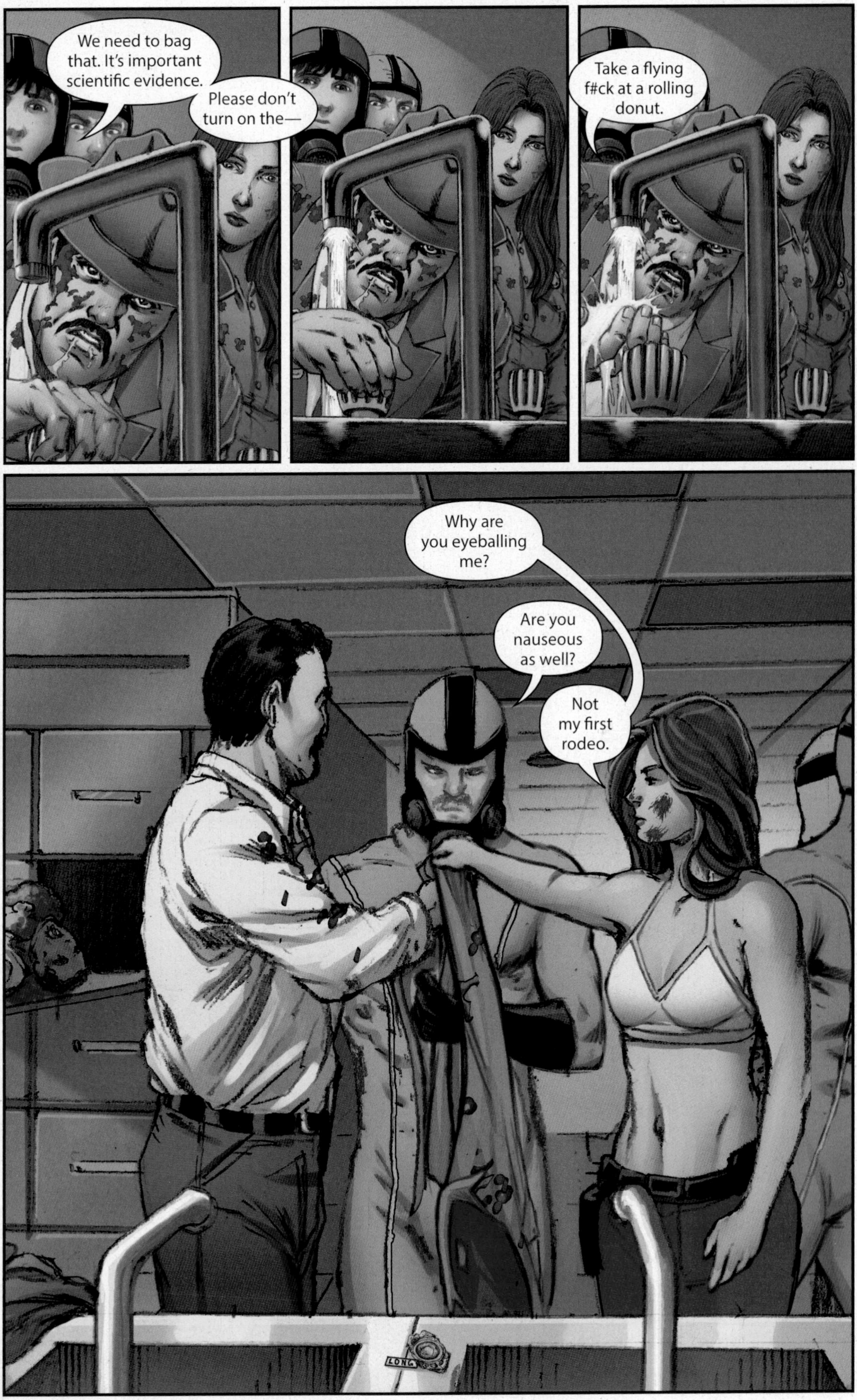
We need to bag that. It's important scientific evidence.
Please don't turn on the—
Take a flying f#ck at a rolling donut.
Why are you eyeballing me?
Are you nauseous as well?
Not my first rodeo.

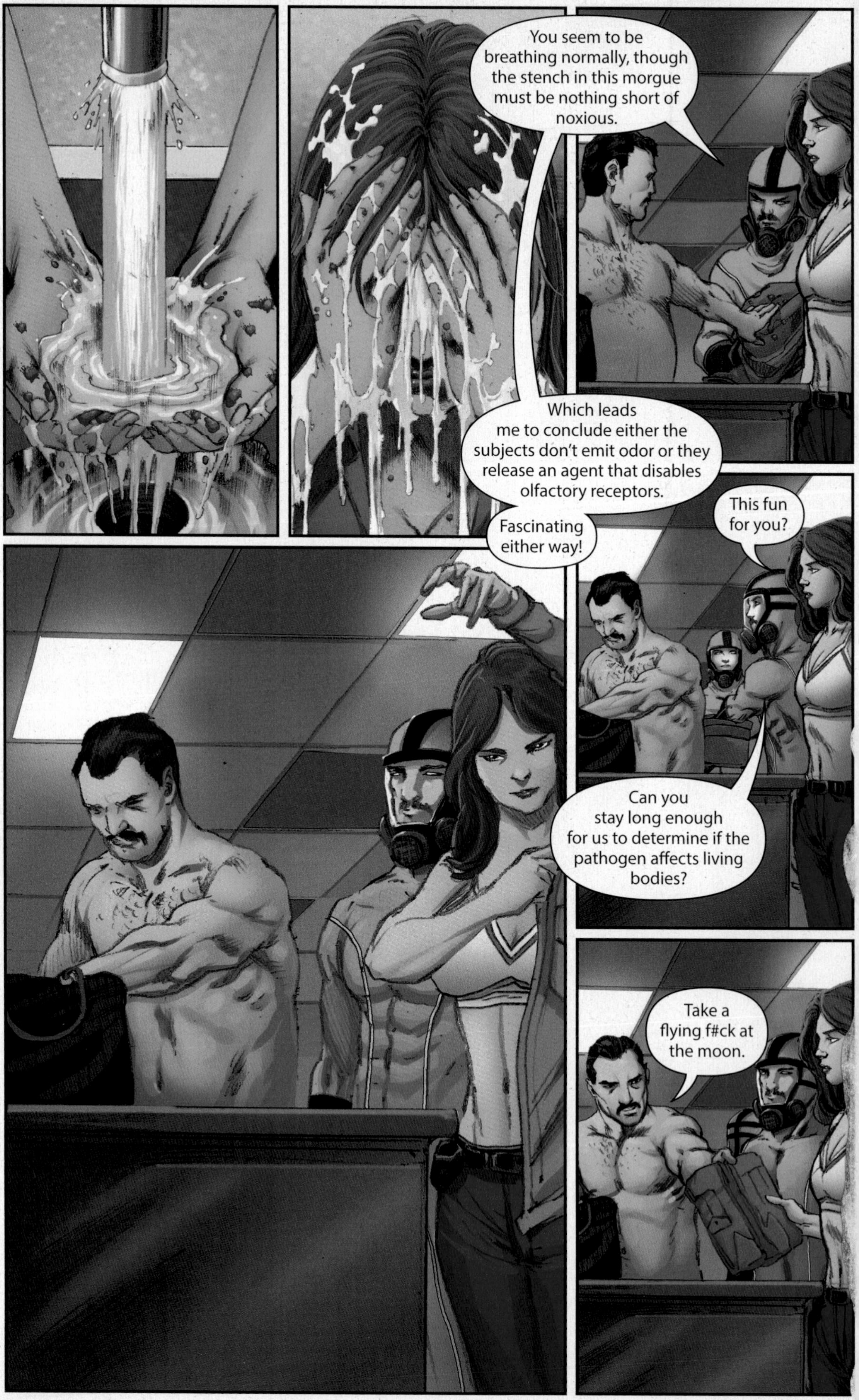
You seem to be breathing normally, though the stench in this morgue must be nothing short of noxious.
Which leads me to conclude either the subjects don't emit odor or they release an agent that disables olfactory receptors.
Fascinating either way!
This fun for you?
Can you stay long enough for us to determine if the pathogen affects living bodies?
Take a flying f#ck at the moon.

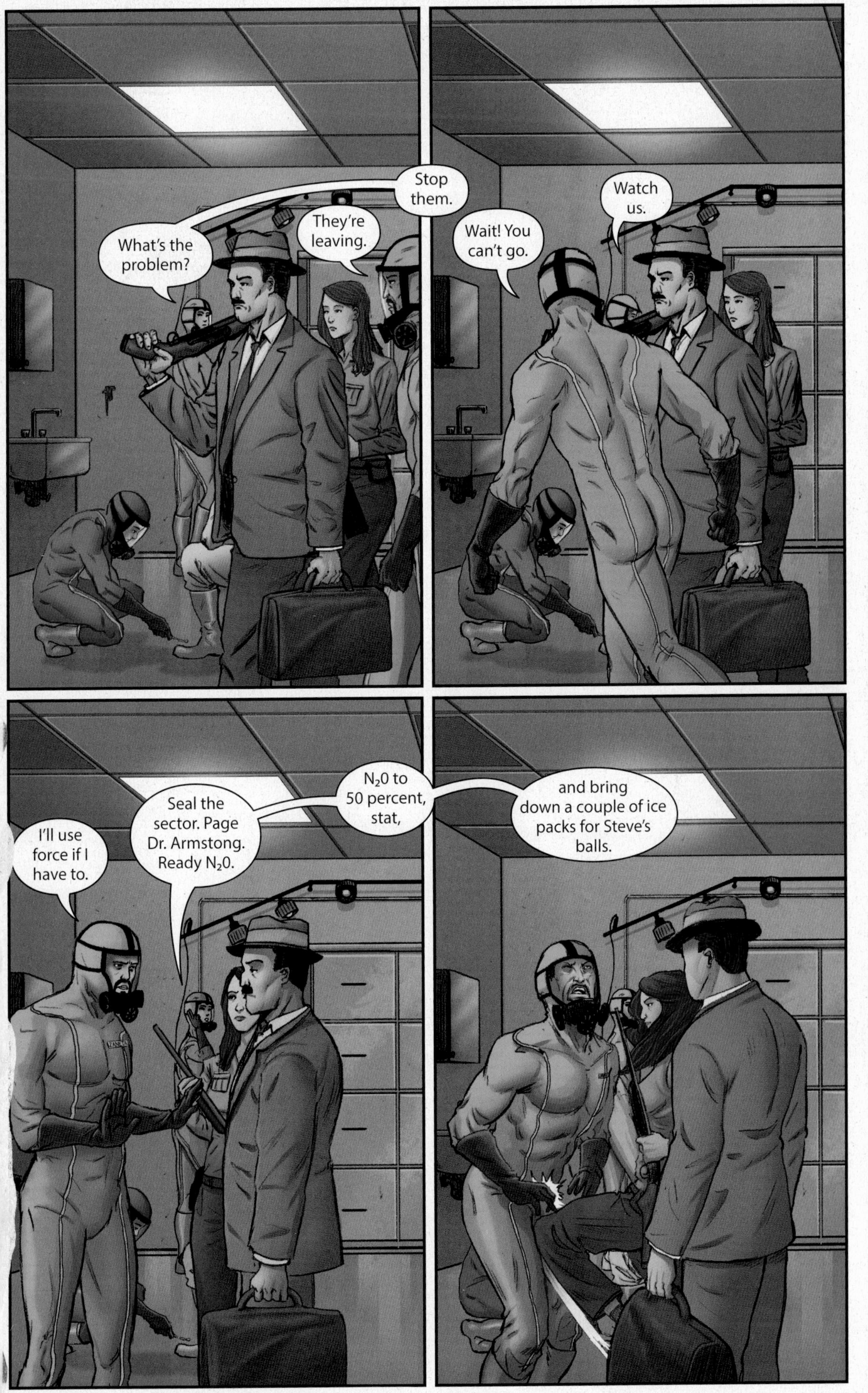
What's the problem?
They're leaving.
Stop them.
Wait! You can't go.
Watch us.
I'll use force if I have to.
Seal the sector. Page Dr. Armstong. Ready N_20.
N_20 to 50 percent, stat,
and bring down a couple of ice packs for Steve's balls.

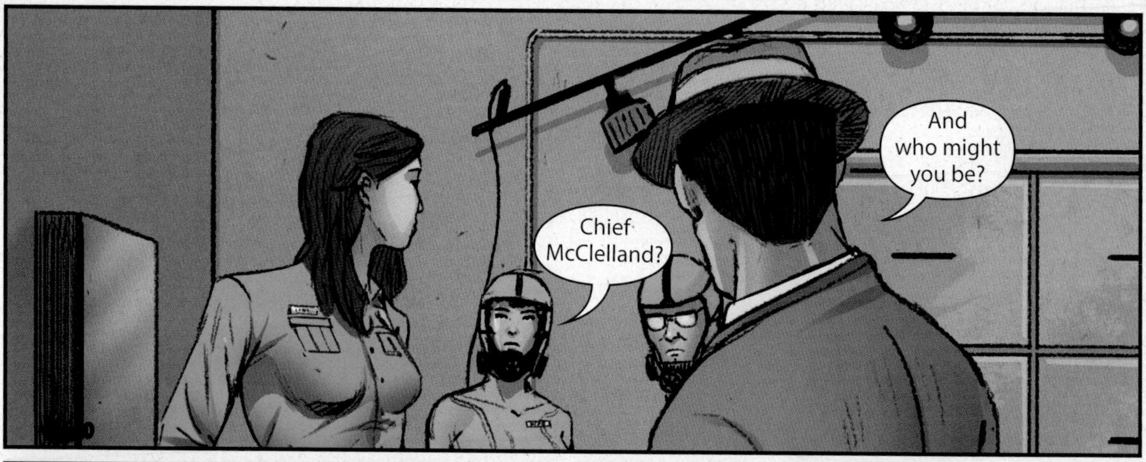
And who might you be?
Chief McClelland?

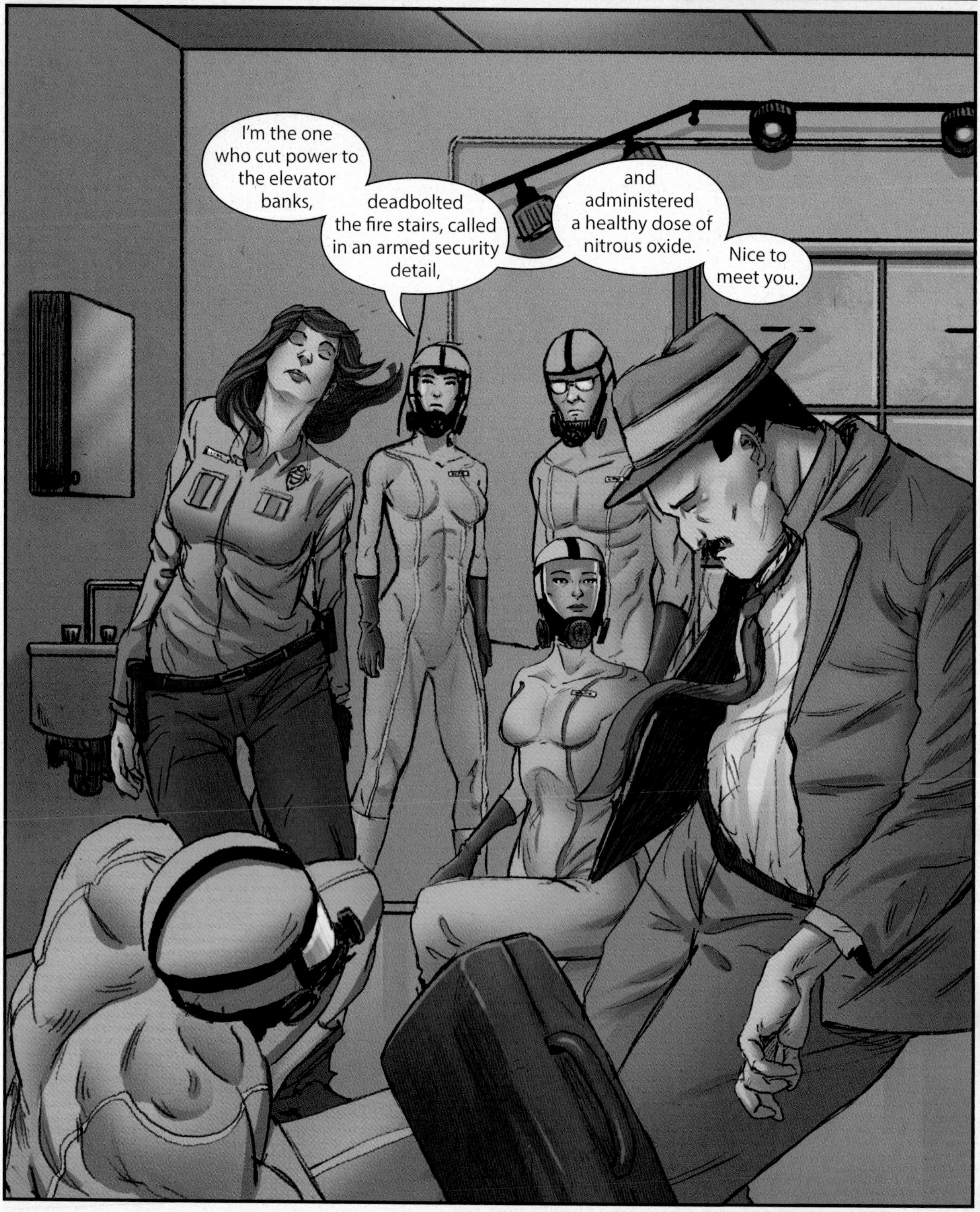
I'm the one who cut power to the elevator banks,
deadbolted the fire stairs, called in an armed security detail,
and administered a healthy dose of nitrous oxide.
Nice to meet you.

NATURE'S ZOMBIES

The modern zombie is usually a cadaver or living human infected with a virus that alters the host's behavior. Our zombie fiction may be closer to reality than imagined. From protozoans to wasps, these parasites manipulate their hosts' behaviors for their benefit (and to their hosts' detriment).

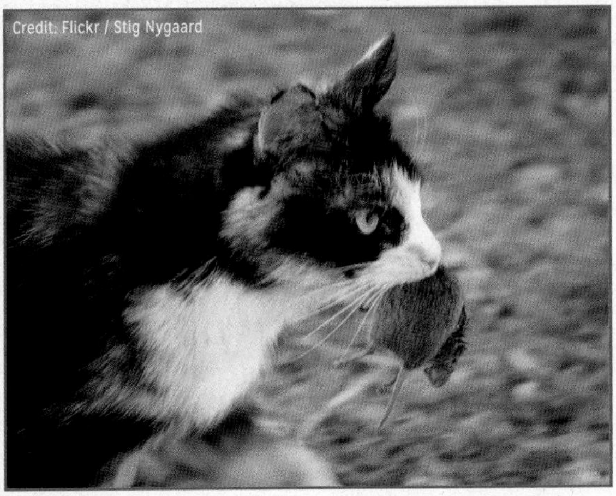

Credit: Flickr / Stig Nygaard

TOXOPLASMA GONDII: A mouse finds itself in the cat's territory; it should be wary from the scent of cat urine. But this mouse is not behaving normally: it is less averse, having been infected with a parasitic protozoan called *T. gondii*. The cat easily snatches up the infected prey. The parasite ends up exactly where it wants to be: in the cat's intestinal tract, which is the only place where it's known to reproduce, and it will spread through feline excrement. While *T. gondii* seems to primarily alter behavior in mice, the parasite can infect almost all warm-blooded animals. An estimated 30 to 50 percent of the global human population may be chronically infected with *T. gondii* after exposure. While infection in humans is mostly asymptomatic, some studies suggest that the parasite may be associated with a number of neurological disorders in humans (e.g., schizophrenia).

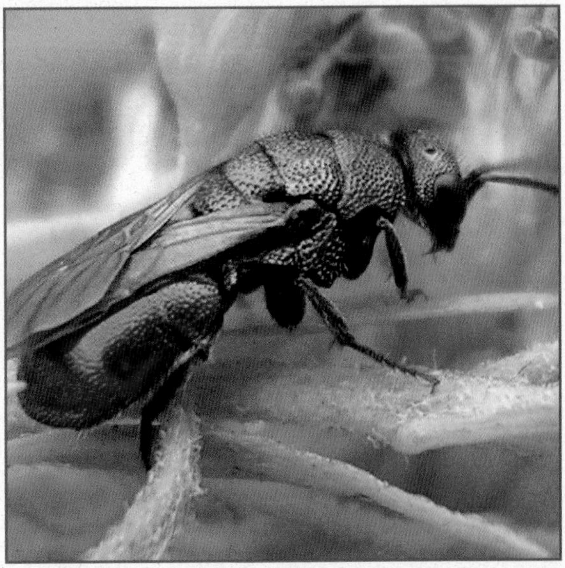

JEWEL WASP OR EMERALD COCKROACH WASP

AMPULEX COMPRESSA: Located in South Asia, Africa, and the Pacific Islands, the female jewel wasp uses a cockroach as its living nursery. First, she paralyzes the roach's front legs; then, she stings the roach's head with a venom disabling the roach's escape reflexes. Instead of running, the roach will groom extensively, and become sluggish. Next, the wasp leads the roach to its burrow by pulling on one of the roach's antennae (much like a leash). Over the next eight days, her larva consumes the roach's organs. The roach stays alive until the larva pupates.

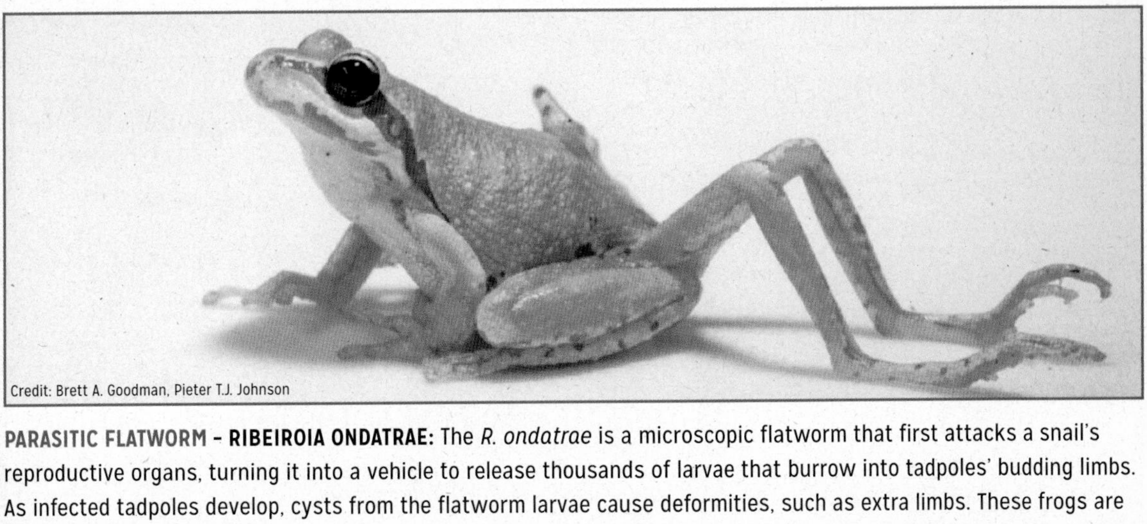

Credit: Brett A. Goodman, Pieter T.J. Johnson

PARASITIC FLATWORM – **RIBEIROIA ONDATRAE:** The *R. ondatrae* is a microscopic flatworm that first attacks a snail's reproductive organs, turning it into a vehicle to release thousands of larvae that burrow into tadpoles' budding limbs. As infected tadpoles develop, cysts from the flatworm larvae cause deformities, such as extra limbs. These frogs are crippled and easy prey for waterbirds. Once consumed, the waterbirds carry the parasites in their stomach to another body of water.

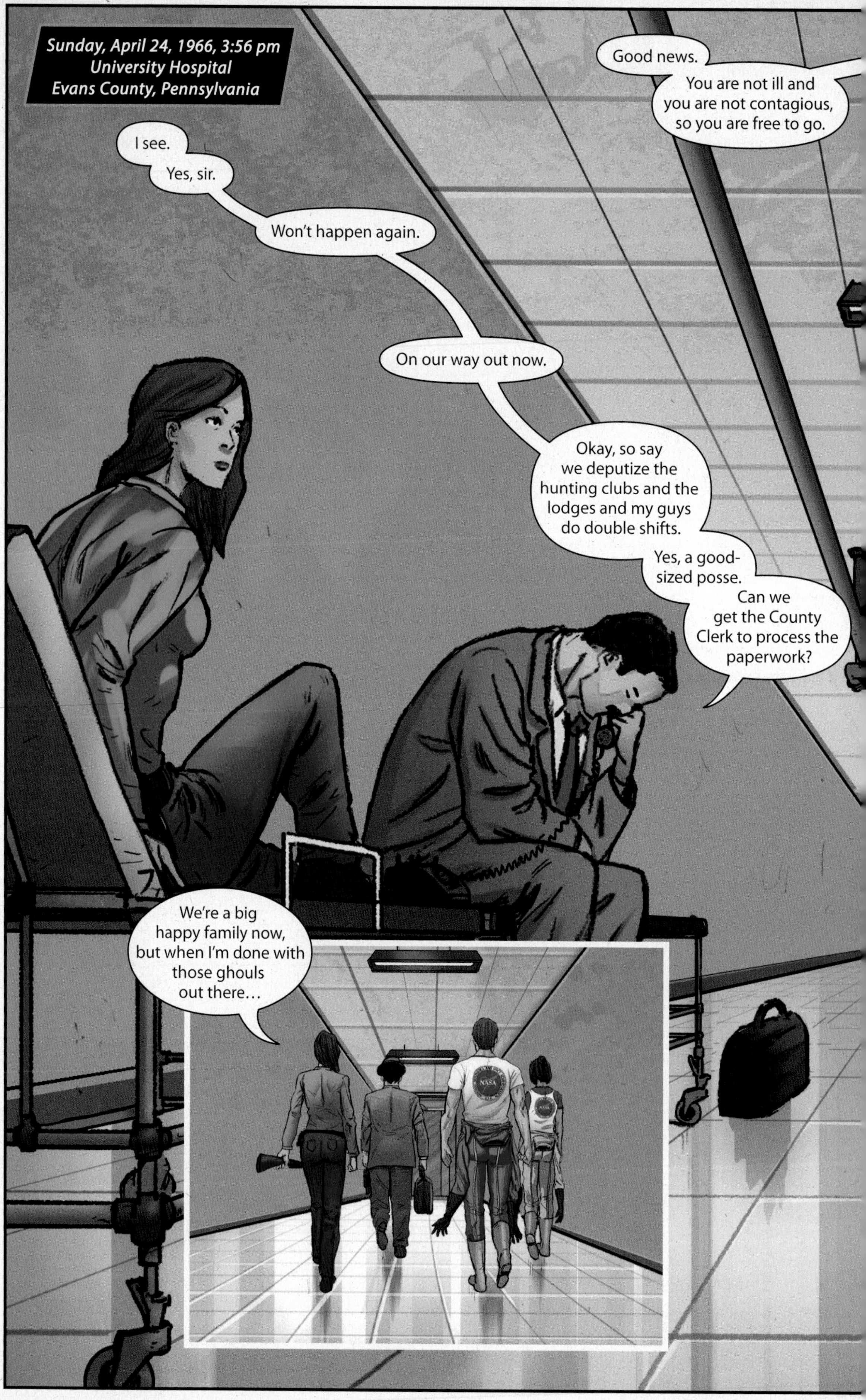
Sunday, April 24, 1966, 3:56 pm
University Hospital
Evans County, Pennsylvania
Good news.
You are not ill and you are not contagious, so you are free to go.
I see.
Yes, sir.
Won't happen again.
On our way out now.
Okay, so say we deputize the hunting clubs and the lodges and my guys do double shifts.
Yes, a good-sized posse.
Can we get the County Clerk to process the paperwork?
We're a big happy family now, but when I'm done with those ghouls out there…
NASA

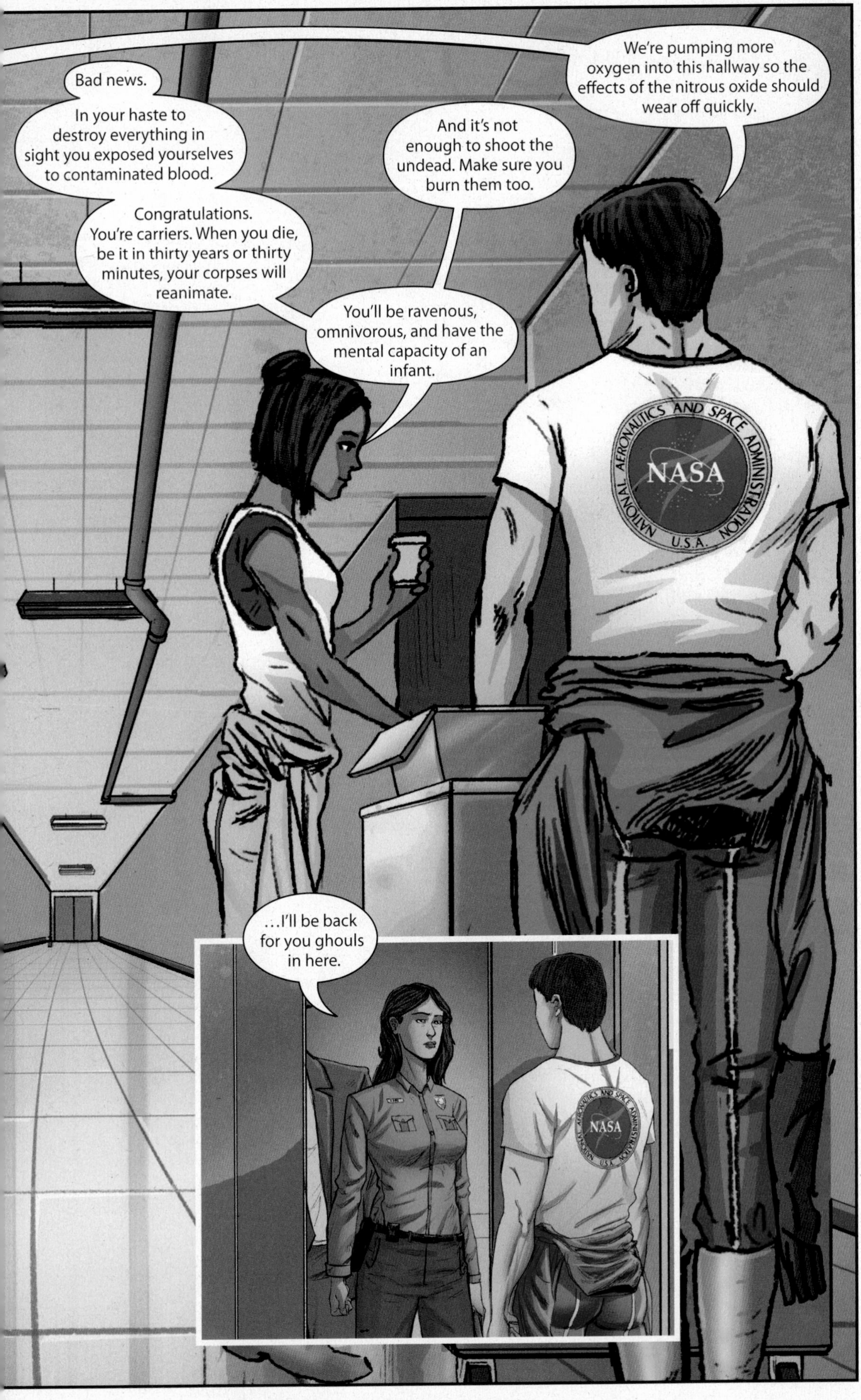
We're pumping more oxygen into this hallway so the effects of the nitrous oxide should wear off quickly.
Bad news.
In your haste to destroy everything in sight you exposed yourselves to contaminated blood.
Congratulations. You're carriers. When you die, be it in thirty years or thirty minutes, your corpses will reanimate.
You'll be ravenous, omnivorous, and have the mental capacity of an infant.
And it's not enough to shoot the undead. Make sure you burn them too.
NATIONAL AERONAUTICS AND SPACE ADMINISTRATION
NASA
U.S.A.
...I'll be back for you ghouls in here.

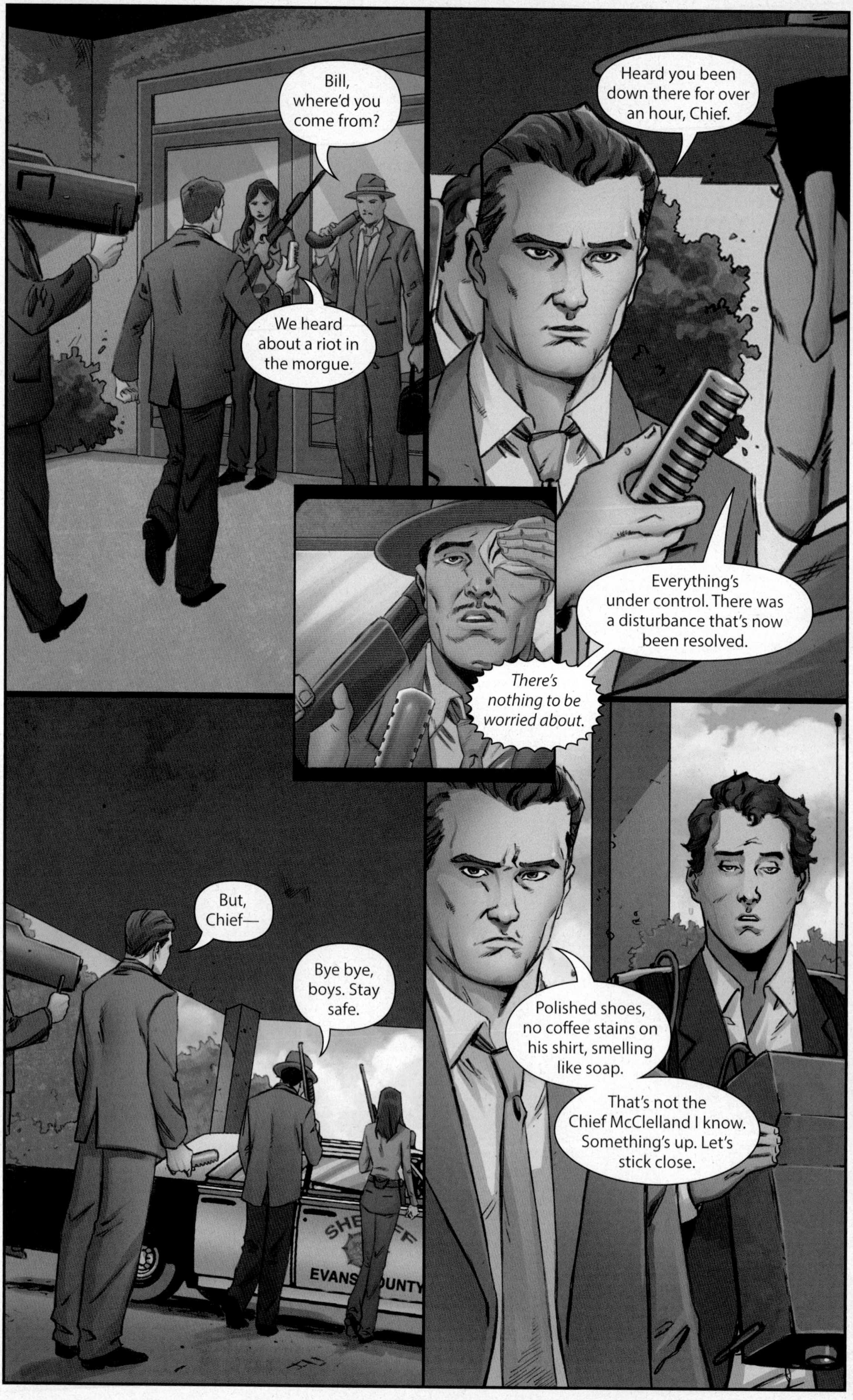
Bill, where'd you come from?
We heard about a riot in the morgue.
Heard you been down there for over an hour, Chief.
Everything's under control. There was a disturbance that's now been resolved.
There's nothing to be worried about.
But, Chief—
Bye bye, boys. Stay safe.
Polished shoes, no coffee stains on his shirt, smelling like soap.
That's not the Chief McClelland I know. Something's up. Let's stick close.
SHERIFF
EVANS COUNTY

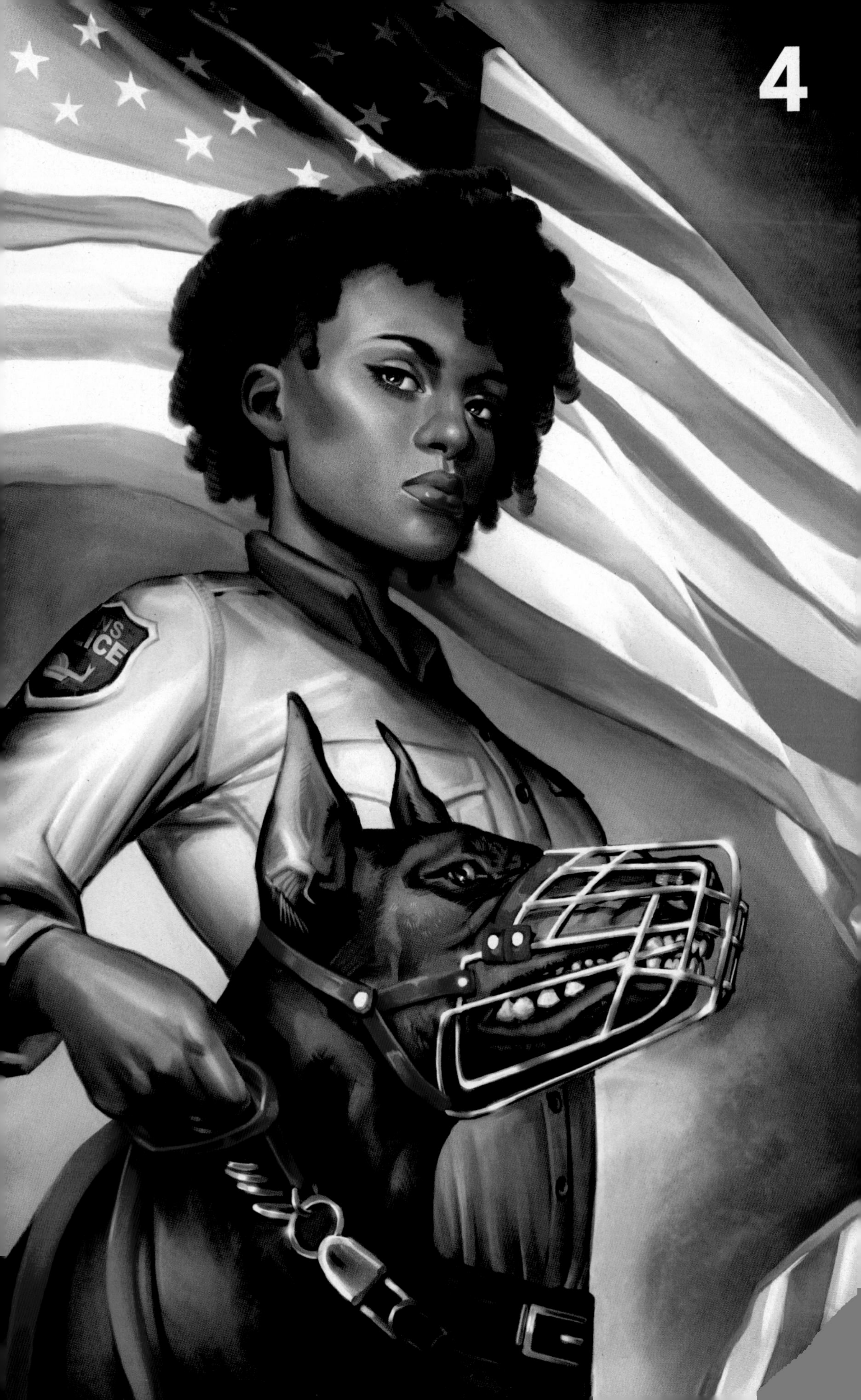
4

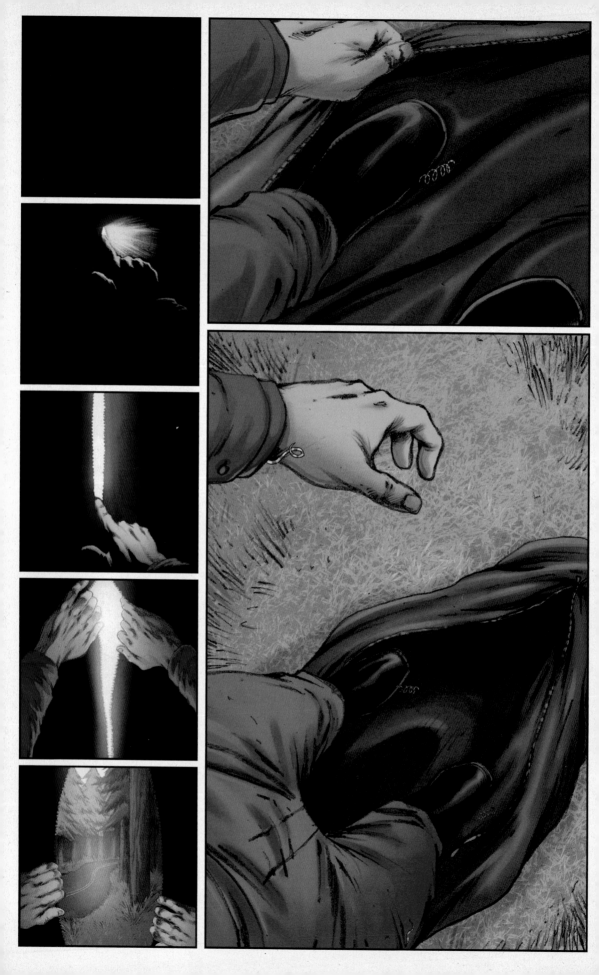

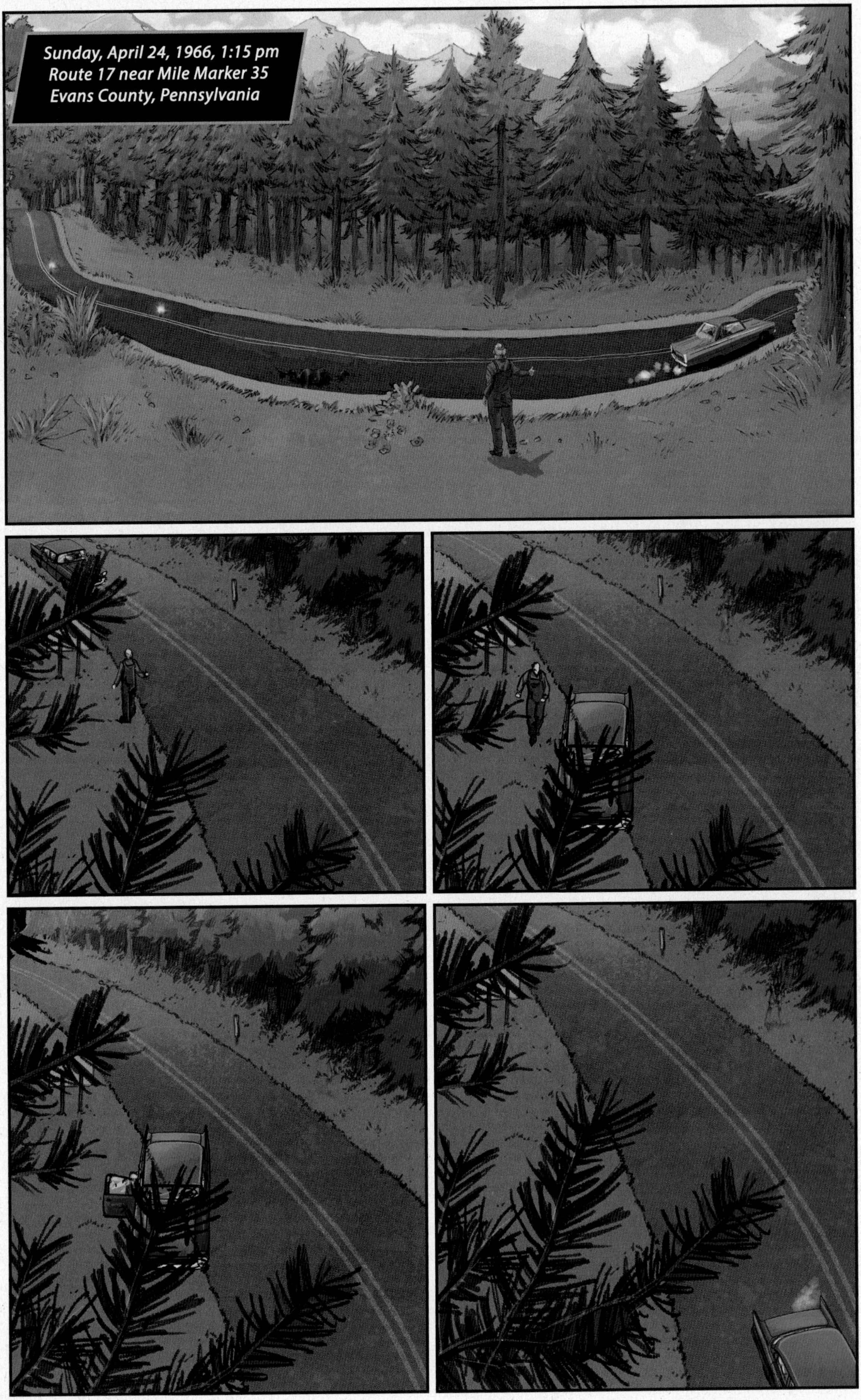
Sunday, April 24, 1966, 1:15 pm
Route 17 near Mile Marker 35
Evans County, Pennsylvania

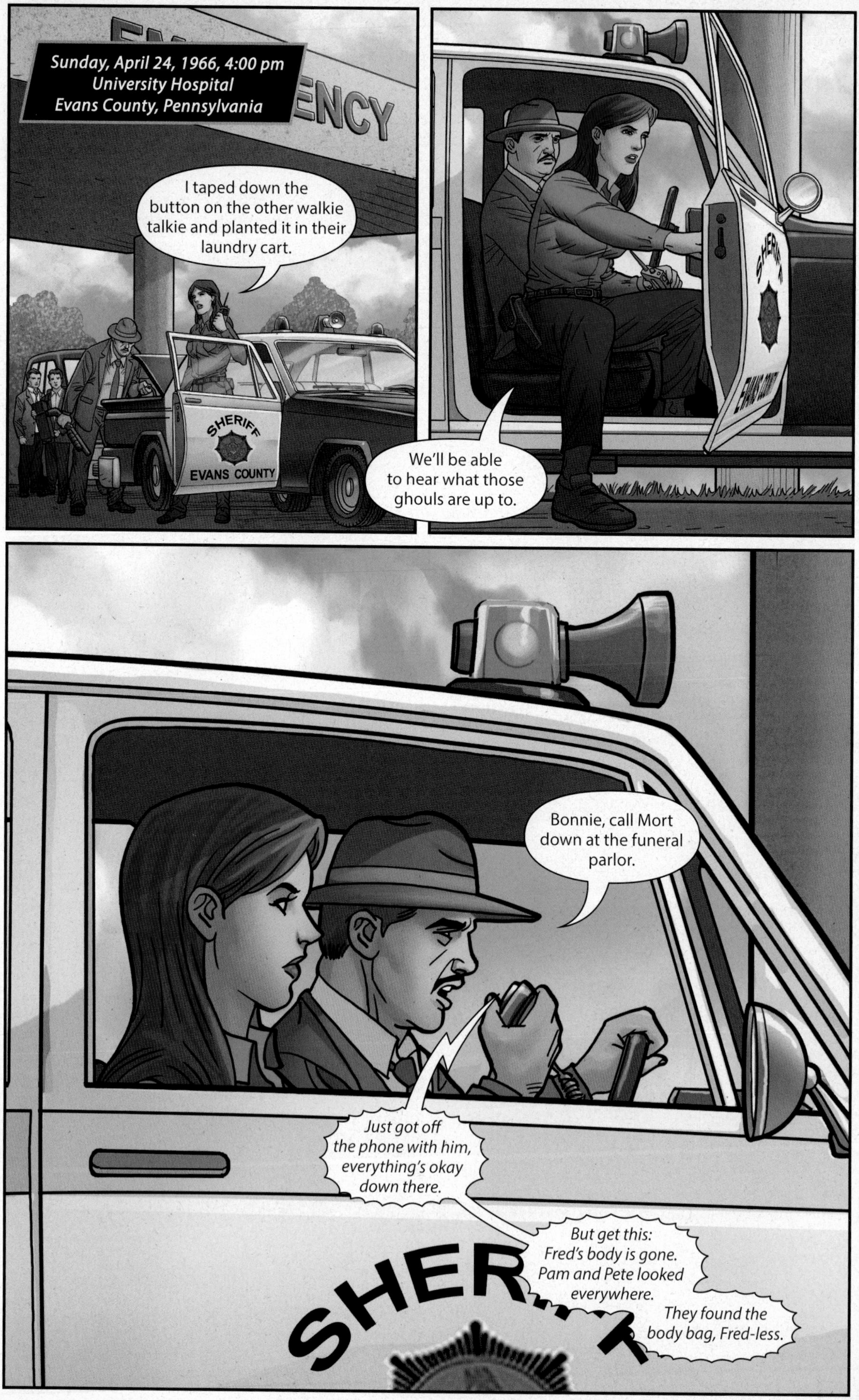
Sunday, April 24, 1966, 4:00 pm
University Hospital
Evans County, Pennsylvania
ENCY
I taped down the button on the other walkie talkie and planted it in their laundry cart.
SHERIFF
EVANS COUNTY
We'll be able to hear what those ghouls are up to.
SHERIFF
EVANS COUNTY
Bonnie, call Mort down at the funeral parlor.
Just got off the phone with him, everything's okay down there.
But get this: Fred's body is gone. Pam and Pete looked everywhere.
They found the body bag, Fred-less.
SHER

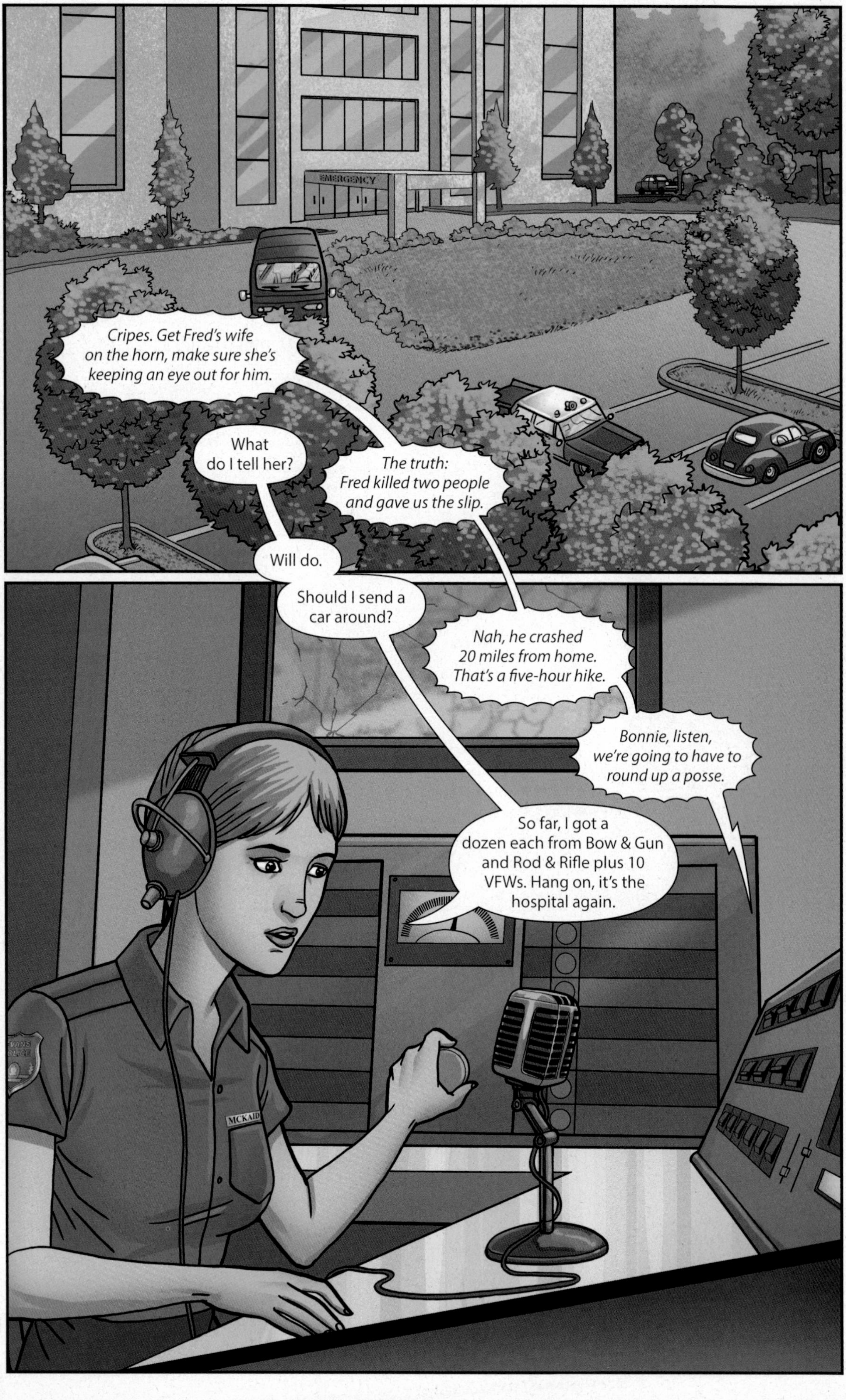
EMERGENCY
Cripes. Get Fred's wife on the horn, make sure she's keeping an eye out for him.
What do I tell her?
The truth: Fred killed two people and gave us the slip.
Will do.
Should I send a car around?
Nah, he crashed 20 miles from home. That's a five-hour hike.
Bonnie, listen, we're going to have to round up a posse.
So far, I got a dozen each from Bow & Gun and Rod & Rifle plus 10 VFWs. Hang on, it's the hospital again.
MCKAID

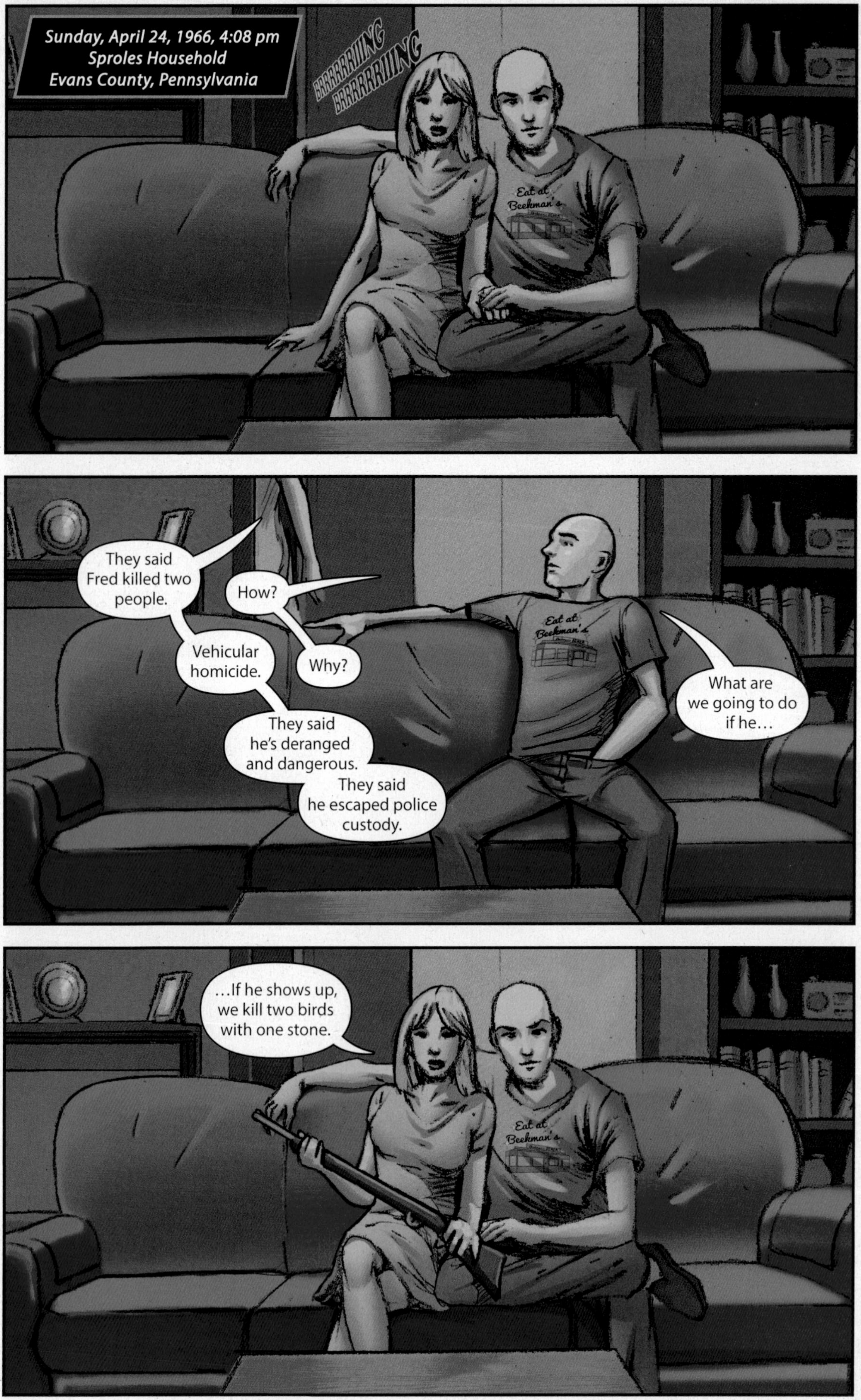
Sunday, April 24, 1966, 4:08 pm
Sproles Household
Evans County, Pennsylvania
BRRRRRRIIING
BRRRRRRIIING
Eat at Beekman's
They said Fred killed two people.
How?
Vehicular homicide.
Why?
They said he's deranged and dangerous.
They said he escaped police custody.
What are we going to do if he…
…If he shows up, we kill two birds with one stone.

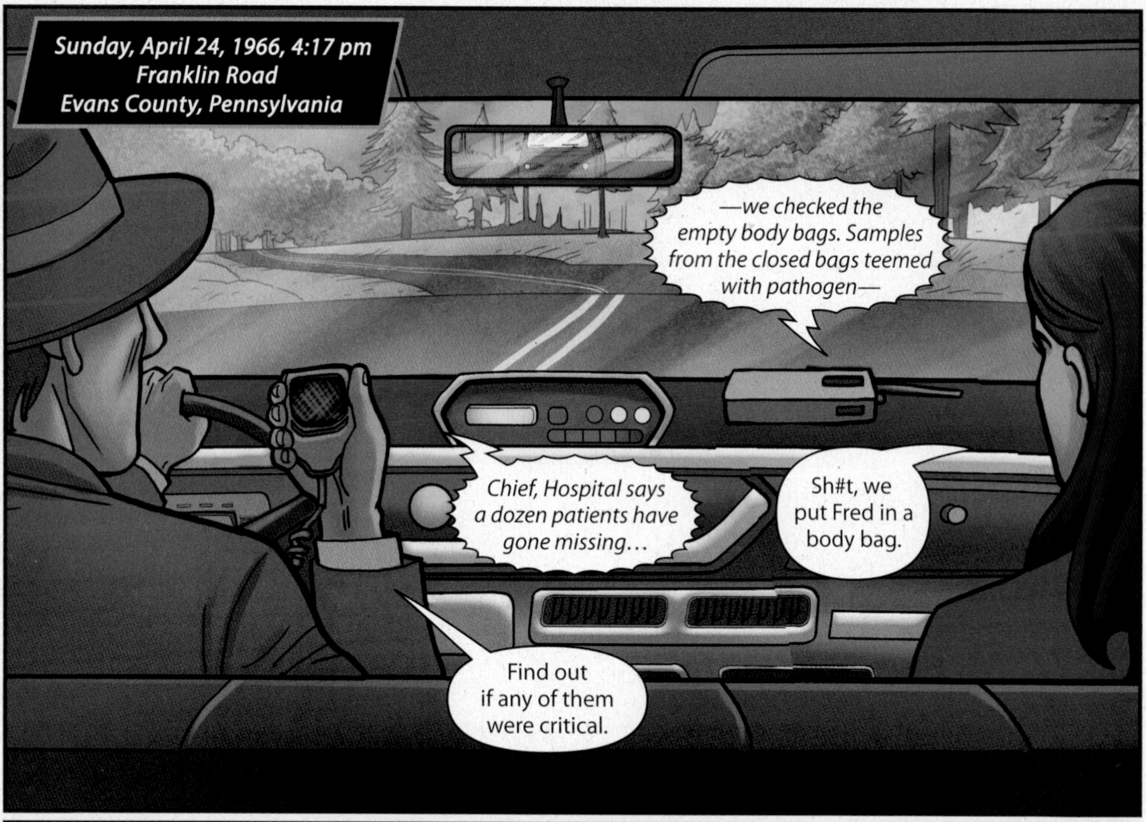
Sunday, April 24, 1966, 4:17 pm
Franklin Road
Evans County, Pennsylvania
—we checked the empty body bags. Samples from the closed bags teemed with pathogen—
Chief, Hospital says a dozen patients have gone missing…
Sh#t, we put Fred in a body bag.
Find out if any of them were critical.

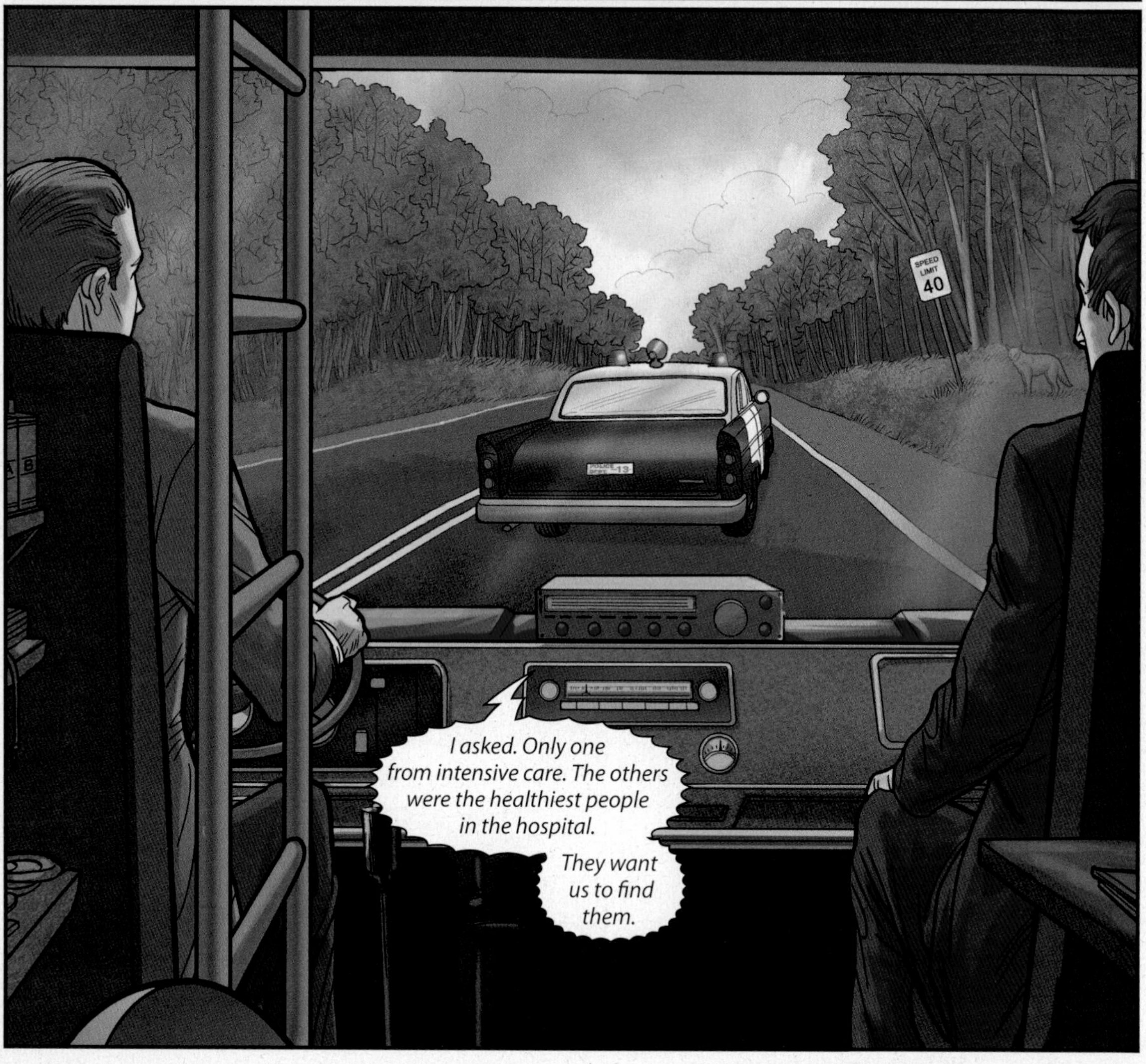
SPEED LIMIT 40
I asked. Only one from intensive care. The others were the healthiest people in the hospital.
They want us to find them.

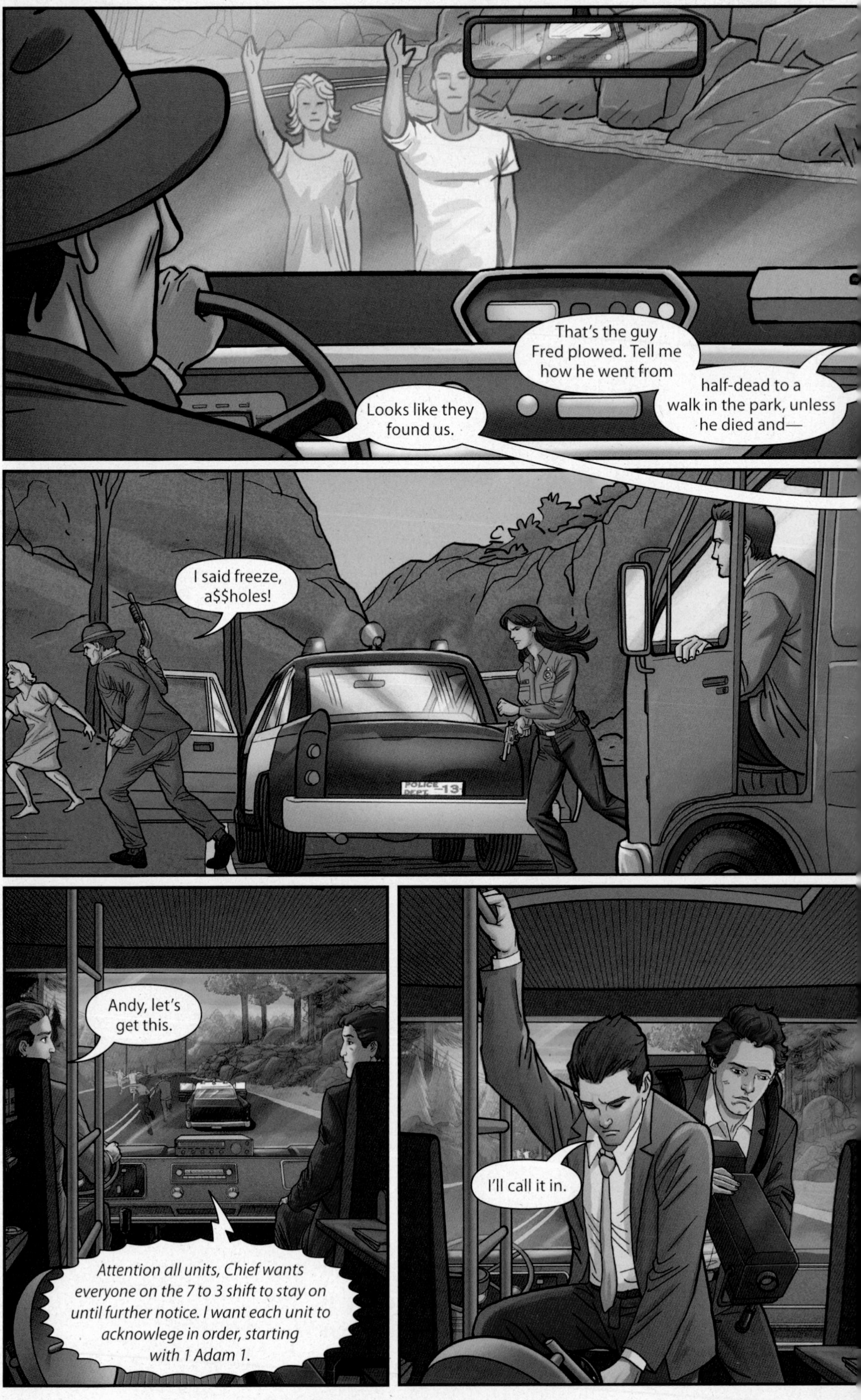
That's the guy Fred plowed. Tell me how he went from
half-dead to a walk in the park, unless he died and—
Looks like they found us.
I said freeze, a$$holes!
Andy, let's get this.
Attention all units, Chief wants everyone on the 7 to 3 shift to stay on until further notice. I want each unit to acknowlege in order, starting with 1 Adam 1.
I'll call it in.
POLICE DEPT. 13

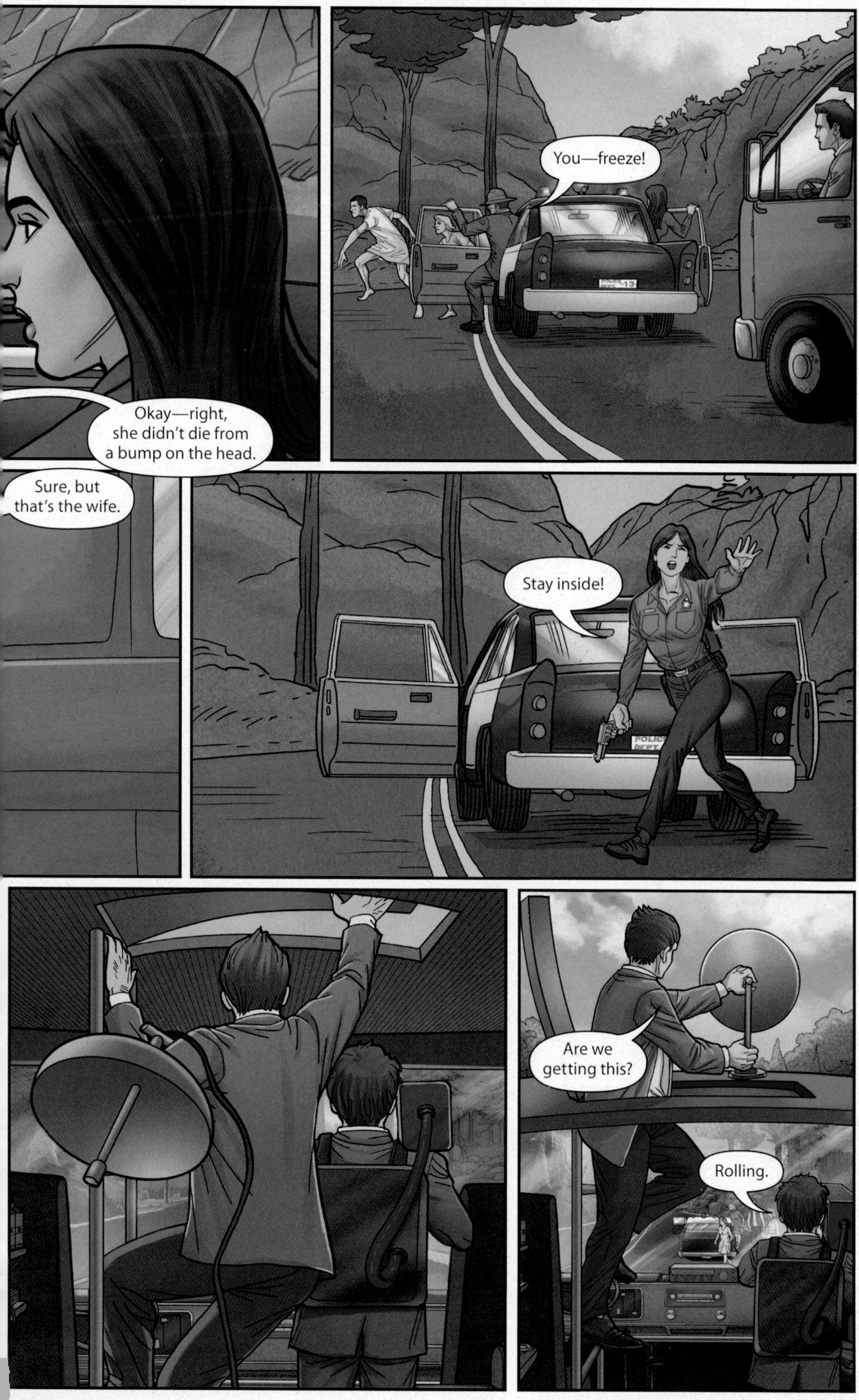
Okay—right,
she didn't die from
a bump on the head.
You—freeze!
Sure, but
that's the wife.
Stay inside!
Are we
getting this?
Rolling.

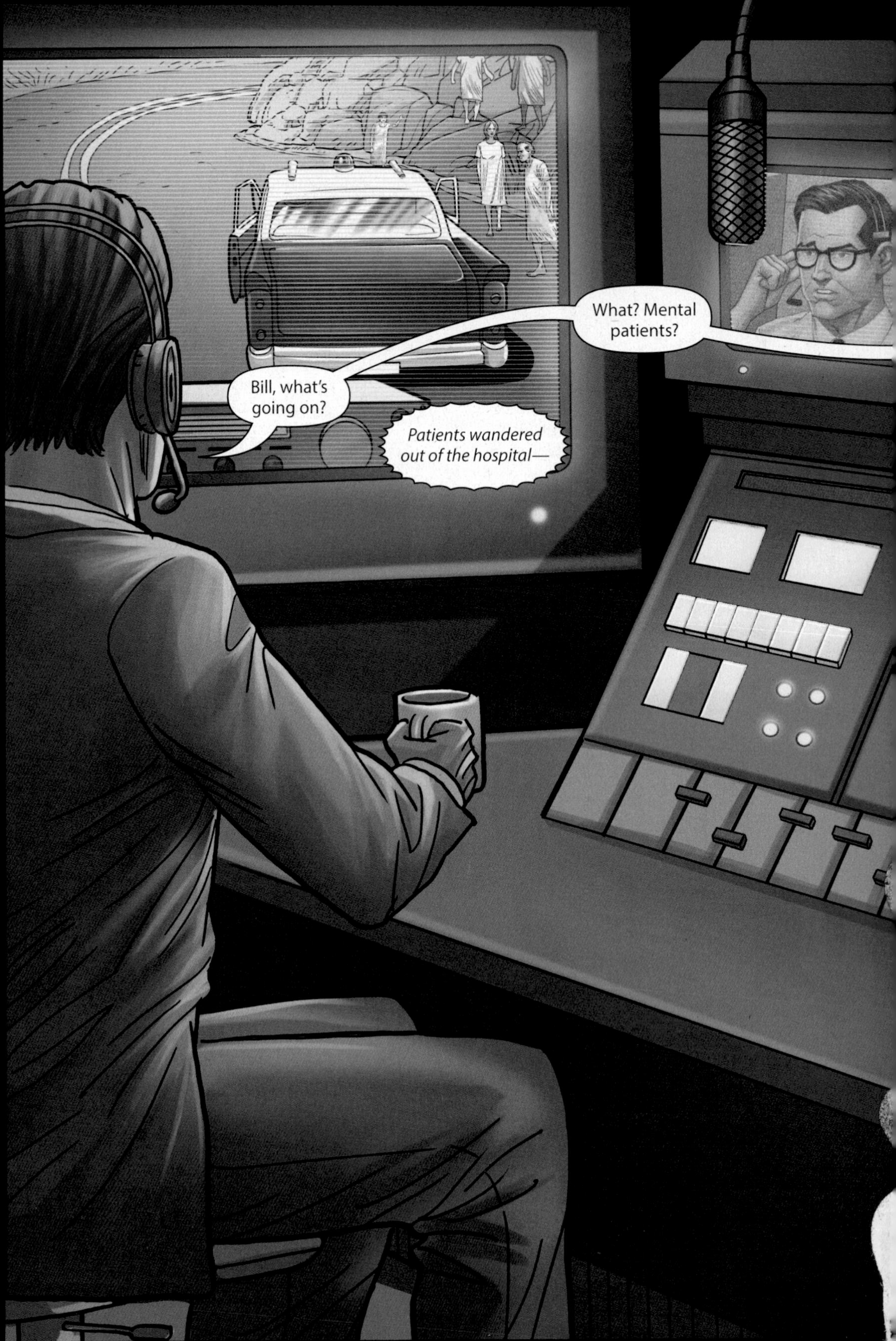
Bill, what's going on?
Patients wandered out of the hospital—
What? Mental patients?

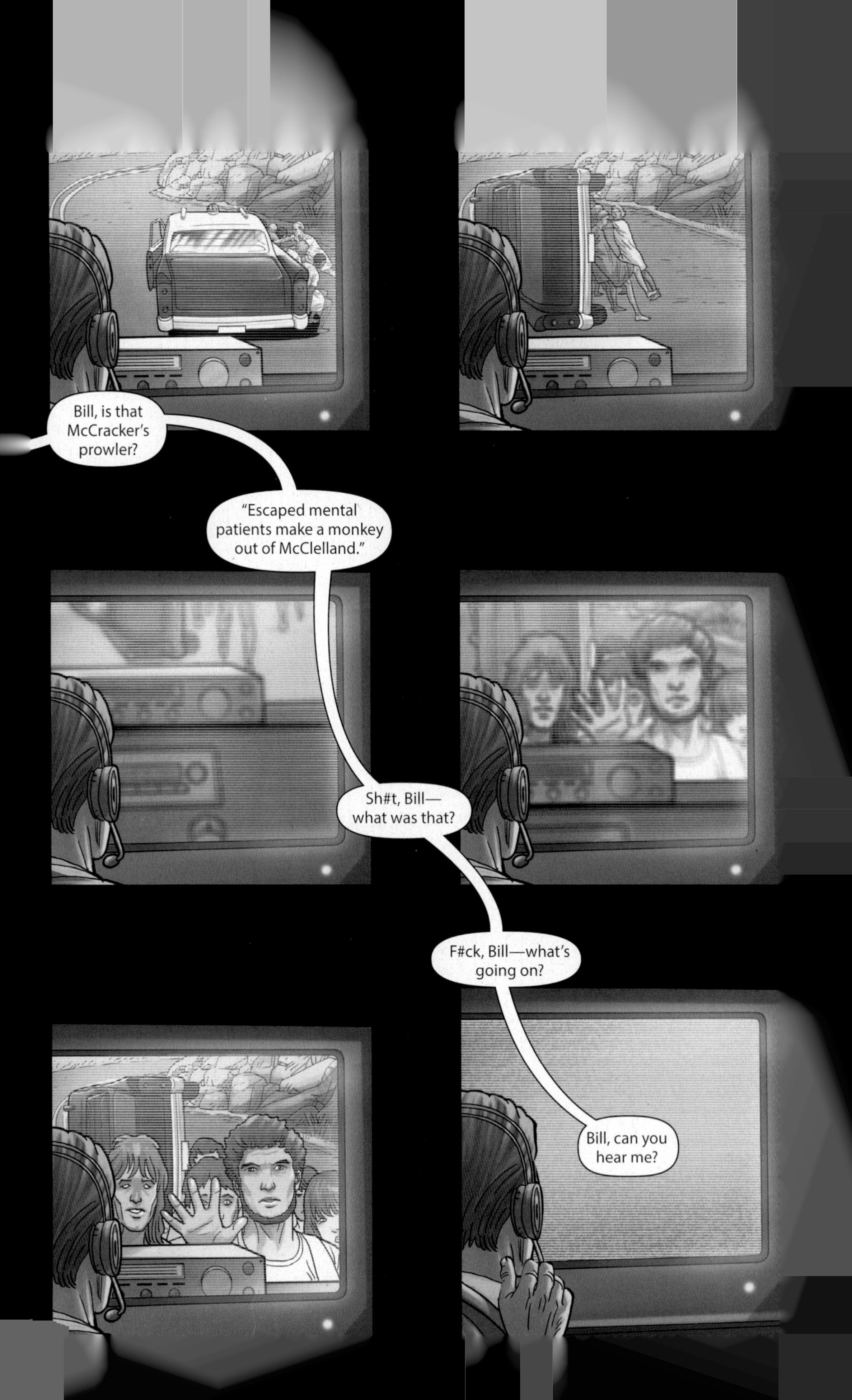

Bill, is that McCracker's prowler?
"Escaped mental patients make a monkey out of McClelland."
Sh#t, Bill—what was that?
F#ck, Bill—what's going on?
Bill, can you hear me?

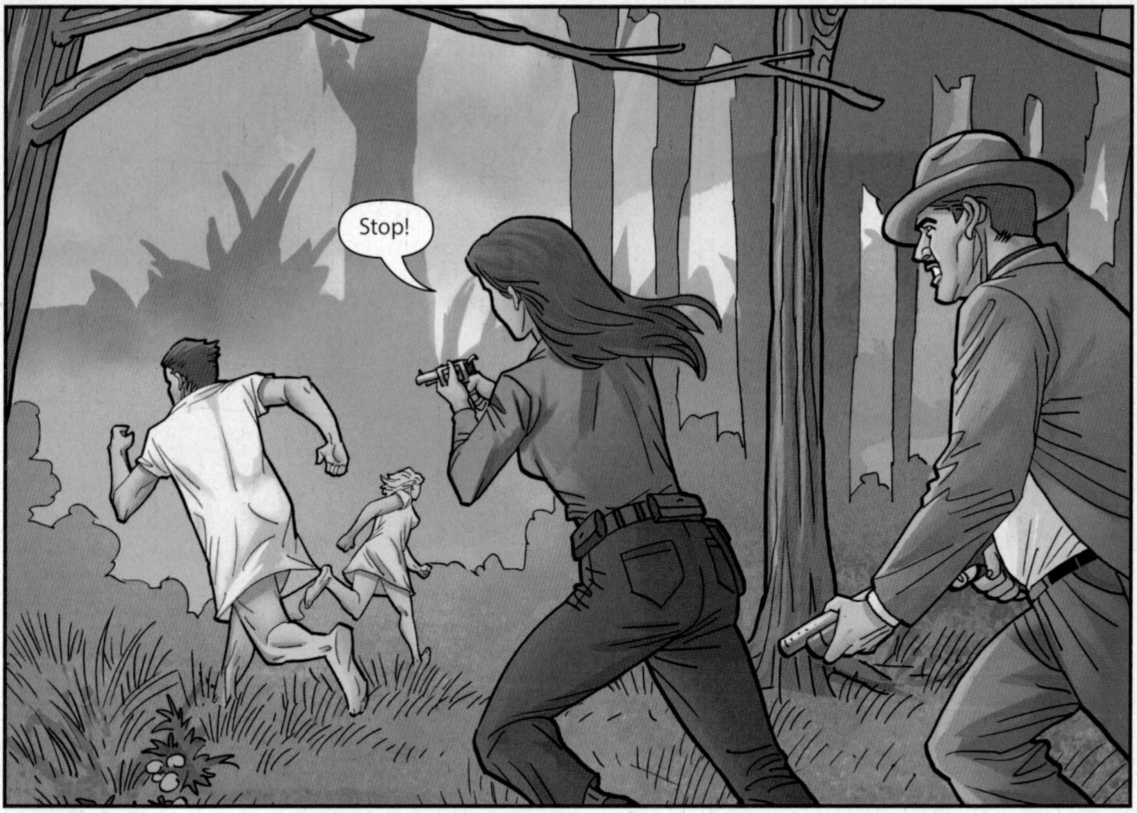
Stop!

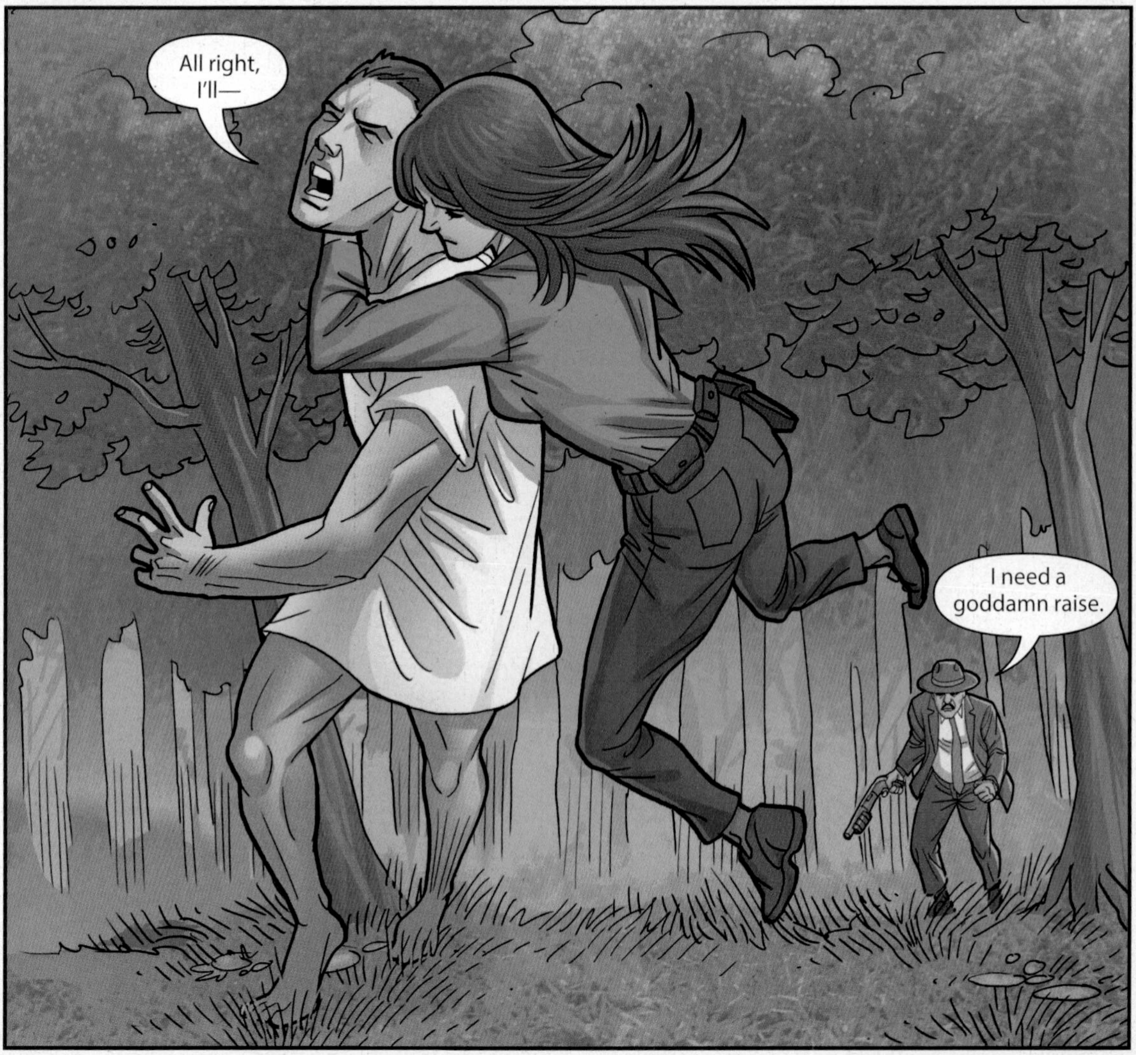
All right, I'll—
I need a goddamn raise.

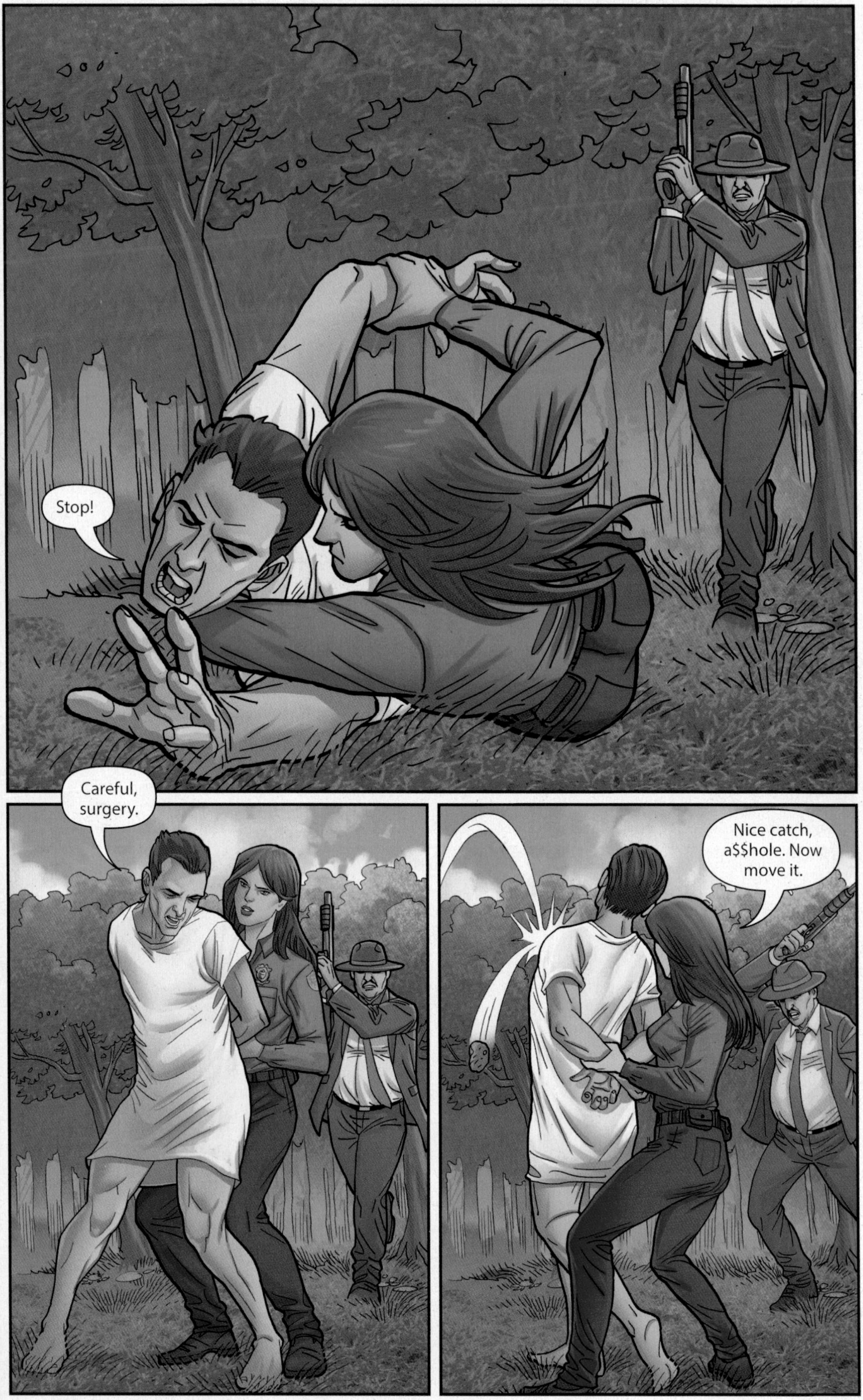

Stop!
Careful, surgery.
Nice catch, a$$hole. Now move it.

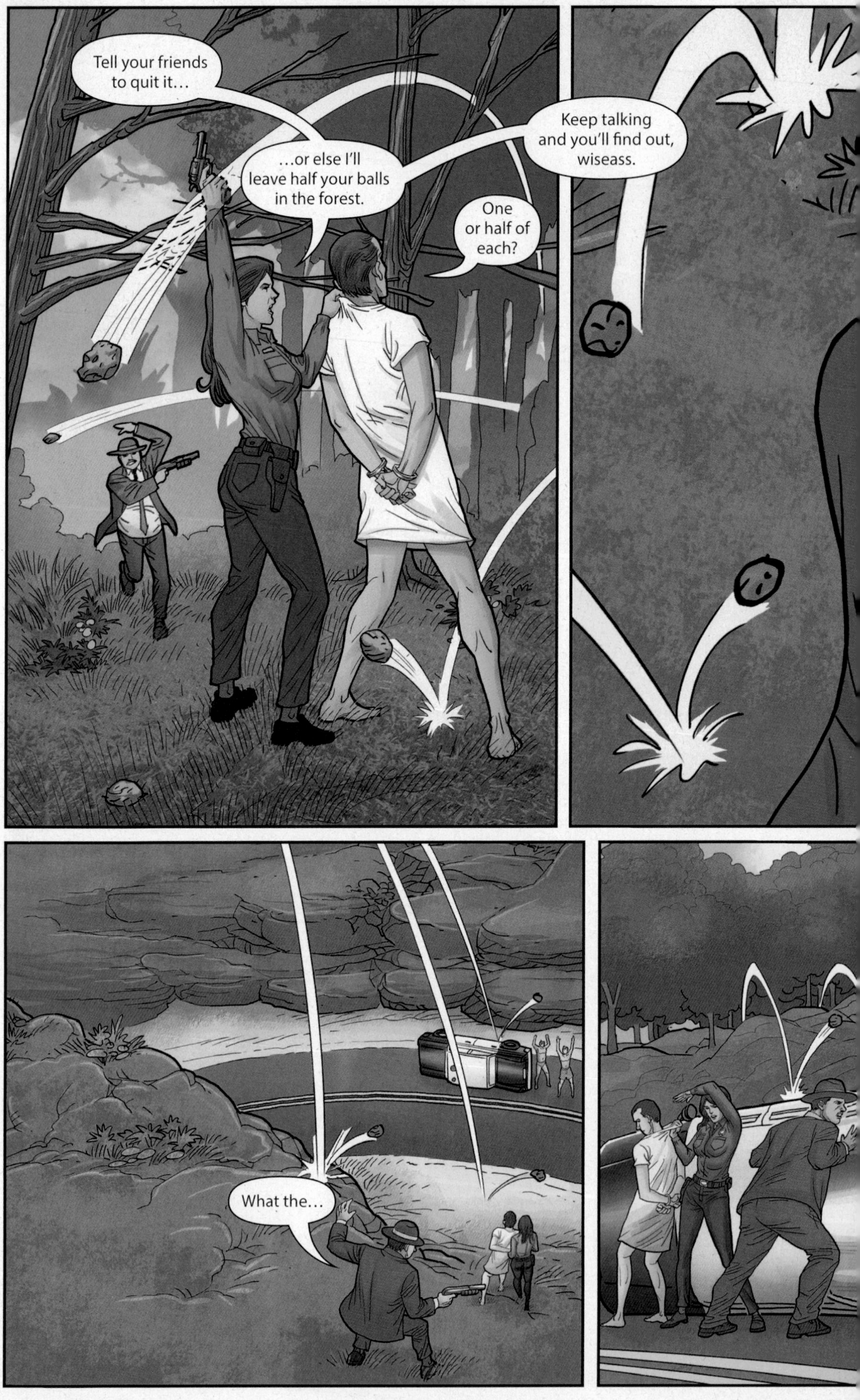
Tell your friends
to quit it…
…or else I'll
leave half your balls
in the forest.
Keep talking
and you'll find out,
wiseass.
One
or half of
each?
What the…

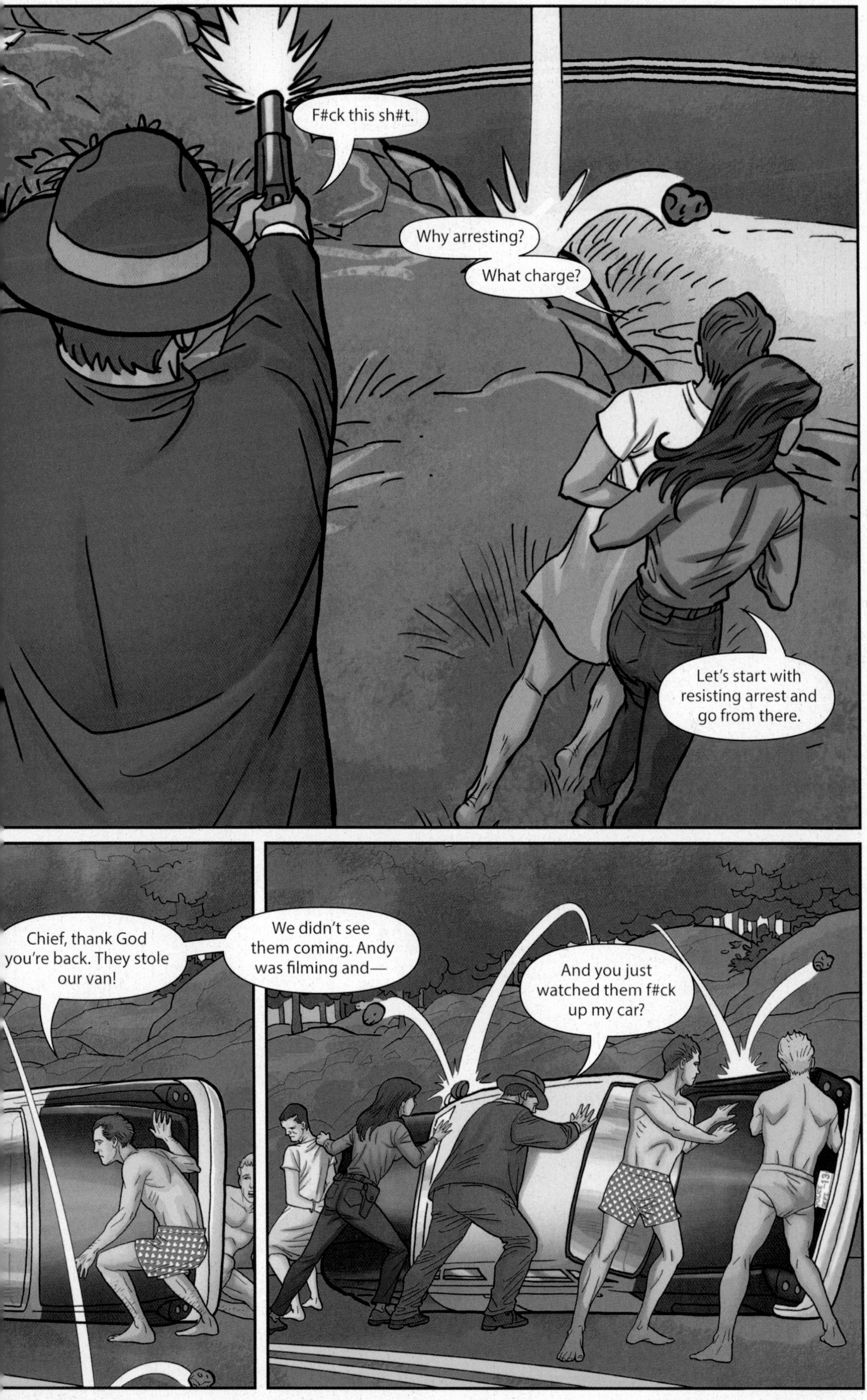
F#ck this sh#t.
Why arresting?
What charge?
Let's start with resisting arrest and go from there.
Chief, thank God you're back. They stole our van!
We didn't see them coming. Andy was filming and—
And you just watched them f#ck up my car?

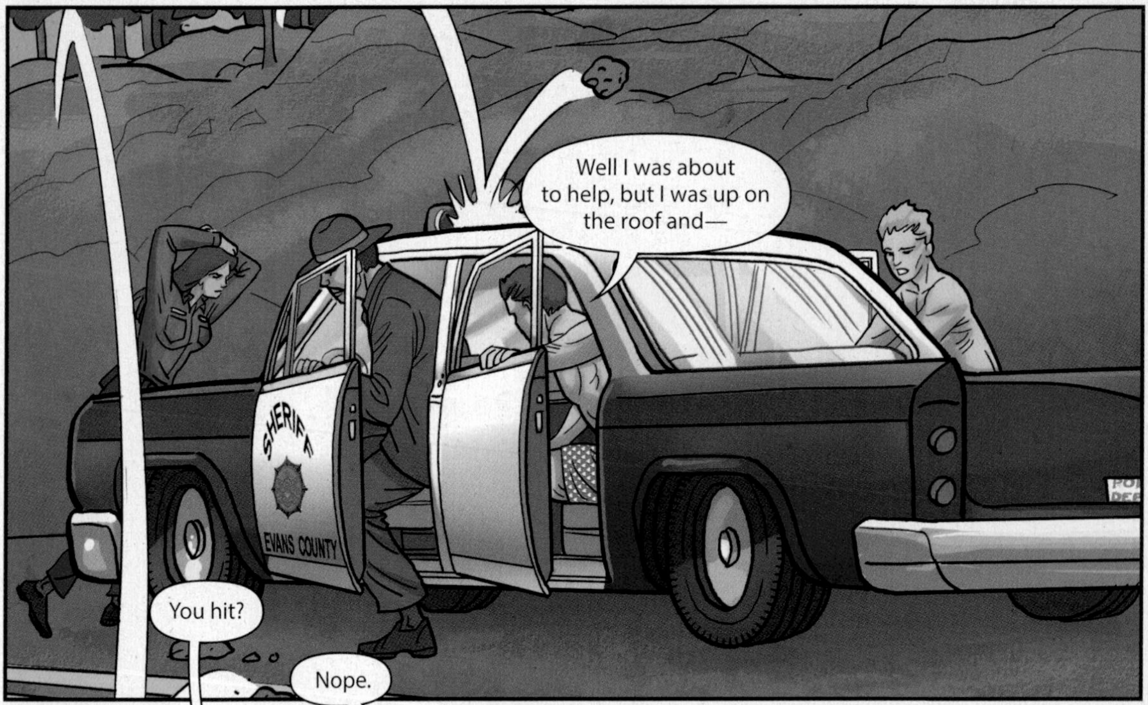
Well I was about
to help, but I was up on
the roof and—
You hit?
Nope.

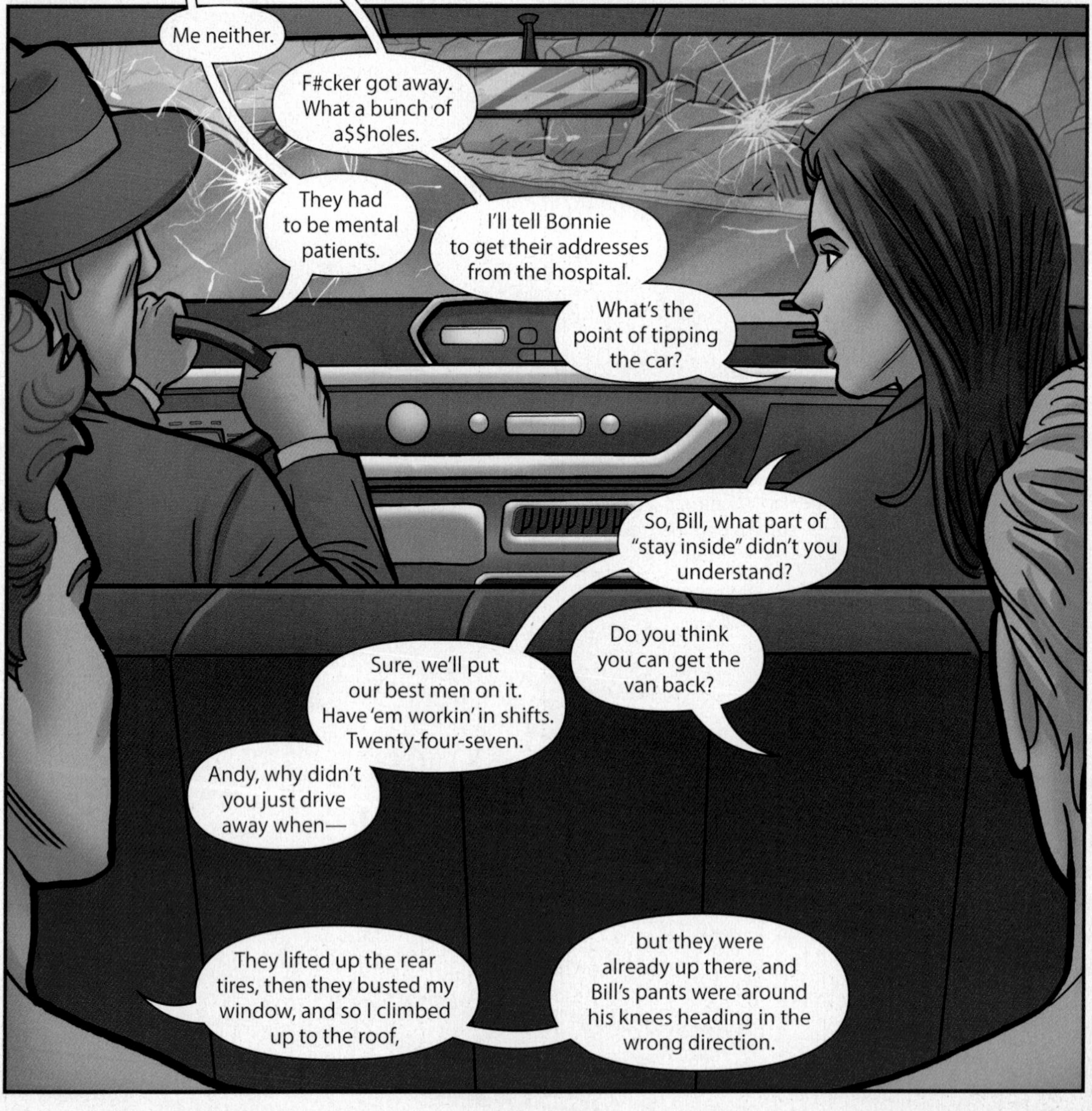
Me neither.
F#cker got away.
What a bunch of
a$$holes.
They had
to be mental
patients.
I'll tell Bonnie
to get their addresses
from the hospital.
What's the
point of tipping
the car?
So, Bill, what part of
"stay inside" didn't you
understand?
Do you think
you can get the
van back?
Sure, we'll put
our best men on it.
Have 'em workin' in shifts.
Twenty-four-seven.
Andy, why didn't
you just drive
away when—
They lifted up the rear
tires, then they busted my
window, and so I climbed
up to the roof,
but they were
already up there, and
Bill's pants were around
his knees heading in the
wrong direction.

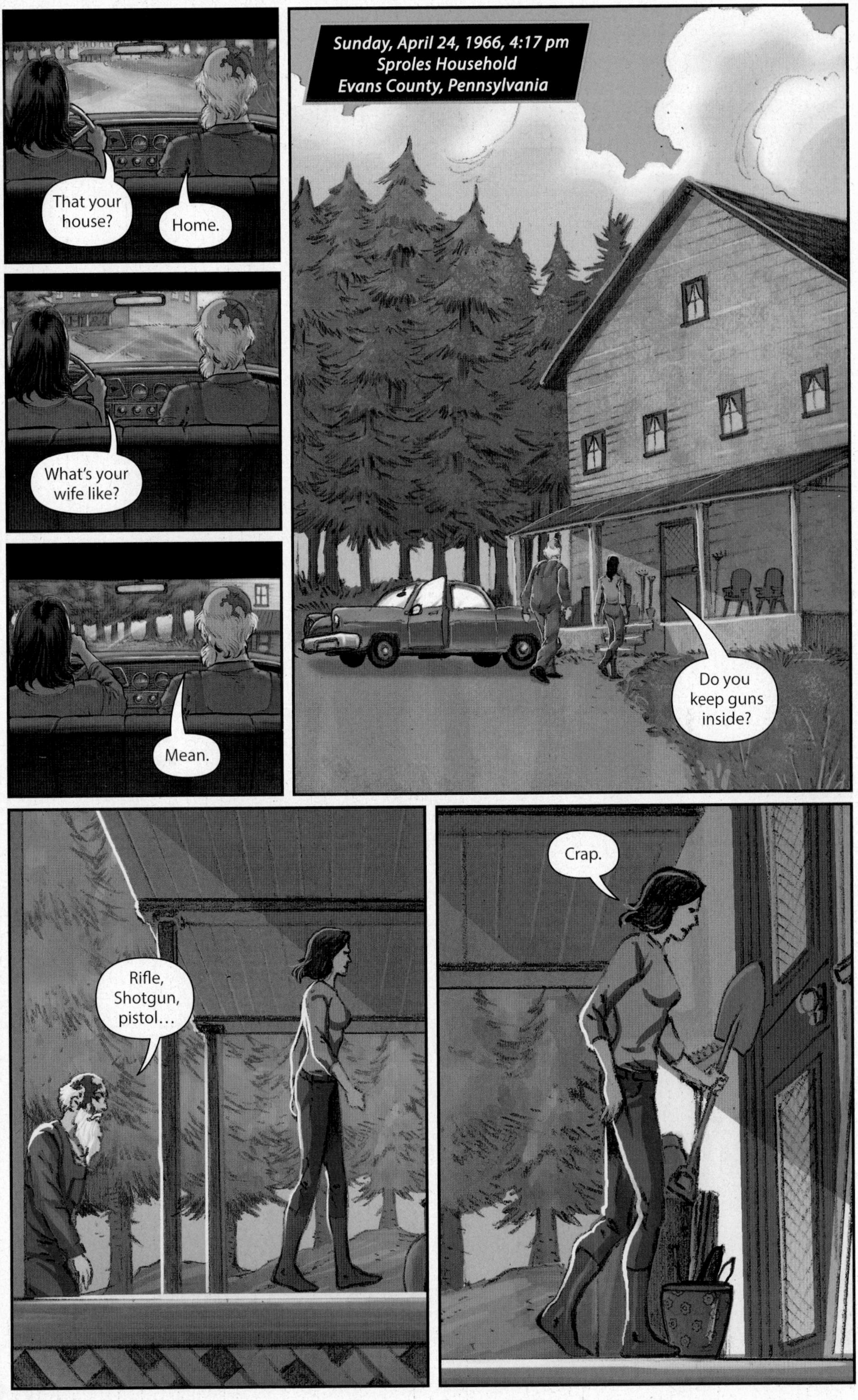
That your house?
Home.
What's your wife like?
Mean.
Sunday, April 24, 1966, 4:17 pm
Sproles Household
Evans County, Pennsylvania
Do you keep guns inside?
Rifle, Shotgun, pistol…
Crap.

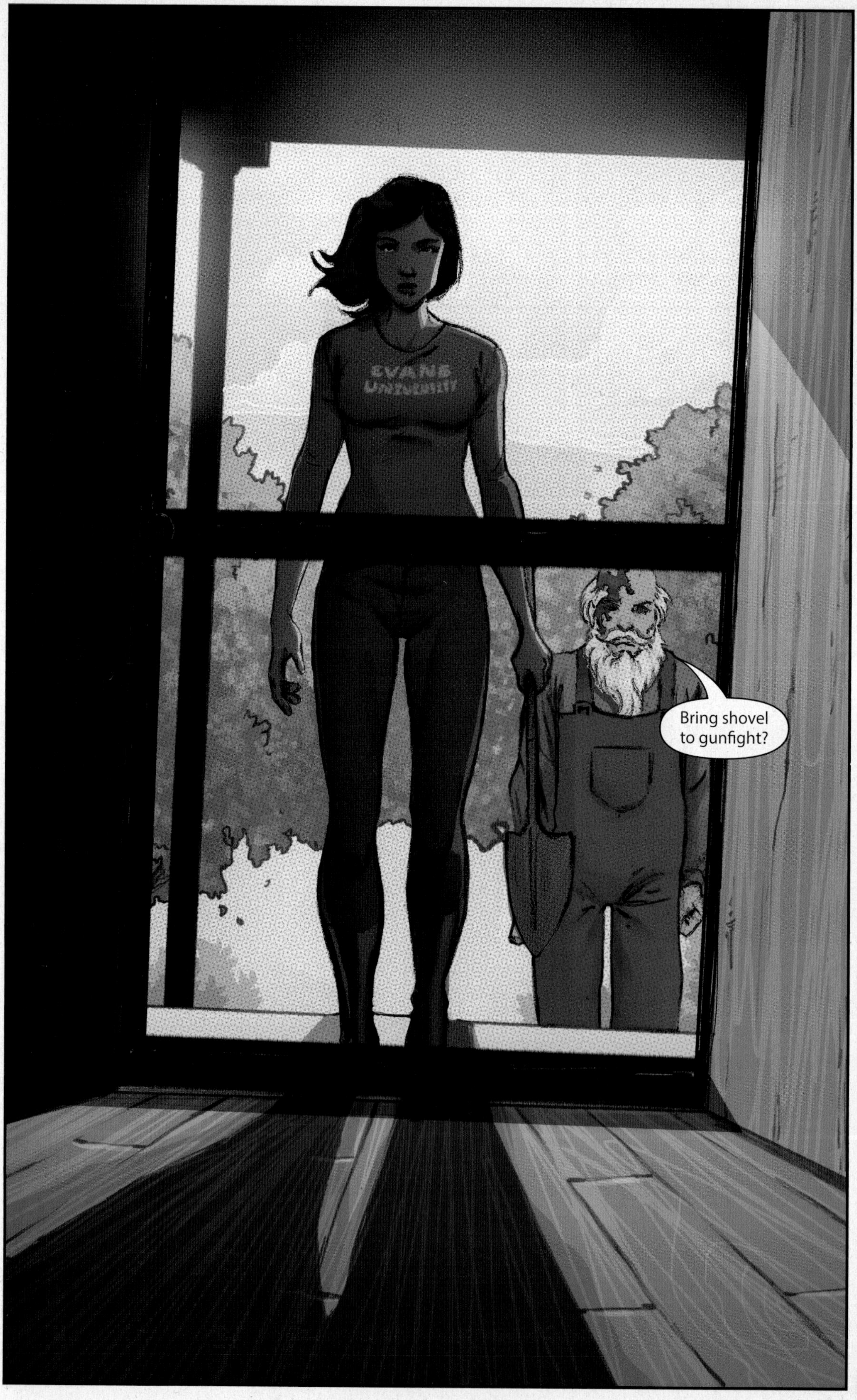
Bring shovel to gunfight?

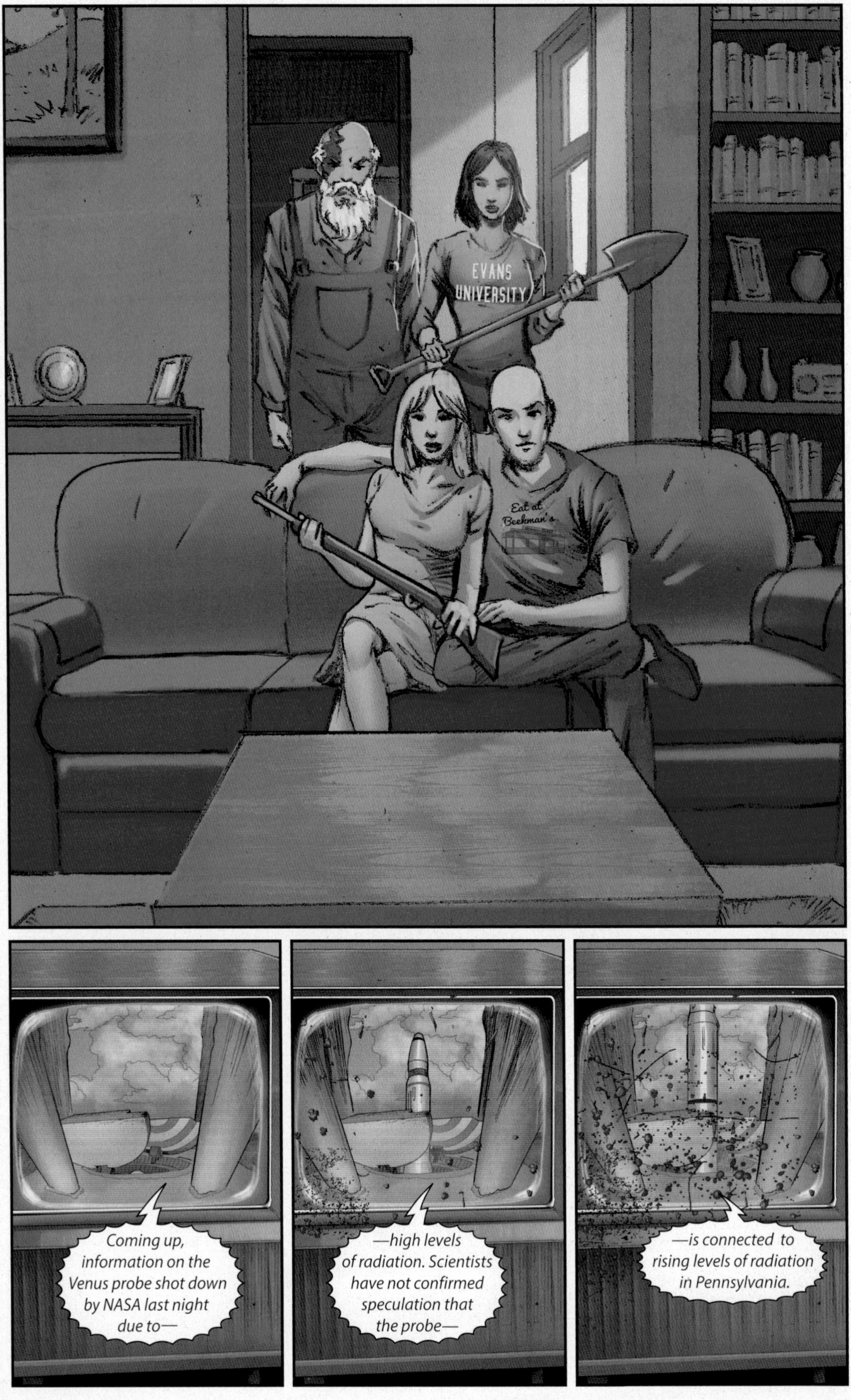
EVANS UNIVERSITY
Eat at Beekman's
Coming up, information on the Venus probe shot down by NASA last night due to—
—high levels of radiation. Scientists have not confirmed speculation that the probe—
—is connected to rising levels of radiation in Pennsylvania.

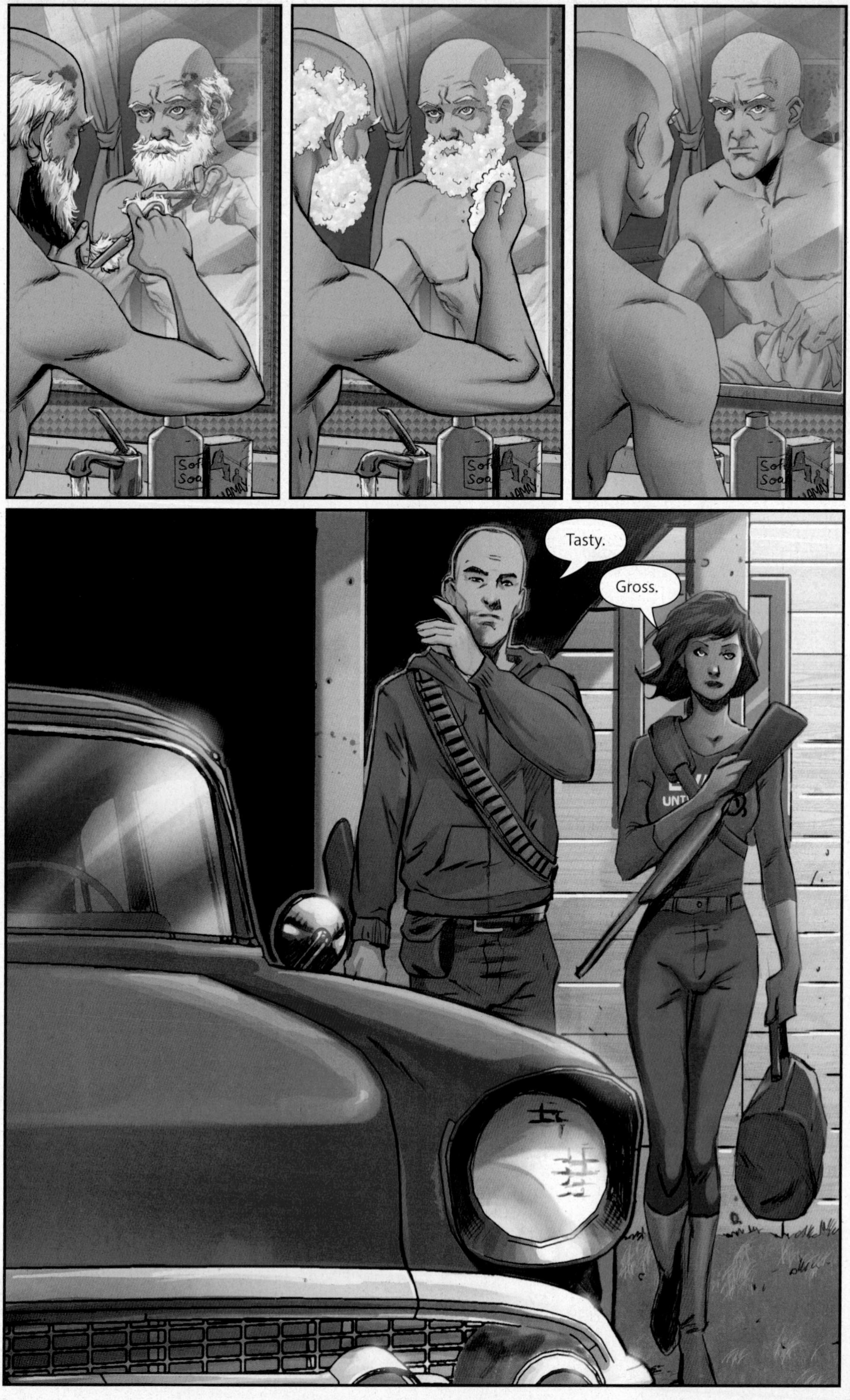
Tasty.
Gross.

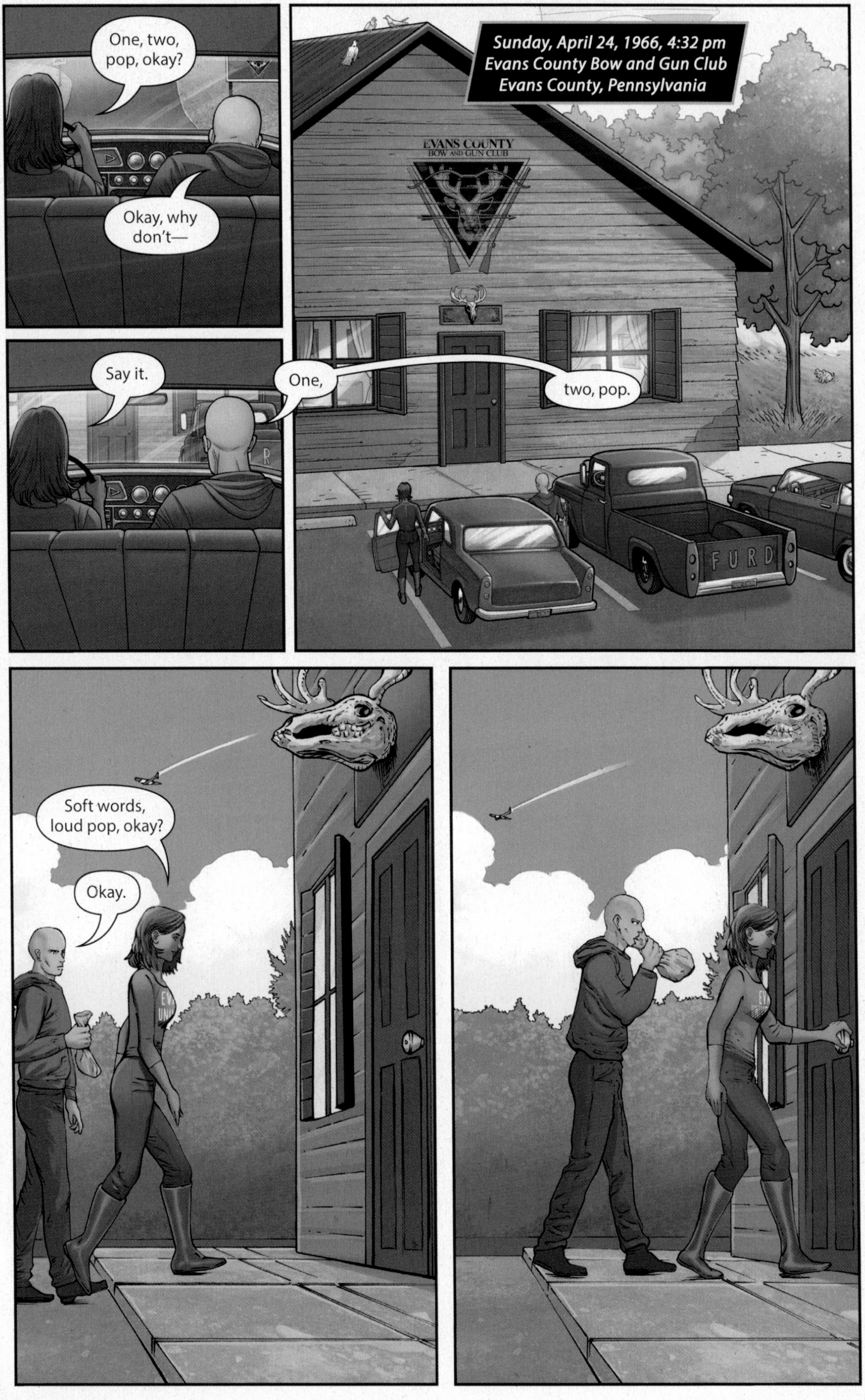
One, two, pop, okay?
Okay, why don't—
Sunday, April 24, 1966, 4:32 pm
Evans County Bow and Gun Club
Evans County, Pennsylvania
EVANS COUNTY
BOW AND GUN CLUB
Say it.
One,
two, pop.
FURD
Soft words, loud pop, okay?
Okay.

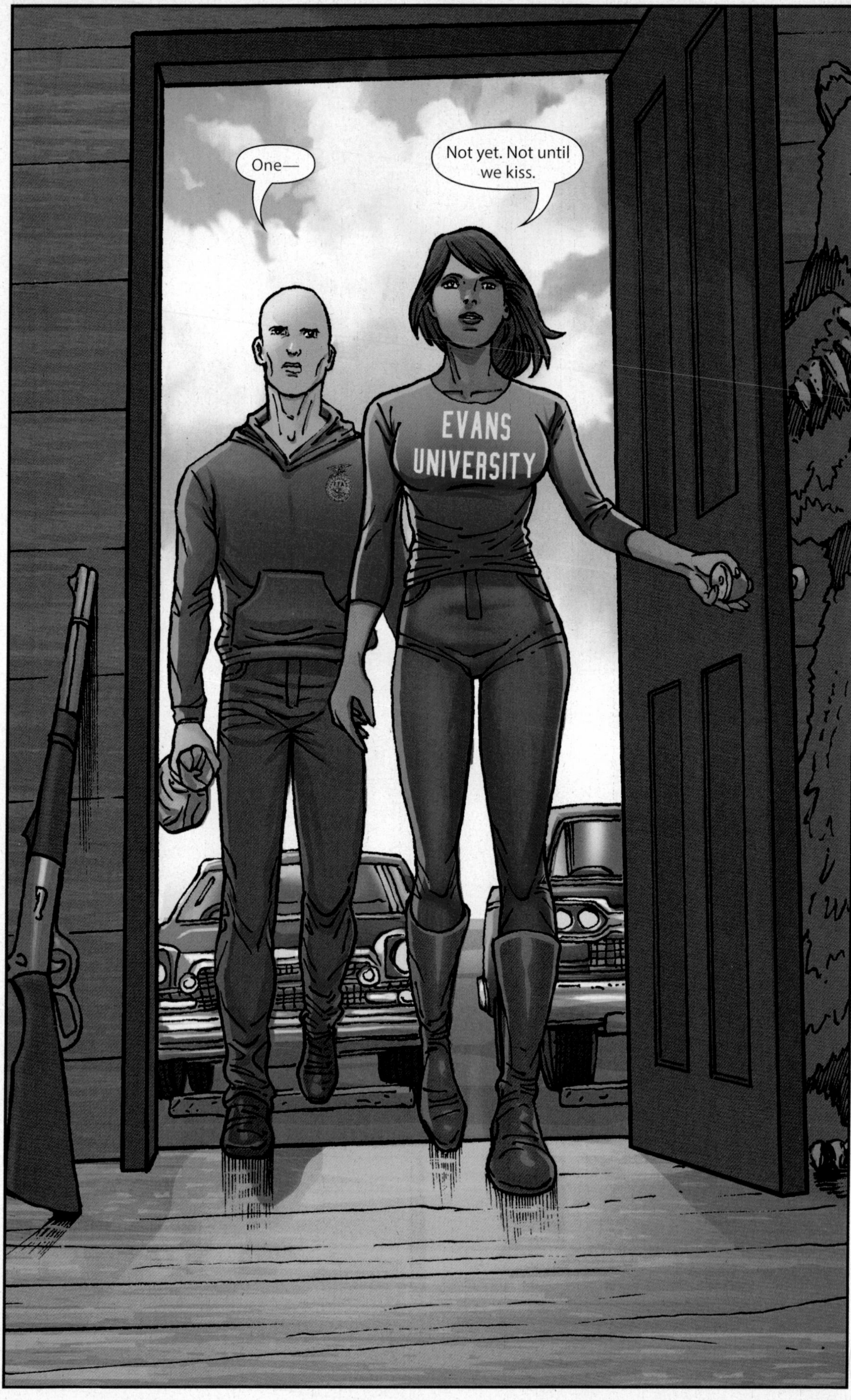
One—
Not yet. Not until we kiss.
EVANS UNIVERSITY

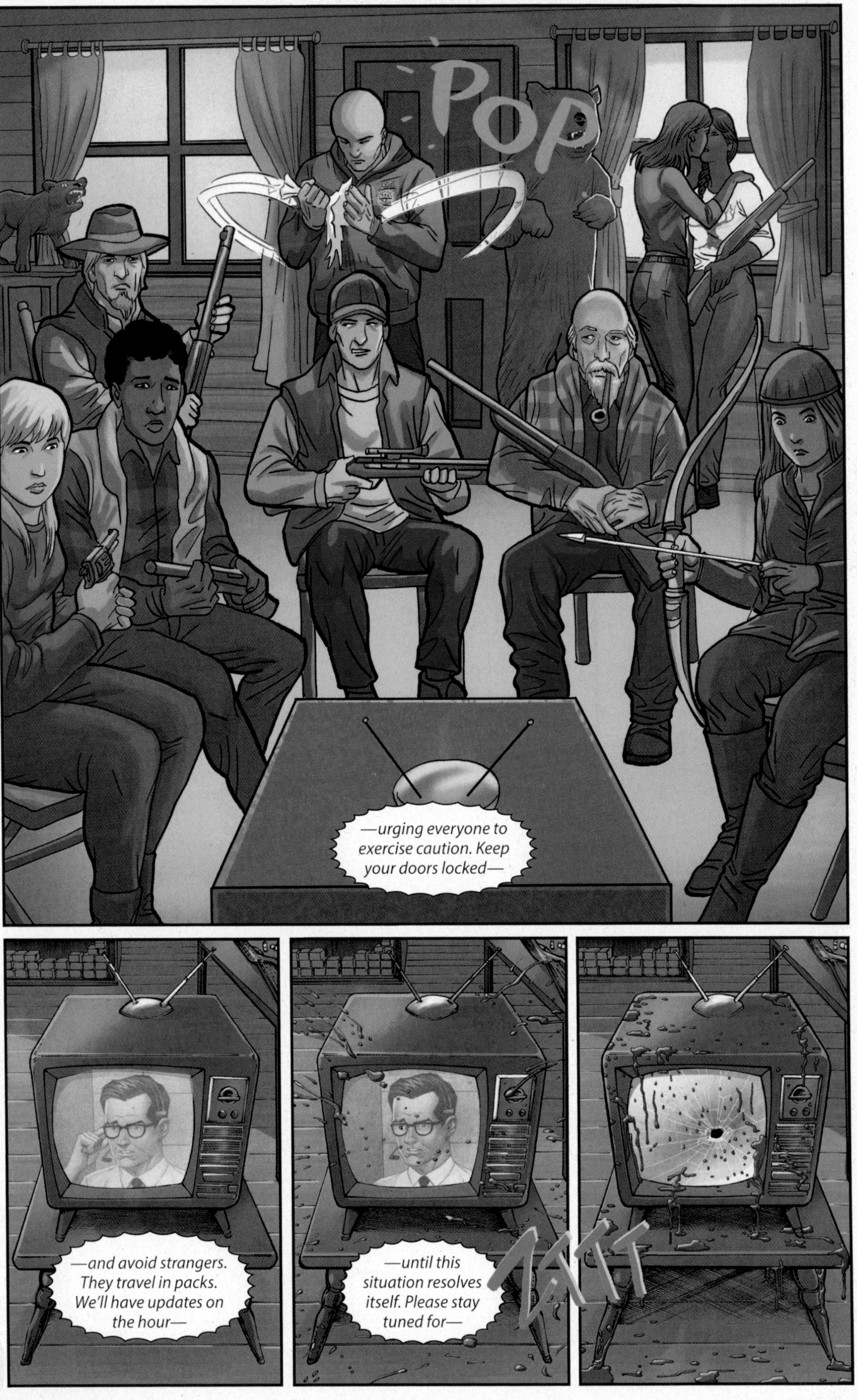
POP
—urging everyone to exercise caution. Keep your doors locked—
—and avoid strangers. They travel in packs. We'll have updates on the hour—
—until this situation resolves itself. Please stay tuned for—
ZTTT

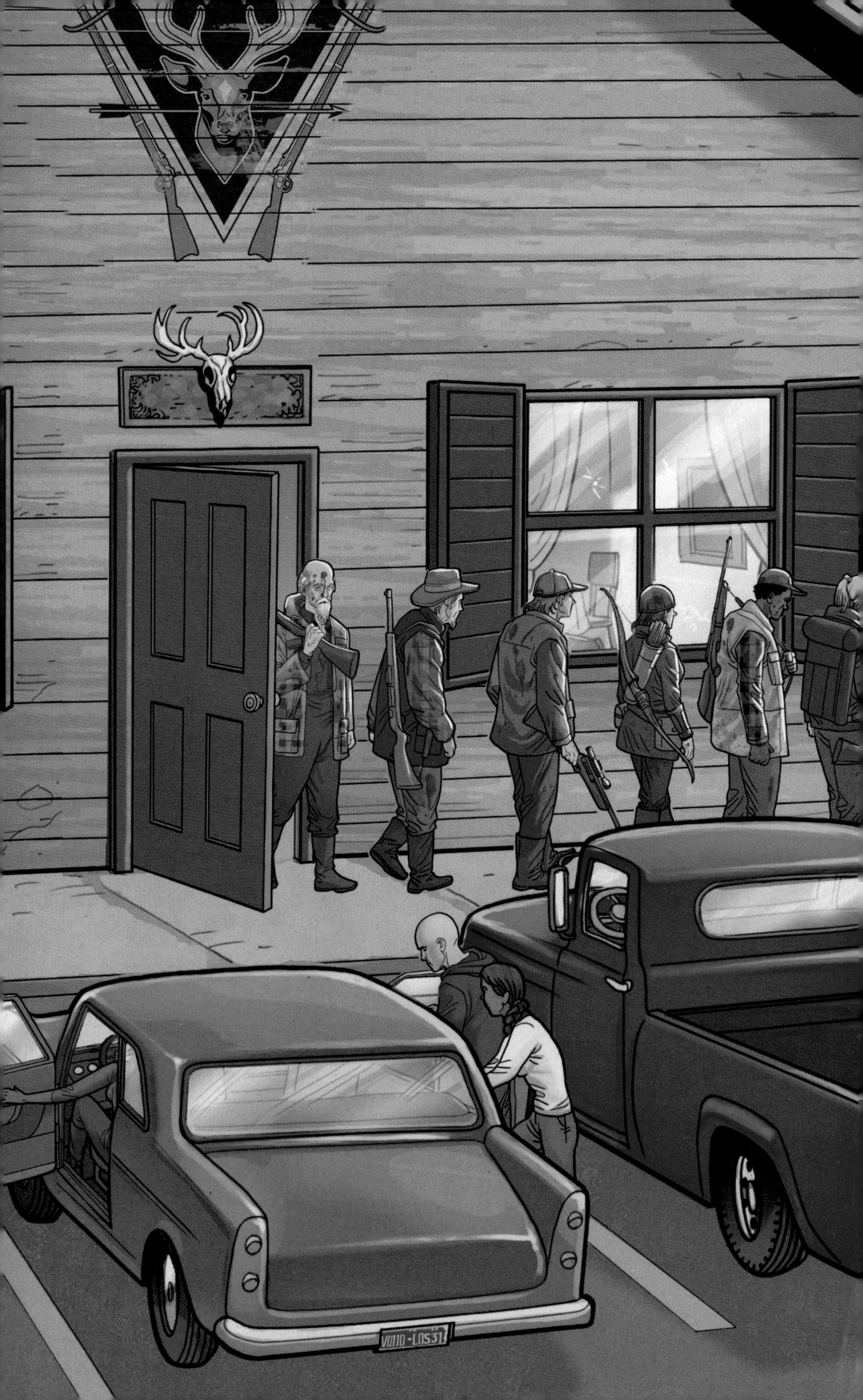
V011D-LOS31

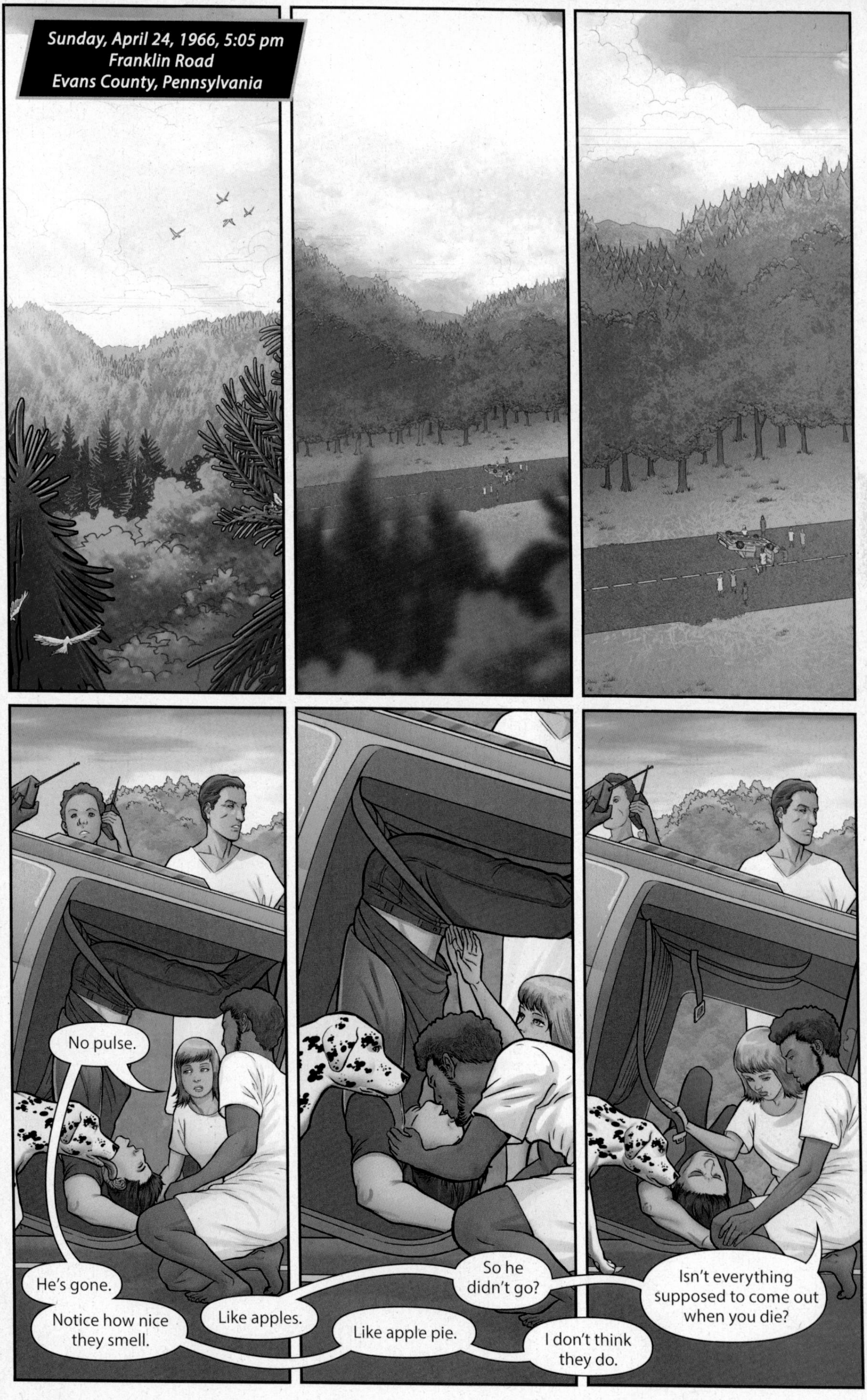
Sunday, April 24, 1966, 5:05 pm
Franklin Road
Evans County, Pennsylvania
No pulse.
He's gone.
Notice how nice they smell.
Like apples.
Like apple pie.
So he didn't go?
Isn't everything supposed to come out when you die?
I don't think they do.

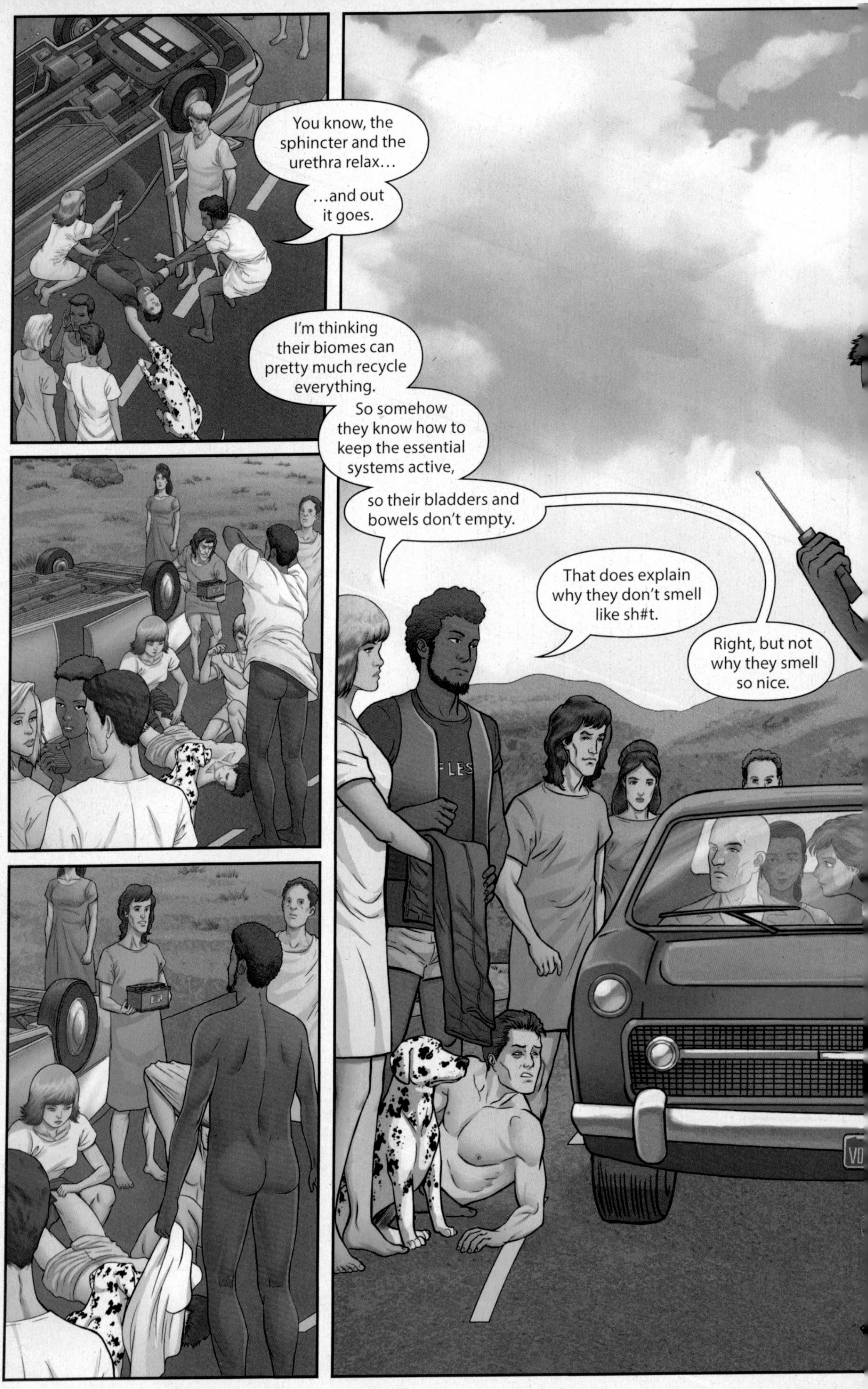
You know, the sphincter and the urethra relax…
…and out it goes.
I'm thinking their biomes can pretty much recycle everything.
So somehow they know how to keep the essential systems active,
so their bladders and bowels don't empty.
That does explain why they don't smell like sh#t.
Right, but not why they smell so nice.

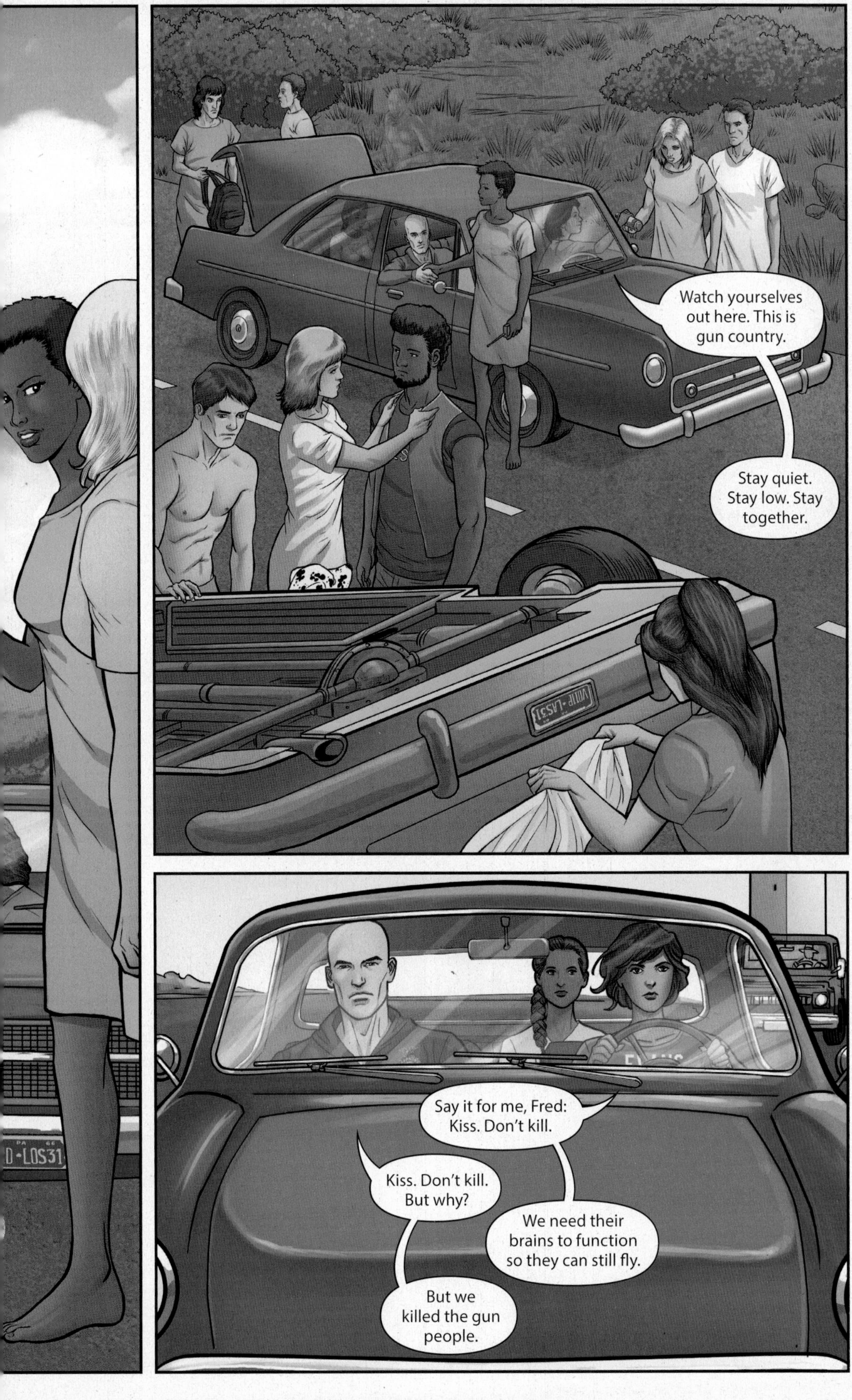
VIIII-LAS31
Watch yourselves out here. This is gun country.
Stay quiet. Stay low. Stay together.
D-LOS31
Say it for me, Fred: Kiss. Don't kill.
Kiss. Don't kill. But why?
We need their brains to function so they can still fly.
But we killed the gun people.

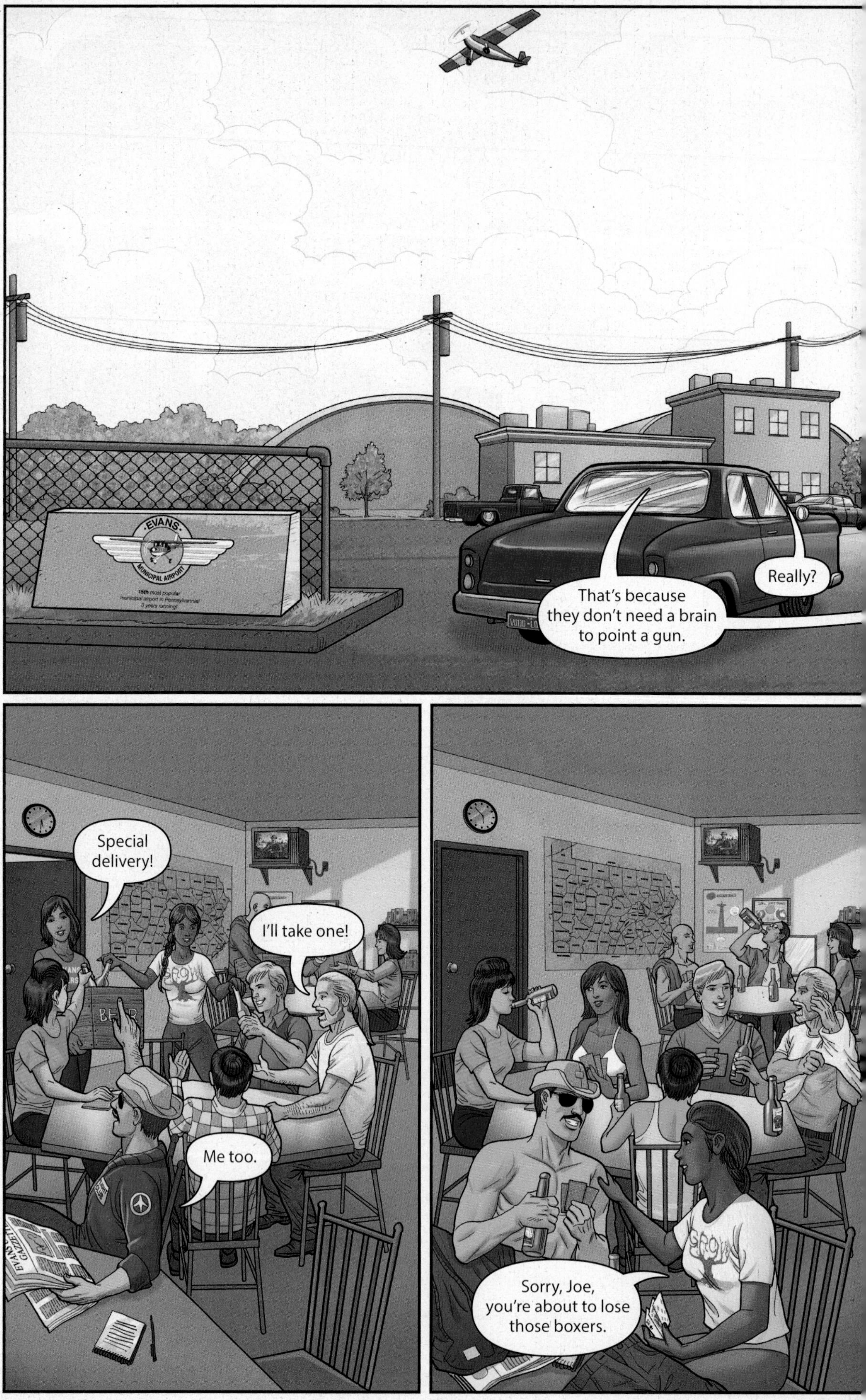
EVANS
MUNICIPAL AIRPORT
15th most popular
municipal airport in Pennsylvania!
3 years running!
That's because they don't need a brain to point a gun.
Really?
Special delivery!
I'll take one!
Me too.
Sorry, Joe, you're about to lose those boxers.

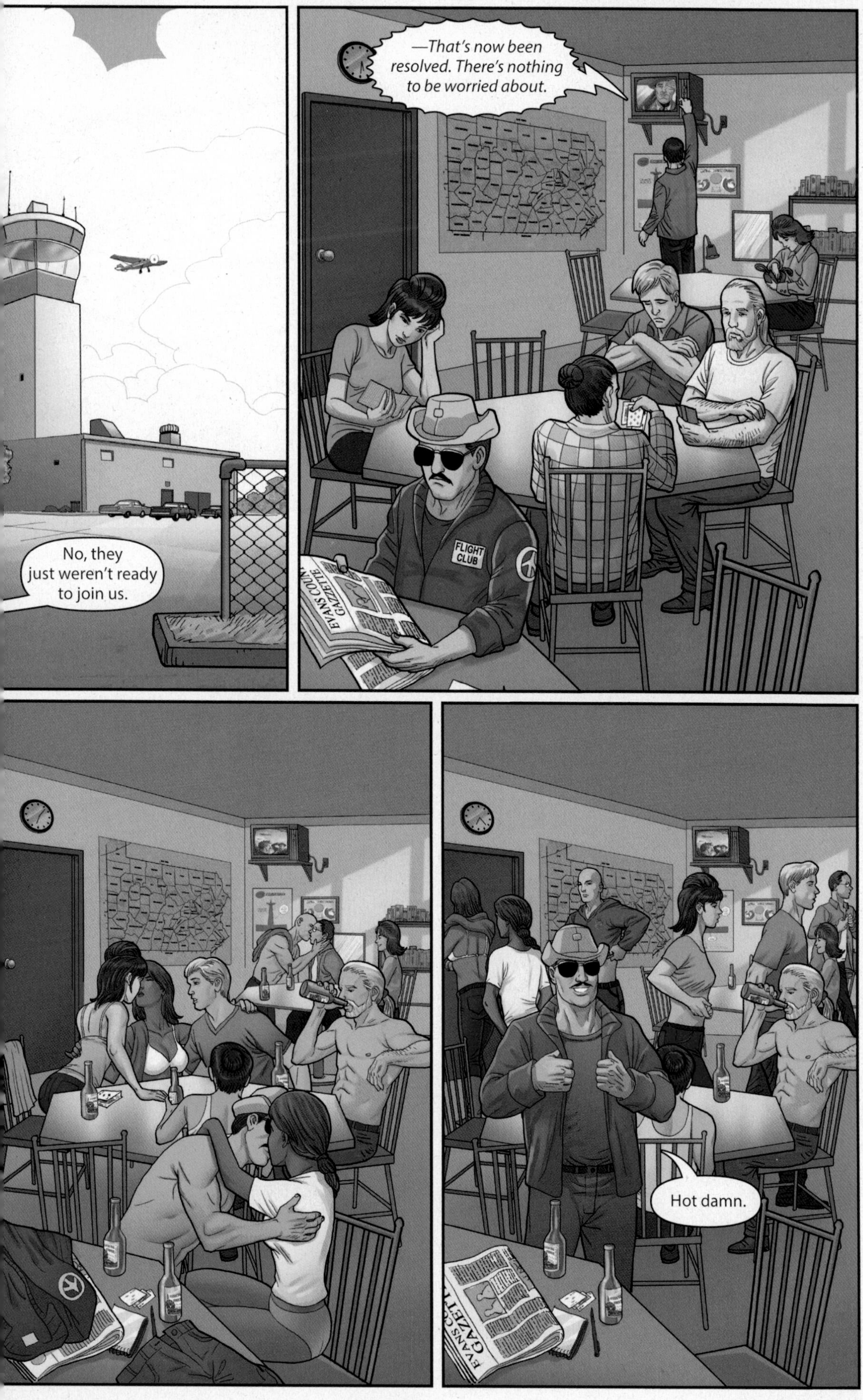
No, they just weren't ready to join us.
—That's now been resolved. There's nothing to be worried about.
FLIGHT CLUB
Hot damn.

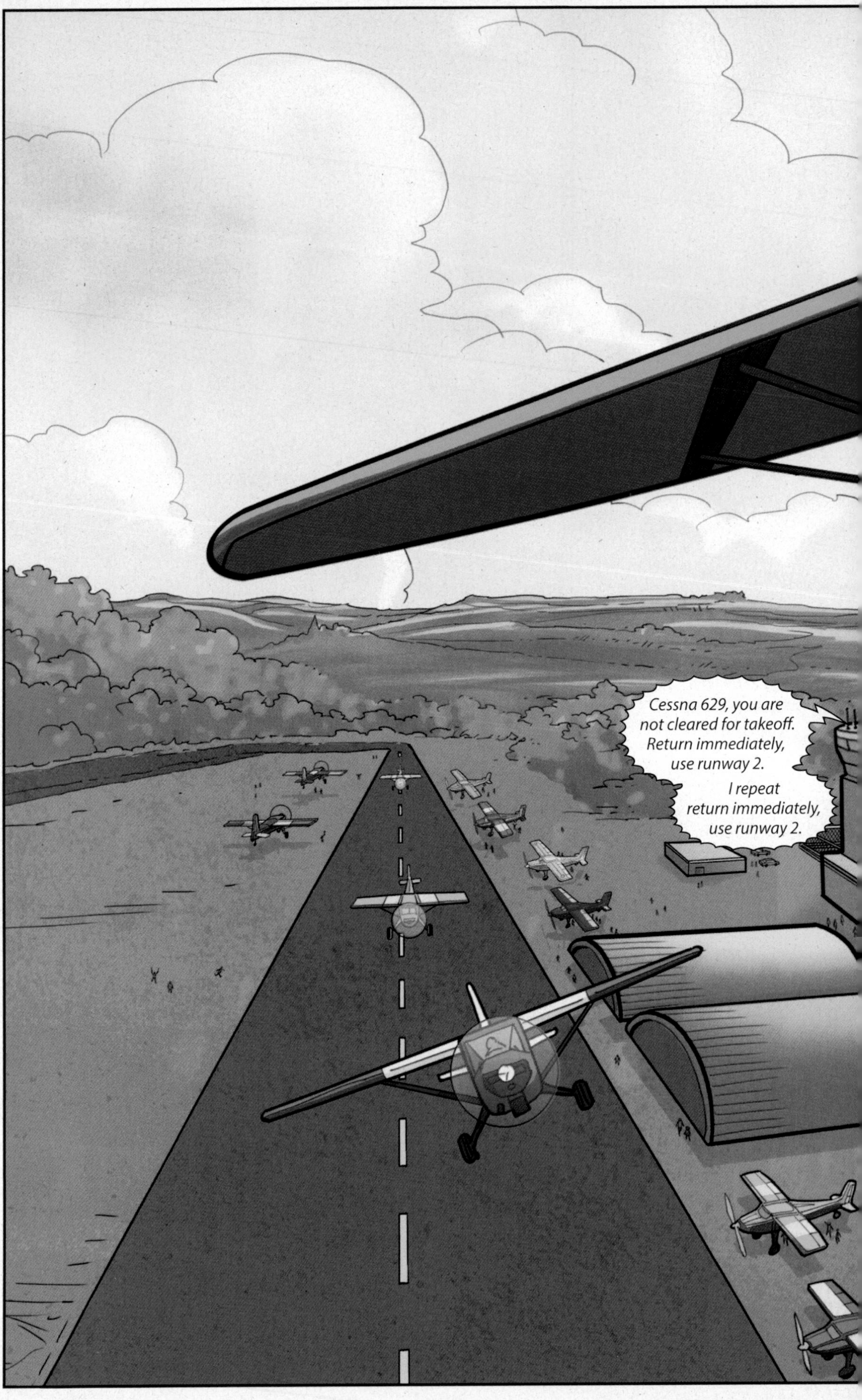
Cessna 629, you are not cleared for takeoff. Return immediately, use runway 2.
I repeat return immediately, use runway 2.

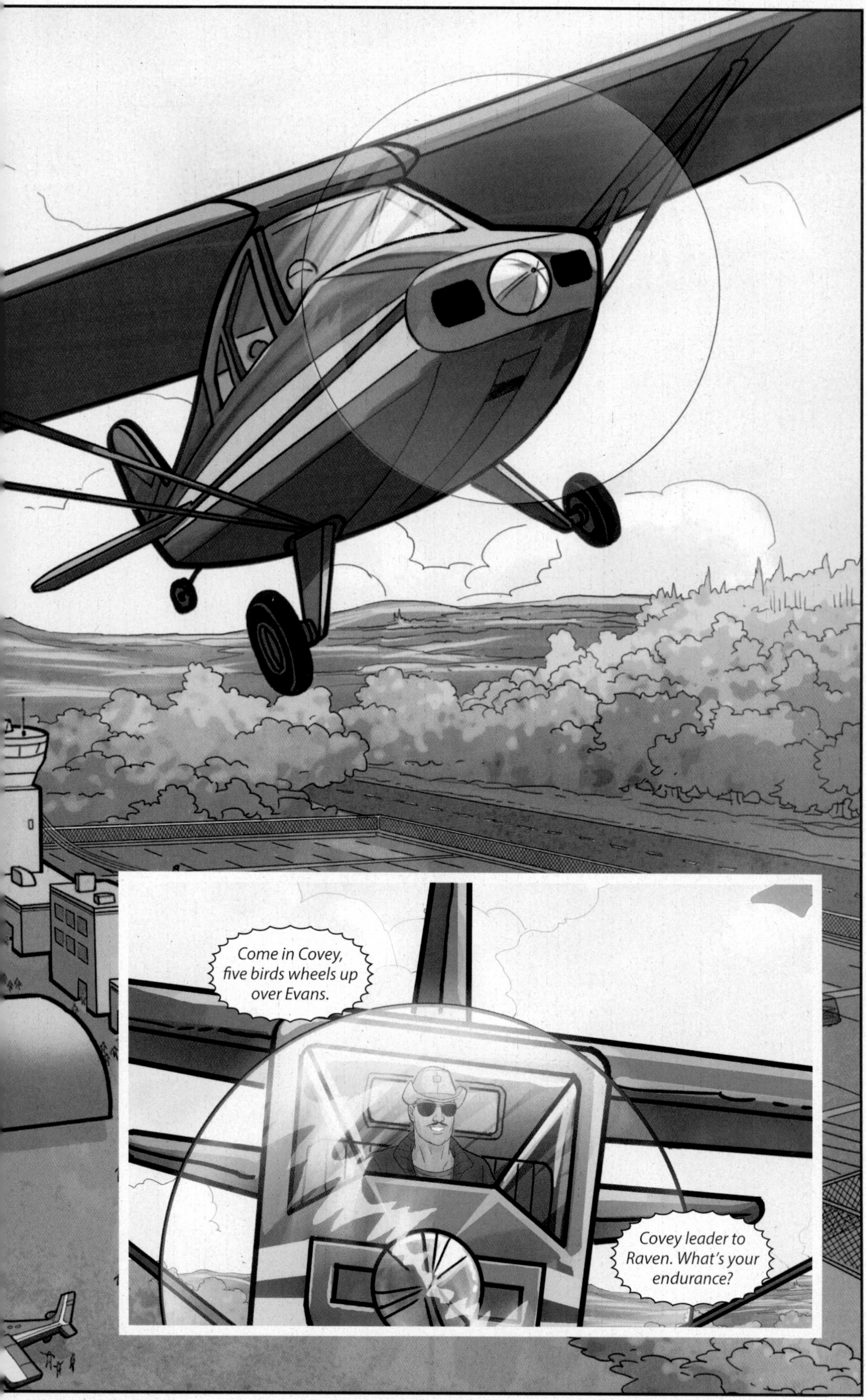
Come in Covey, five birds wheels up over Evans.
Covey leader to Raven. What's your endurance?

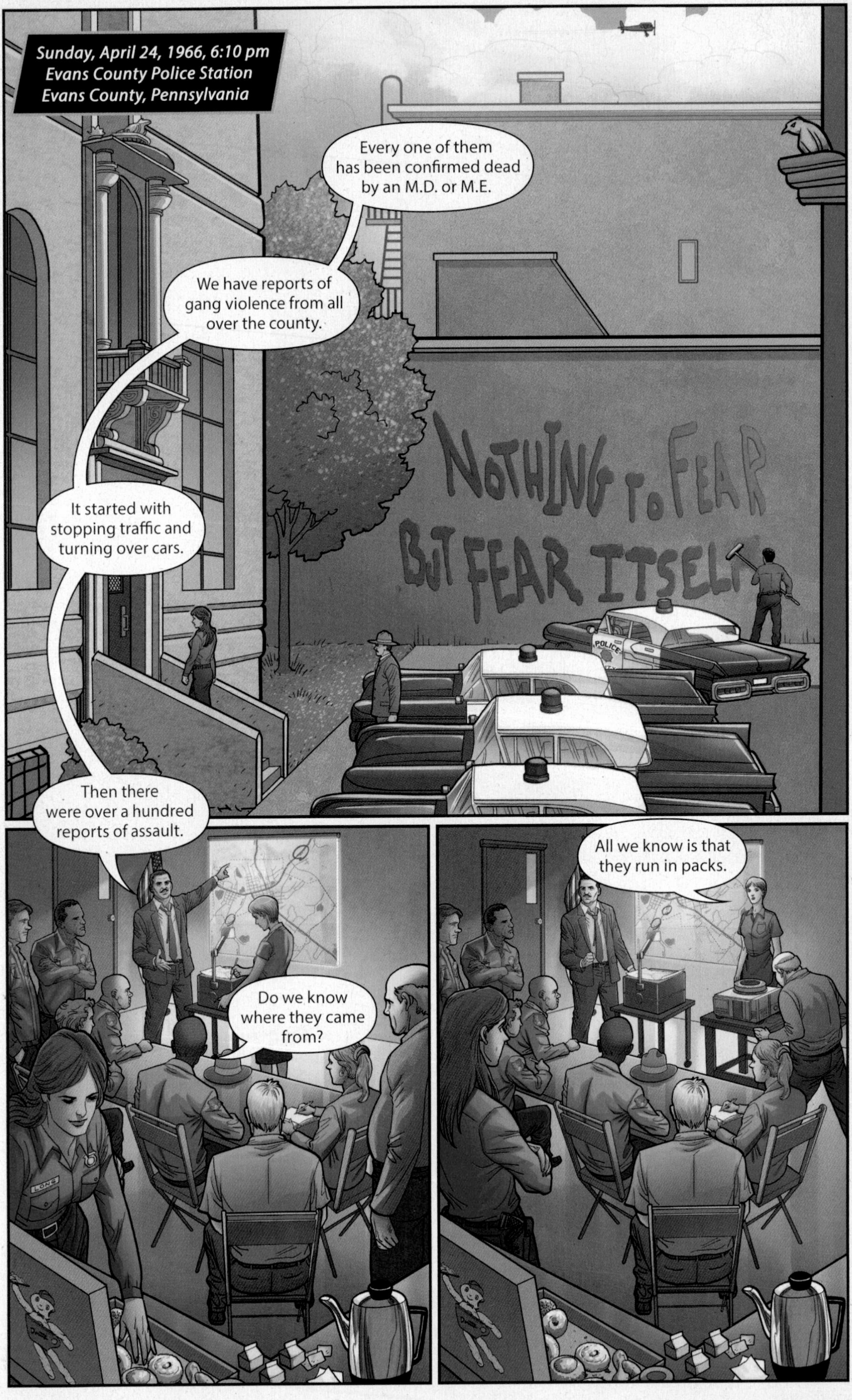

Sunday, April 24, 1966, 6:10 pm
Evans County Police Station
Evans County, Pennsylvania
Every one of them has been confirmed dead by an M.D. or M.E.
We have reports of gang violence from all over the county.
NOTHING TO FEAR
BUT FEAR ITSEL
POLICE
It started with stopping traffic and turning over cars.
Then there were over a hundred reports of assault.
Do we know where they came from?
LONG
All we know is that they run in packs.

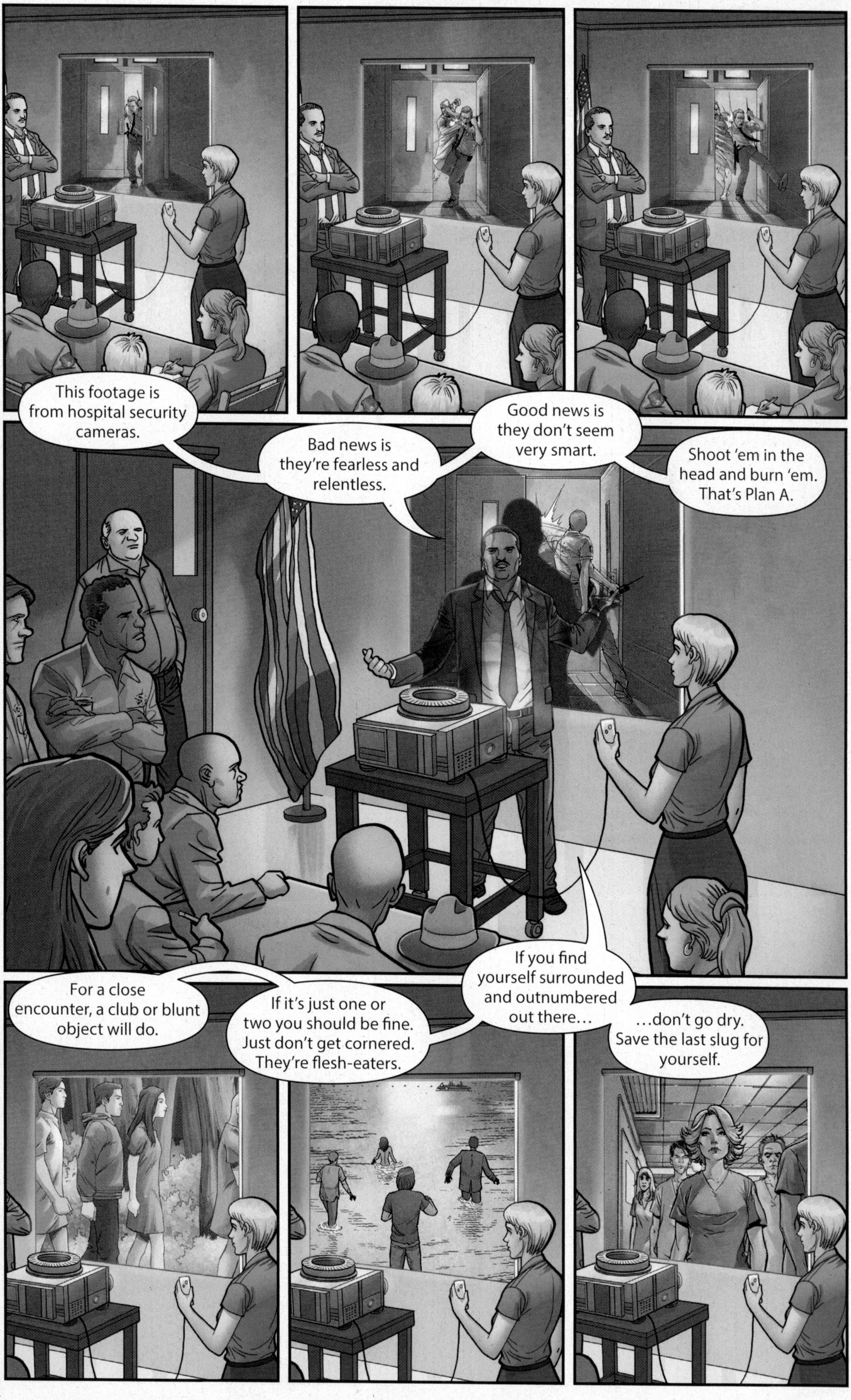
This footage is from hospital security cameras.
Bad news is they're fearless and relentless.
Good news is they don't seem very smart.
Shoot 'em in the head and burn 'em. That's Plan A.
For a close encounter, a club or blunt object will do.
If it's just one or two you should be fine. Just don't get cornered. They're flesh-eaters.
If you find yourself surrounded and outnumbered out there…
…don't go dry. Save the last slug for yourself.

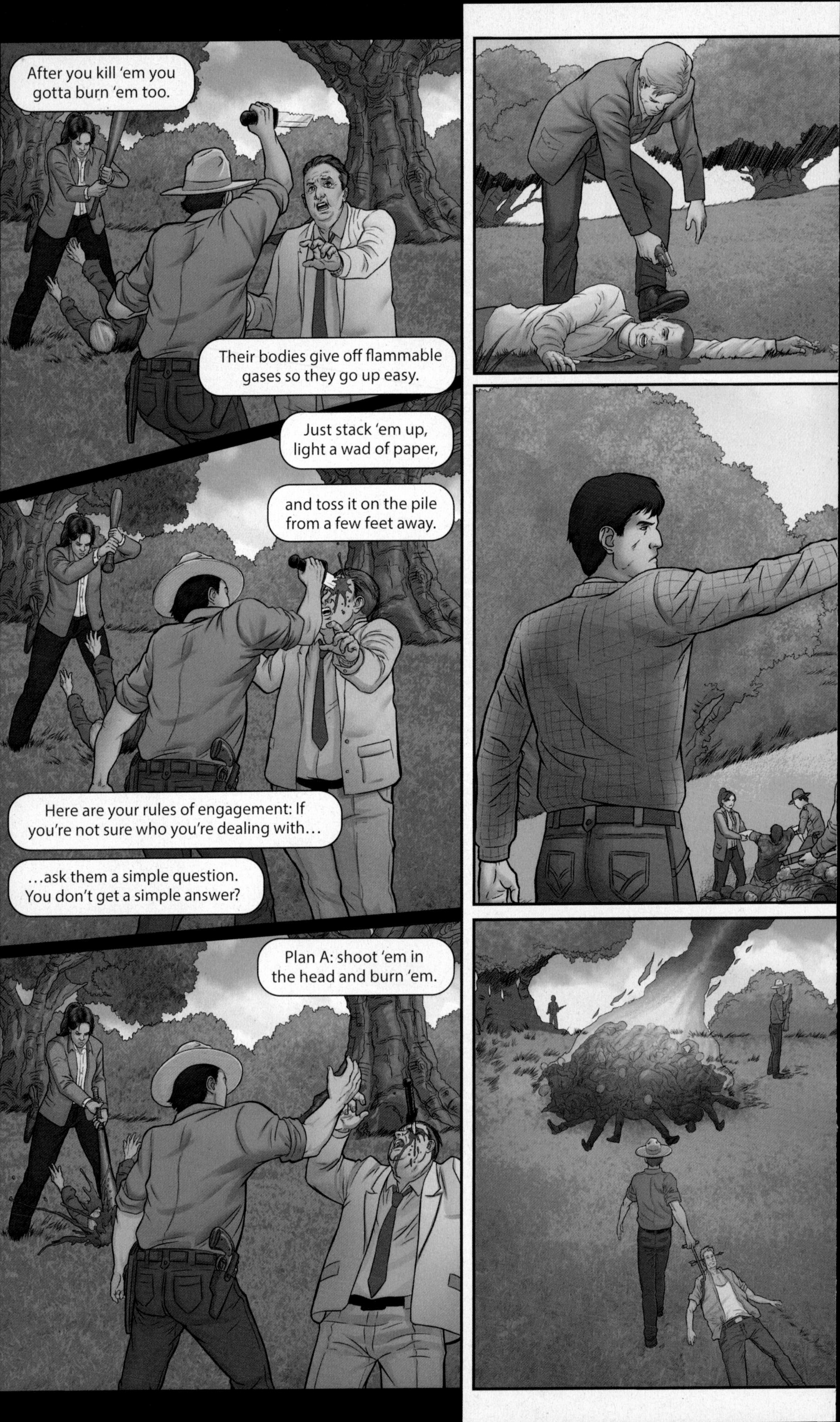
After you kill 'em you gotta burn 'em too.
Their bodies give off flammable gases so they go up easy.
Just stack 'em up, light a wad of paper,
and toss it on the pile from a few feet away.
Here are your rules of engagement: If you're not sure who you're dealing with…
…ask them a simple question. You don't get a simple answer?
Plan A: shoot 'em in the head and burn 'em.

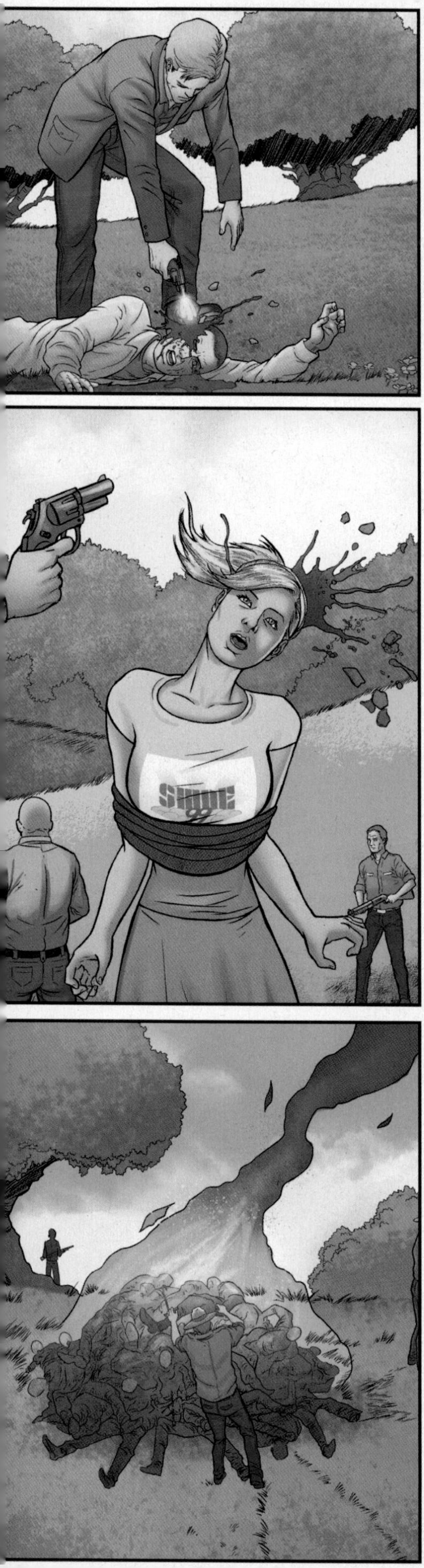

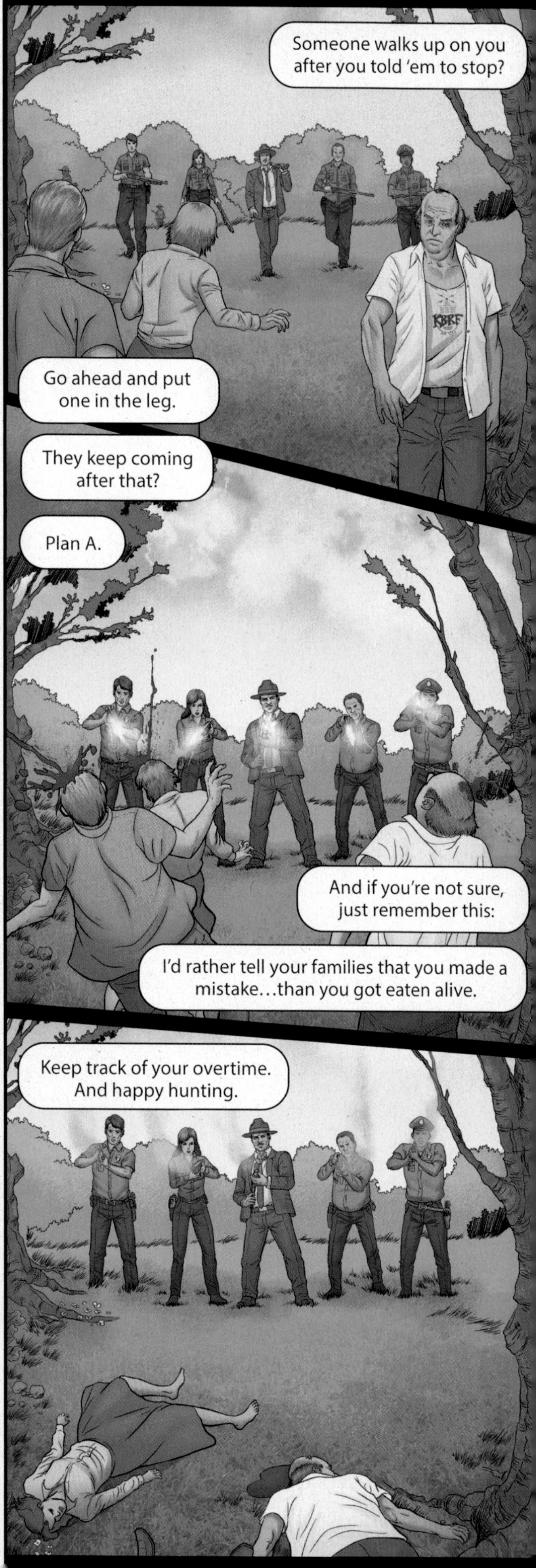
Someone walks up on you after you told 'em to stop?
Go ahead and put one in the leg.
They keep coming after that?
Plan A.
And if you're not sure, just remember this:
I'd rather tell your families that you made a mistake…than you got eaten alive.
Keep track of your overtime. And happy hunting.

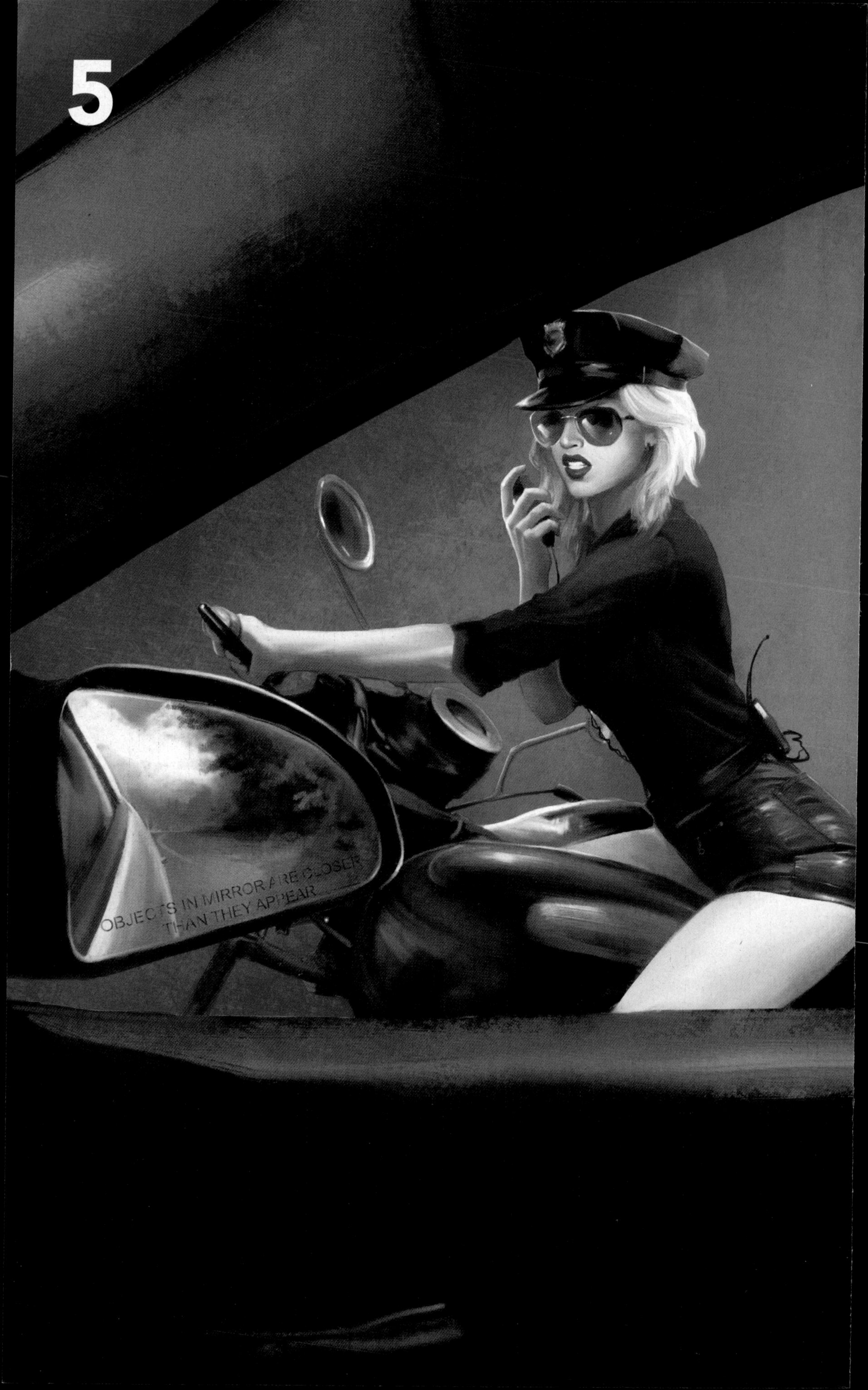
5
OBJECTS IN MIRROR ARE CLOSER
THAN THEY APPEAR

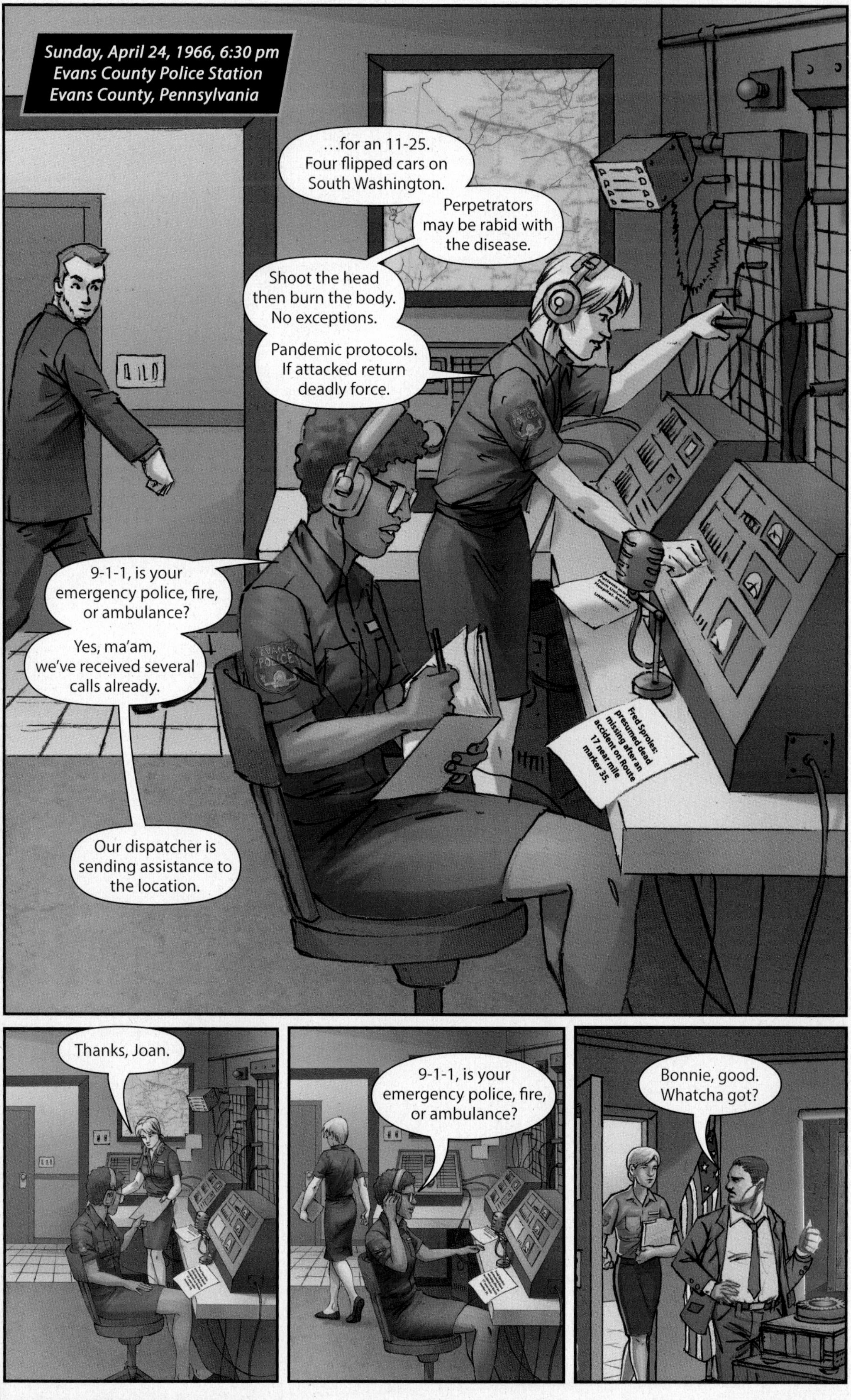
Sunday, April 24, 1966, 6:30 pm
Evans County Police Station
Evans County, Pennsylvania
…for an 11-25. Four flipped cars on South Washington.
Perpetrators may be rabid with the disease.
Shoot the head then burn the body. No exceptions.
Pandemic protocols. If attacked return deadly force.
9-1-1, is your emergency police, fire, or ambulance?
Yes, ma'am, we've received several calls already.
Our dispatcher is sending assistance to the location.
Fred Sproles: presumed dead missing after an accident on Route 17 near mile marker 35.
Thanks, Joan.
9-1-1, is your emergency police, fire, or ambulance?
Bonnie, good. Whatcha got?

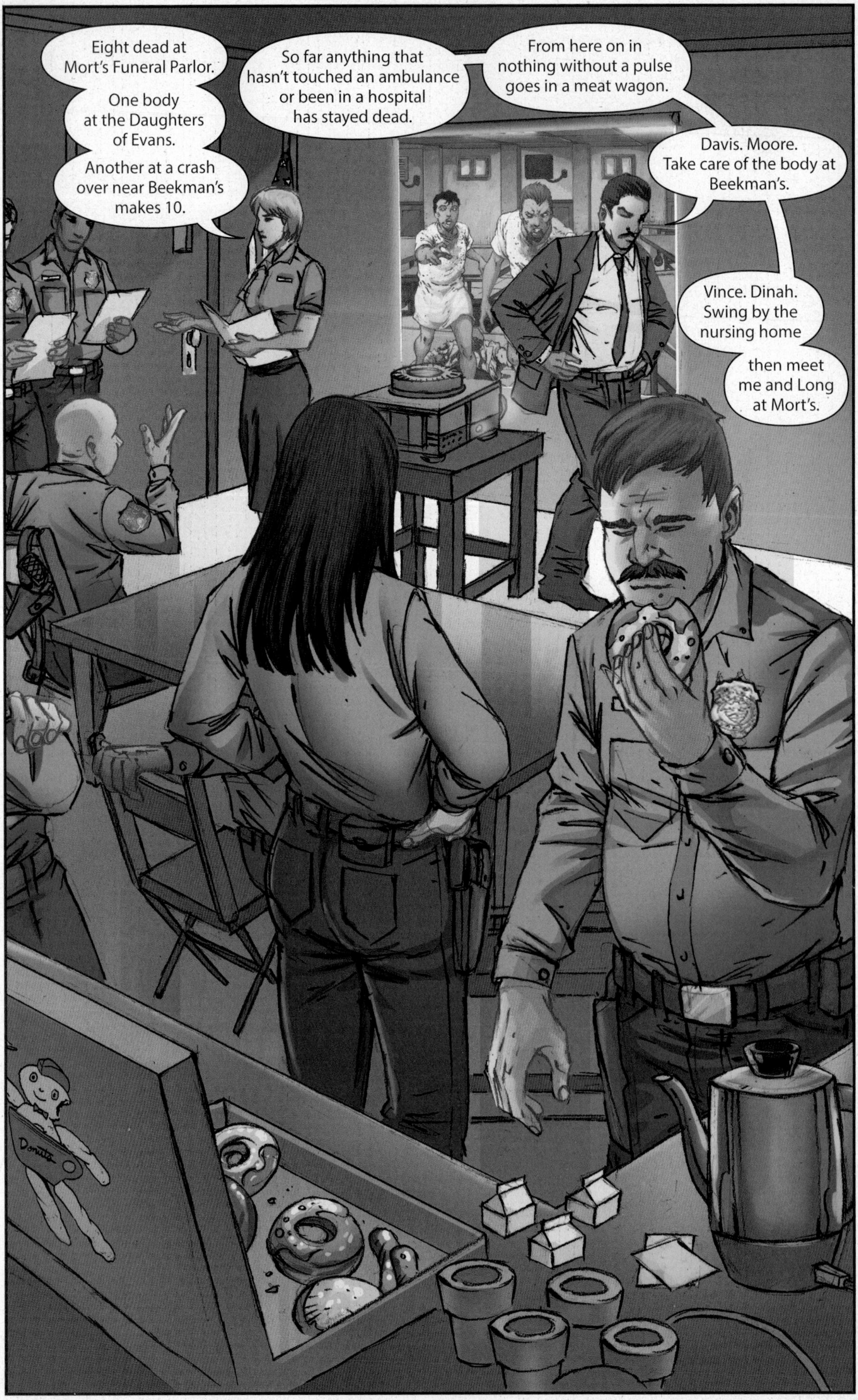

Eight dead at Mort's Funeral Parlor.
One body at the Daughters of Evans.
Another at a crash over near Beekman's makes 10.
So far anything that hasn't touched an ambulance or been in a hospital has stayed dead.
From here on in nothing without a pulse goes in a meat wagon.
Davis. Moore. Take care of the body at Beekman's.
Vince. Dinah. Swing by the nursing home
then meet me and Long at Mort's.
Donuts

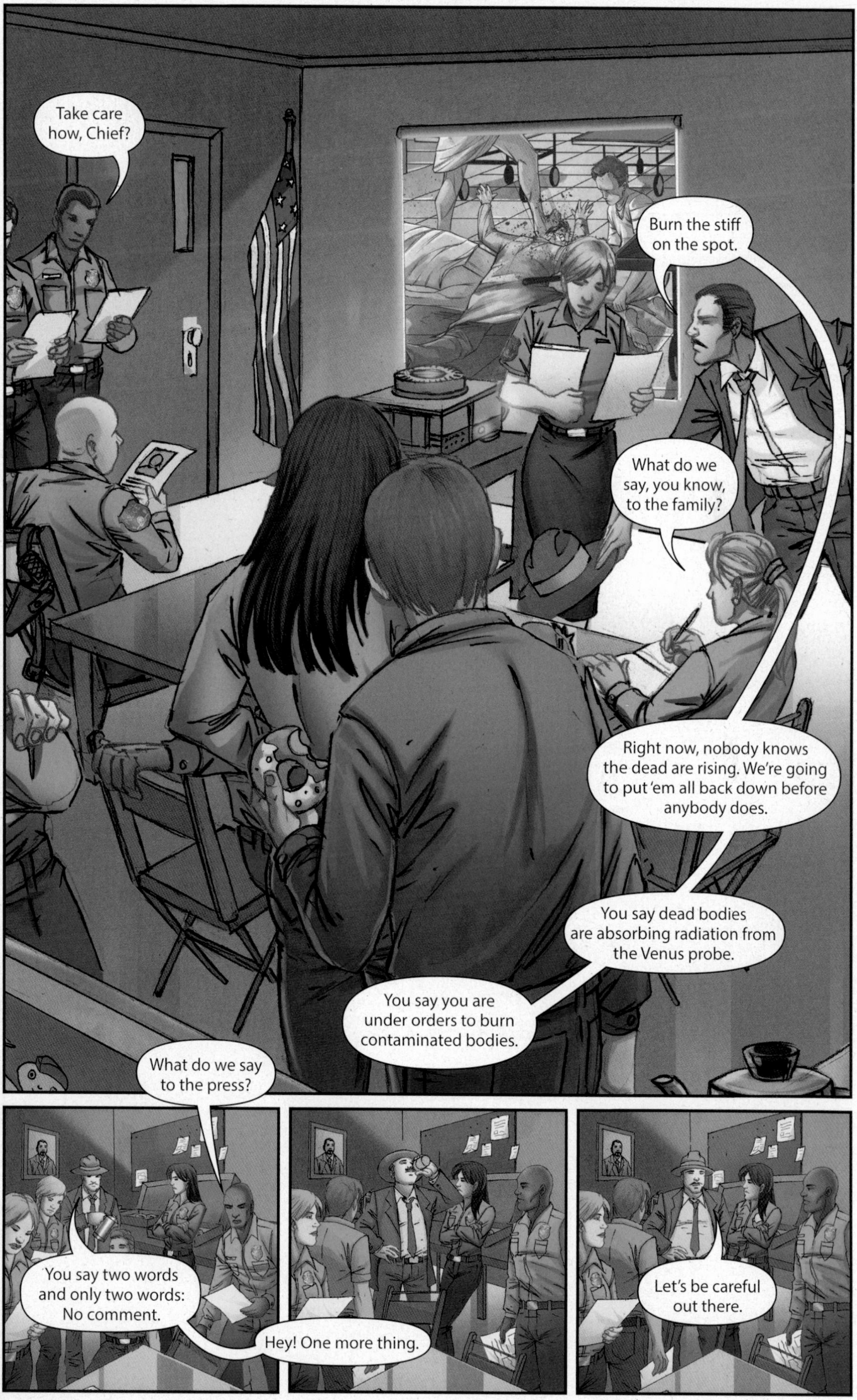
Take care how, Chief?
Burn the stiff on the spot.
What do we say, you know, to the family?
Right now, nobody knows the dead are rising. We're going to put 'em all back down before anybody does.
You say dead bodies are absorbing radiation from the Venus probe.
You say you are under orders to burn contaminated bodies.
What do we say to the press?
You say two words and only two words: No comment.
Hey! One more thing.
Let's be careful out there.

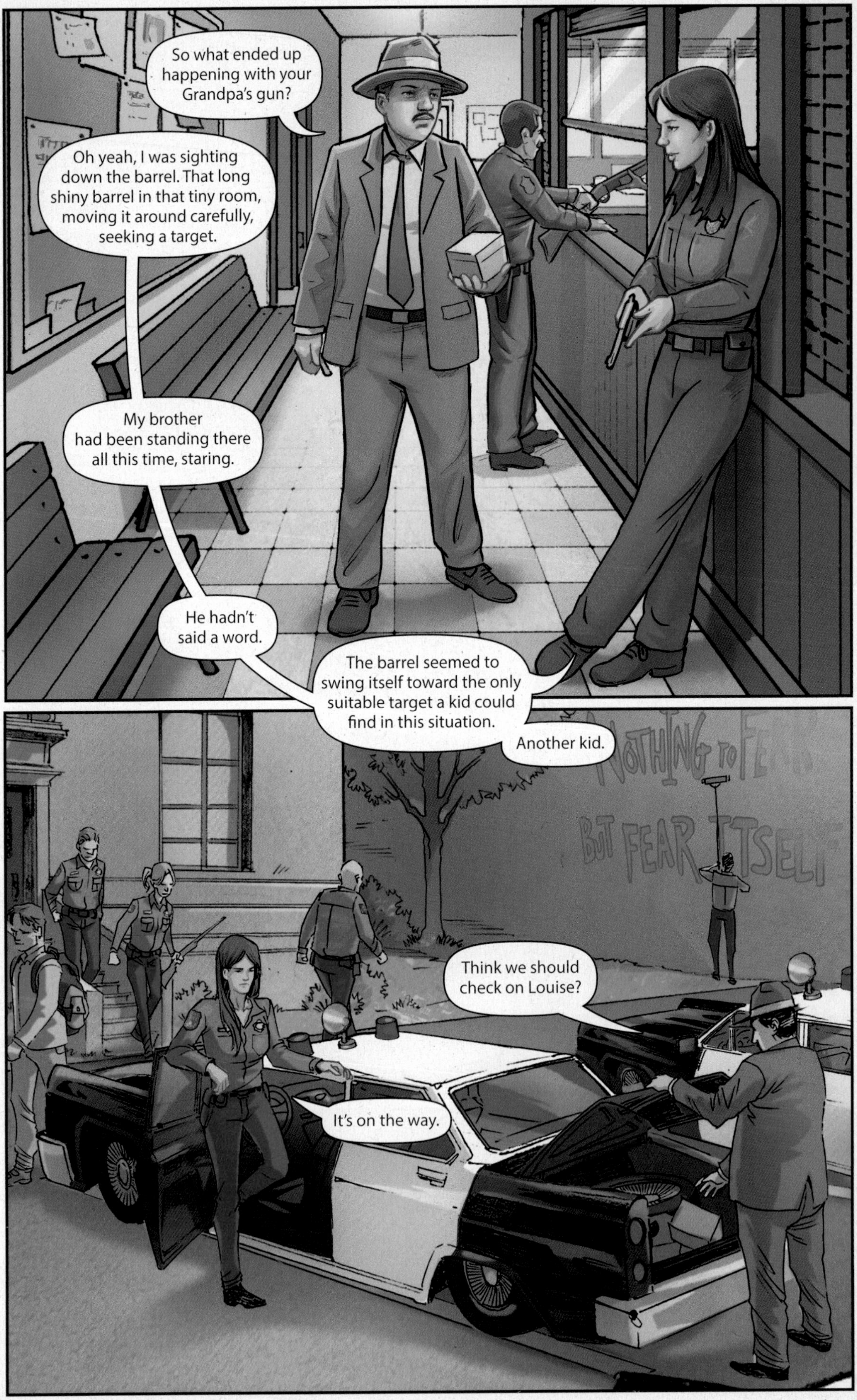
So what ended up happening with your Grandpa's gun?
Oh yeah, I was sighting down the barrel. That long shiny barrel in that tiny room, moving it around carefully, seeking a target.
My brother had been standing there all this time, staring.
He hadn't said a word.
The barrel seemed to swing itself toward the only suitable target a kid could find in this situation.
Another kid.
NOTHING TO FE
BUT FEAR ITSEL
Think we should check on Louise?
It's on the way.

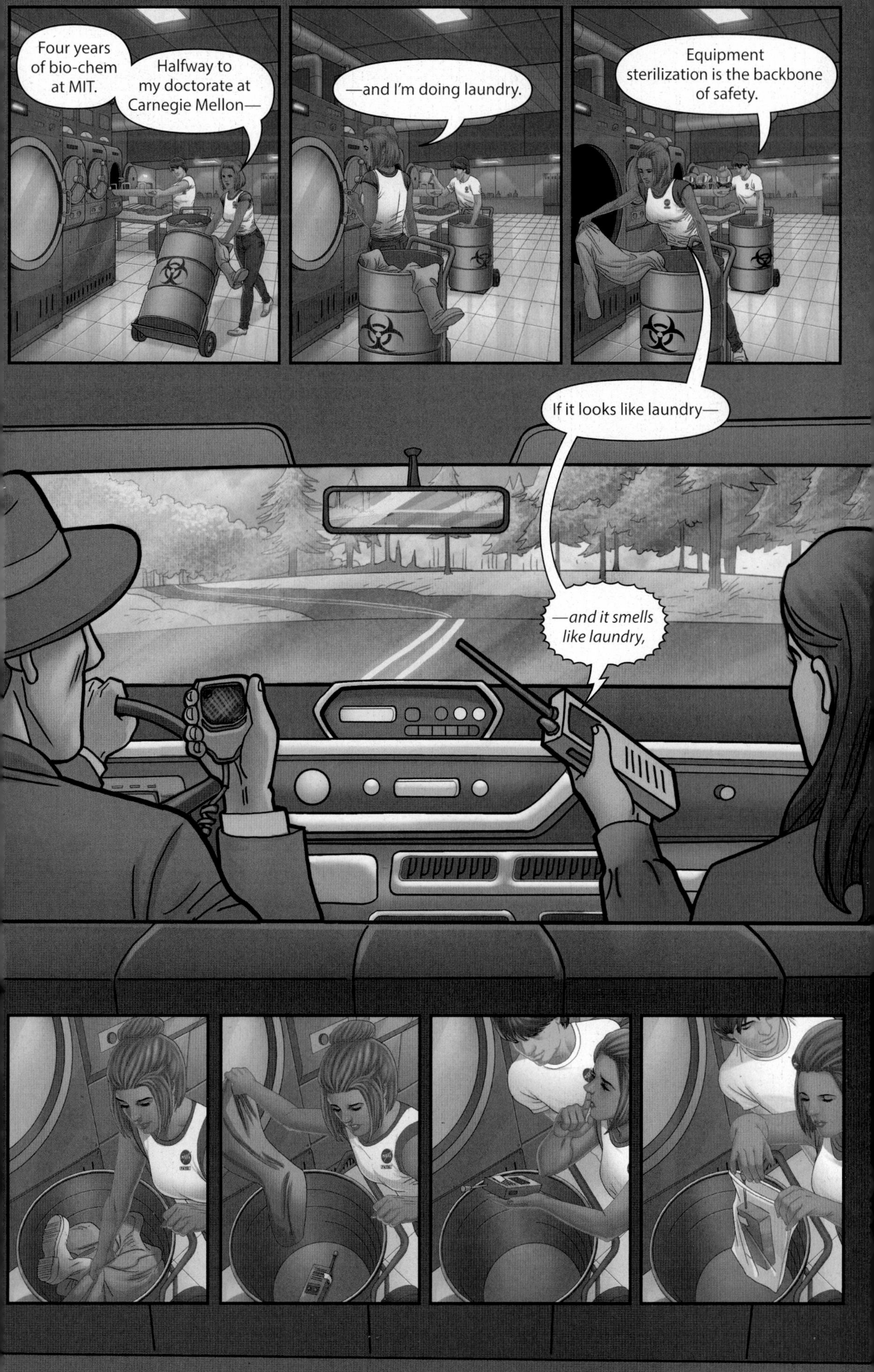
Four years of bio-chem at MIT.
Halfway to my doctorate at Carnegie Mellon—
—and I'm doing laundry.
Equipment sterilization is the backbone of safety.
If it looks like laundry—
—and it smells like laundry,

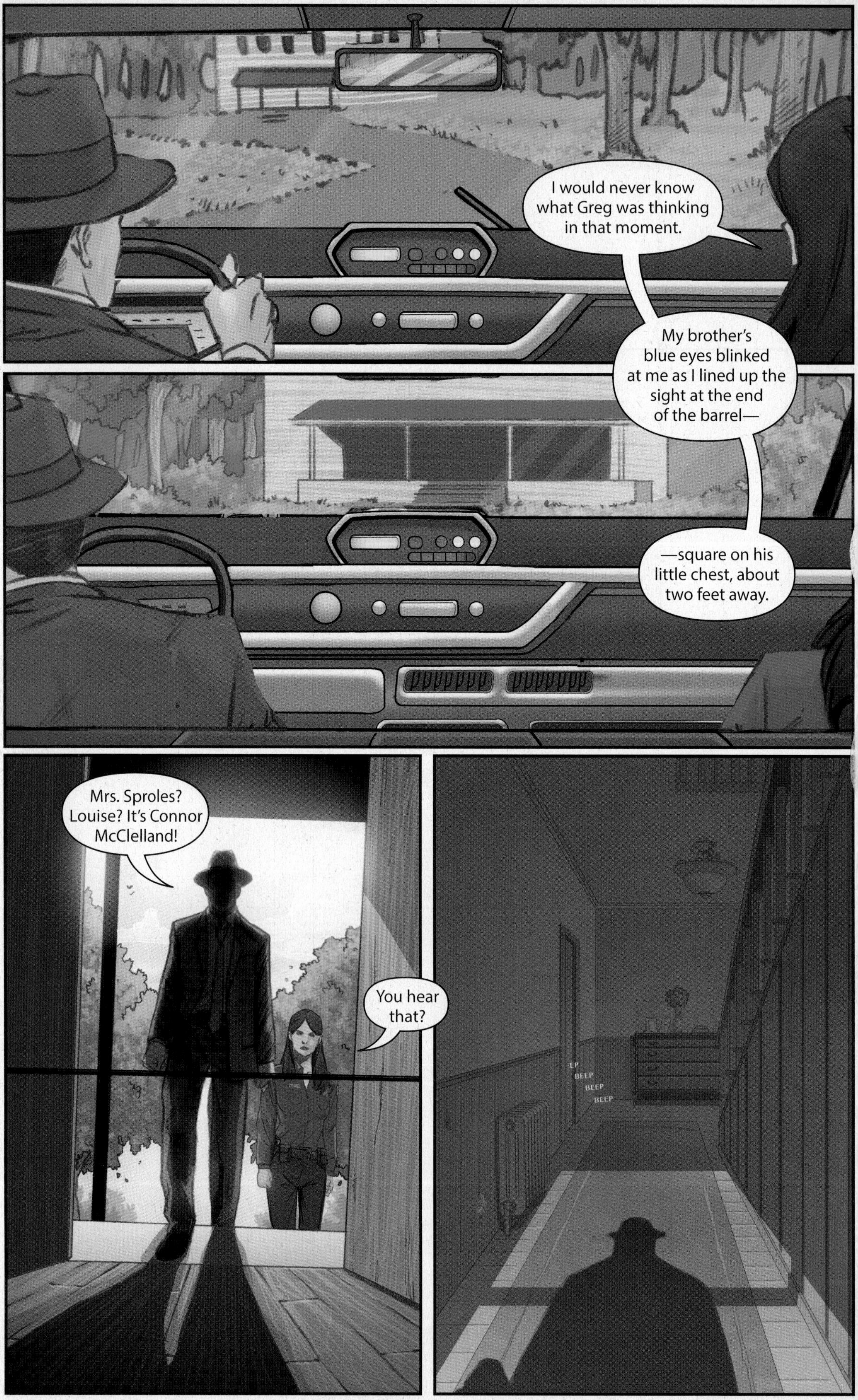
I would never know what Greg was thinking in that moment.
My brother's blue eyes blinked at me as I lined up the sight at the end of the barrel—
—square on his little chest, about two feet away.
Mrs. Sproles? Louise? It's Connor McClelland!
You hear that?
EP
BEEP
BEEP
BEEP

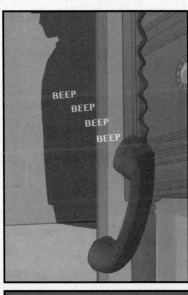
BEEP
BEEP
BEEP
BEEP

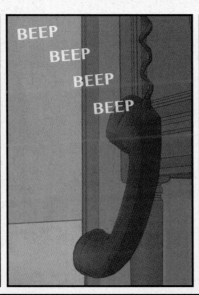
BEEP
BEEP
BEEP
BEEP

BEEP
BEEP
BEEP

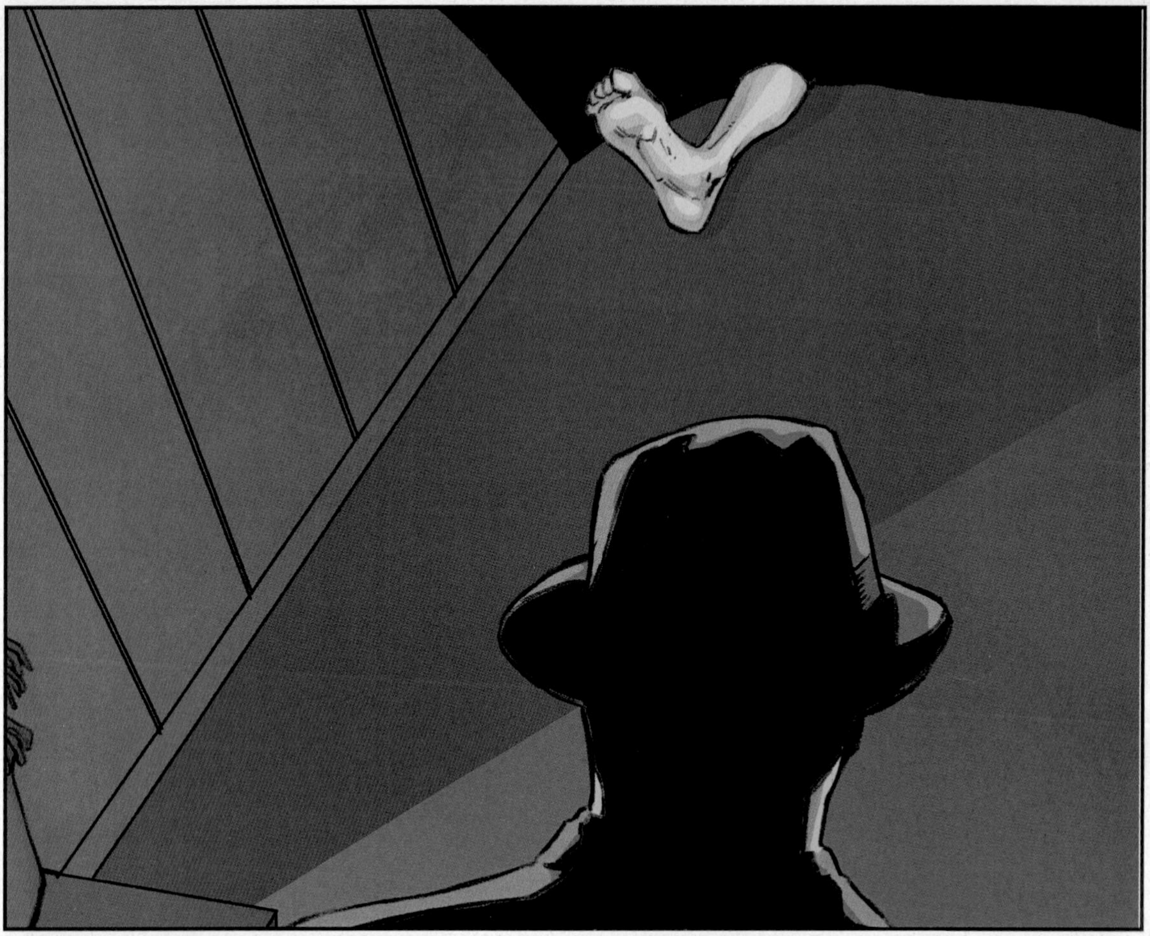

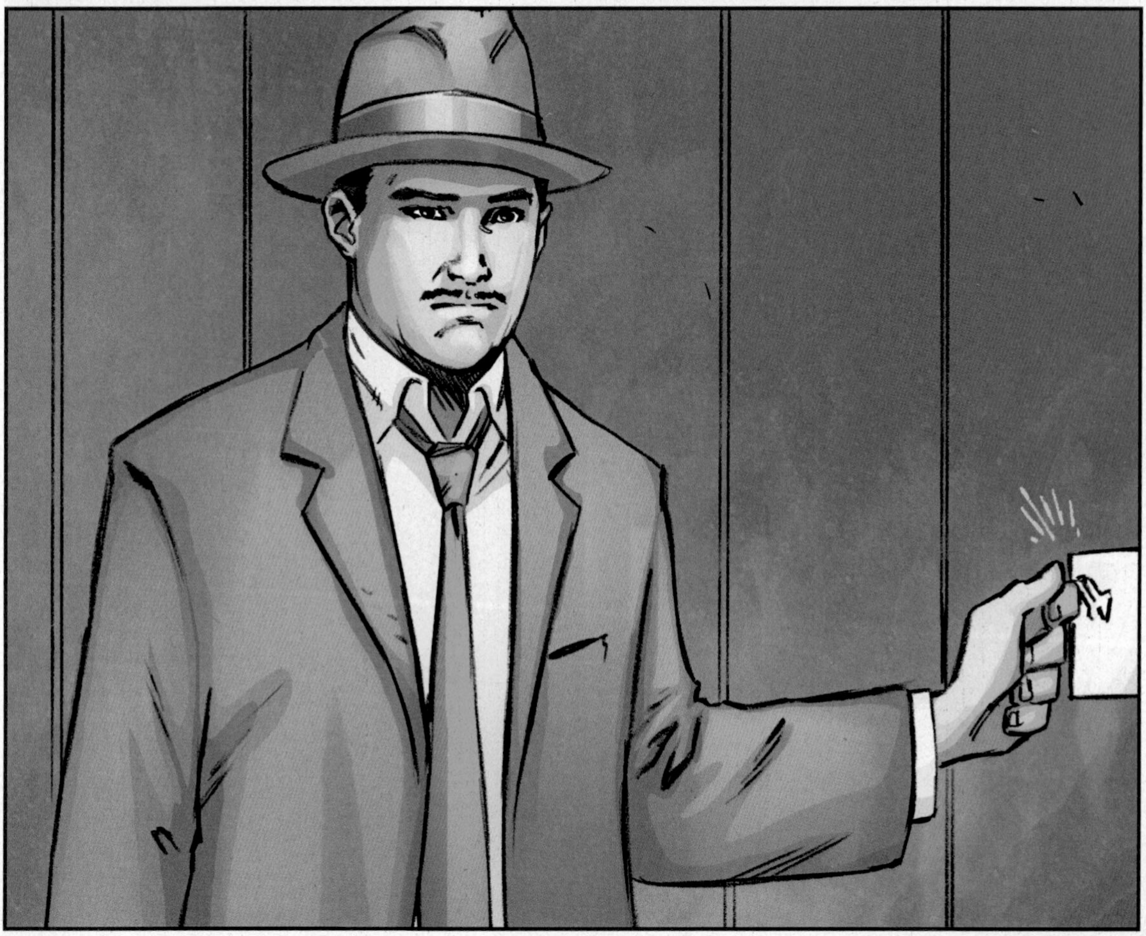

DOUBLE TAKE MANUAL OF STYLE

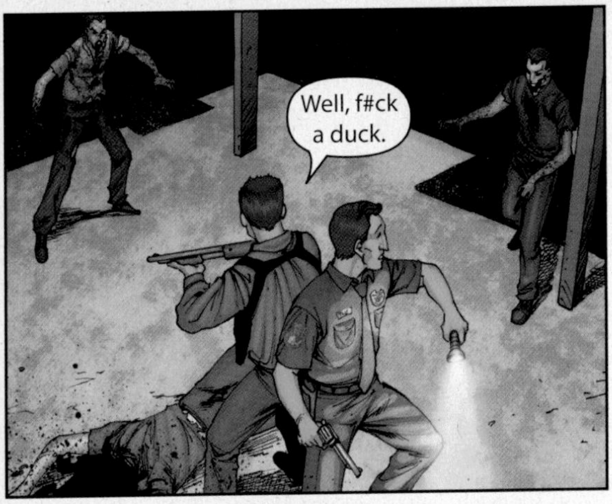
Well, f#ck a duck.

F#ck a Duck

First use: In Henry Miller's *Tropic of Cancer* (1934): the narrator saw another author's title that he wished he'd come up with and exclaimed, "Well, f#ck a duck! I congratulate him just the same."

Etymology: The original inspiration may have been "duckf#cker," which refers to a person aboard a transatlantic ship who is responsible for keeping the domestic animals alive (and not pleasuring them in exotic ways).

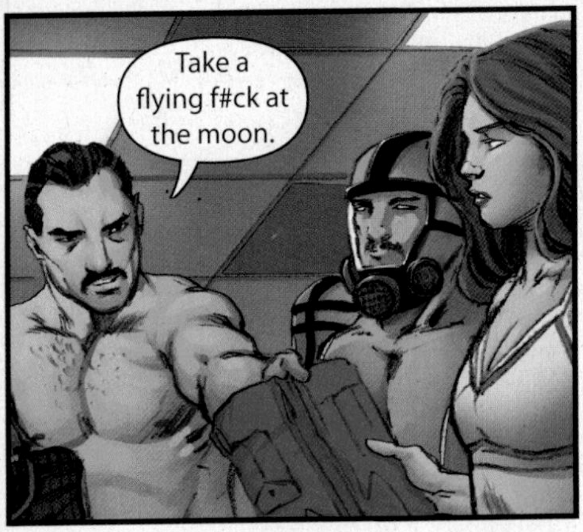
Take a flying f#ck at the moon.

Take a flying f#ck at a rolling donut

First use: Kurt Vonnegut used the phrase verbatim in *Slaughterhouse-Five* (1969) and again in *Slapstick* (1976): "Go take a flying f#ck at a rolling doughnut.... Go take a flying f#ck at the moon."

Etymology: Variations of the phrase date back to 1926: American author and US Army Colonel L.H. Nason used the phrase in *Chevrons*, a novel about life in the Field Artillery during WWI ("Me, I'd tell'em to take a flyin' fling at the moon."). "Flying f#ck" originally meant "sex had on horseback." The phrase appeared in 1800 in a broadside ballad called "New Feats of Horsemanship":

Well mounted on a mettled steed
Famed for his strength as well as speed
Corinna and her favorite buck
Are pleas'd to have a flying f#ck.

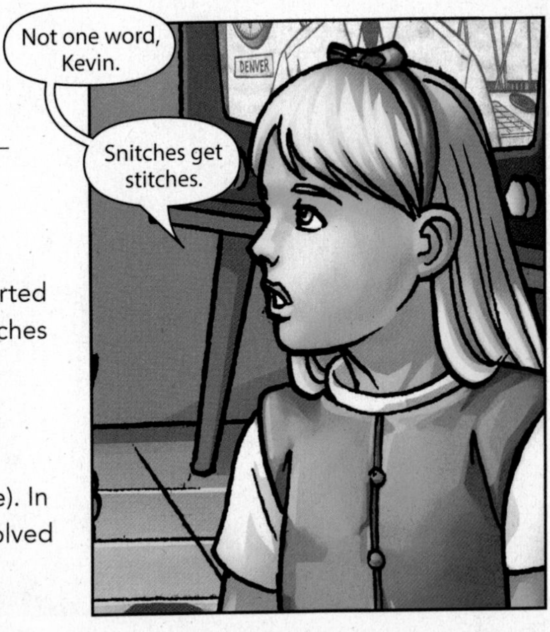
Not one word, Kevin.
DENVER
Snitches get stitches.

Snitches get stitches

First use: Possibly in the streets of late 1980s New York City; around this time, newspapers in NYC started using this phrase in articles. Other phrasings: "Snitches get stitches and end up in ditches."

Etymology: "Snitch" as slang for "informer" dates back to 1785. In the late 1600s, "snitch" originally meant a "fillip on the nose" (i.e., a flick on the nose). In the early 18th century, the meaning of "snitch" evolved to mean "nose," a symbol of intrusion into others' business ("nosy").

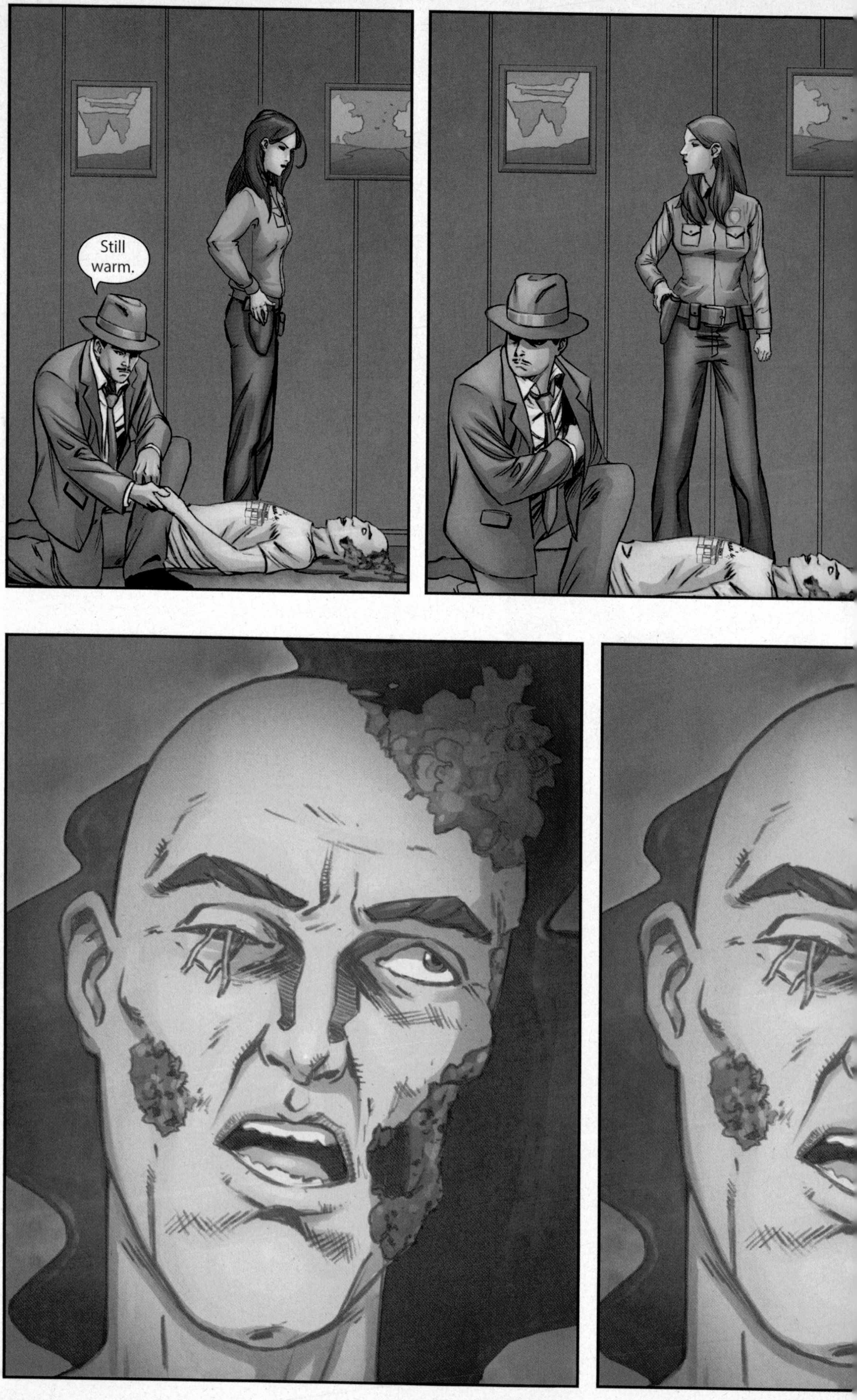
Still warm.

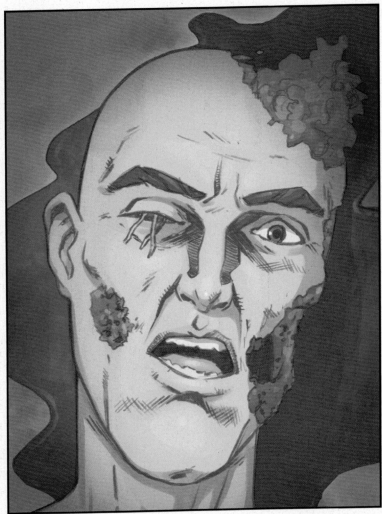

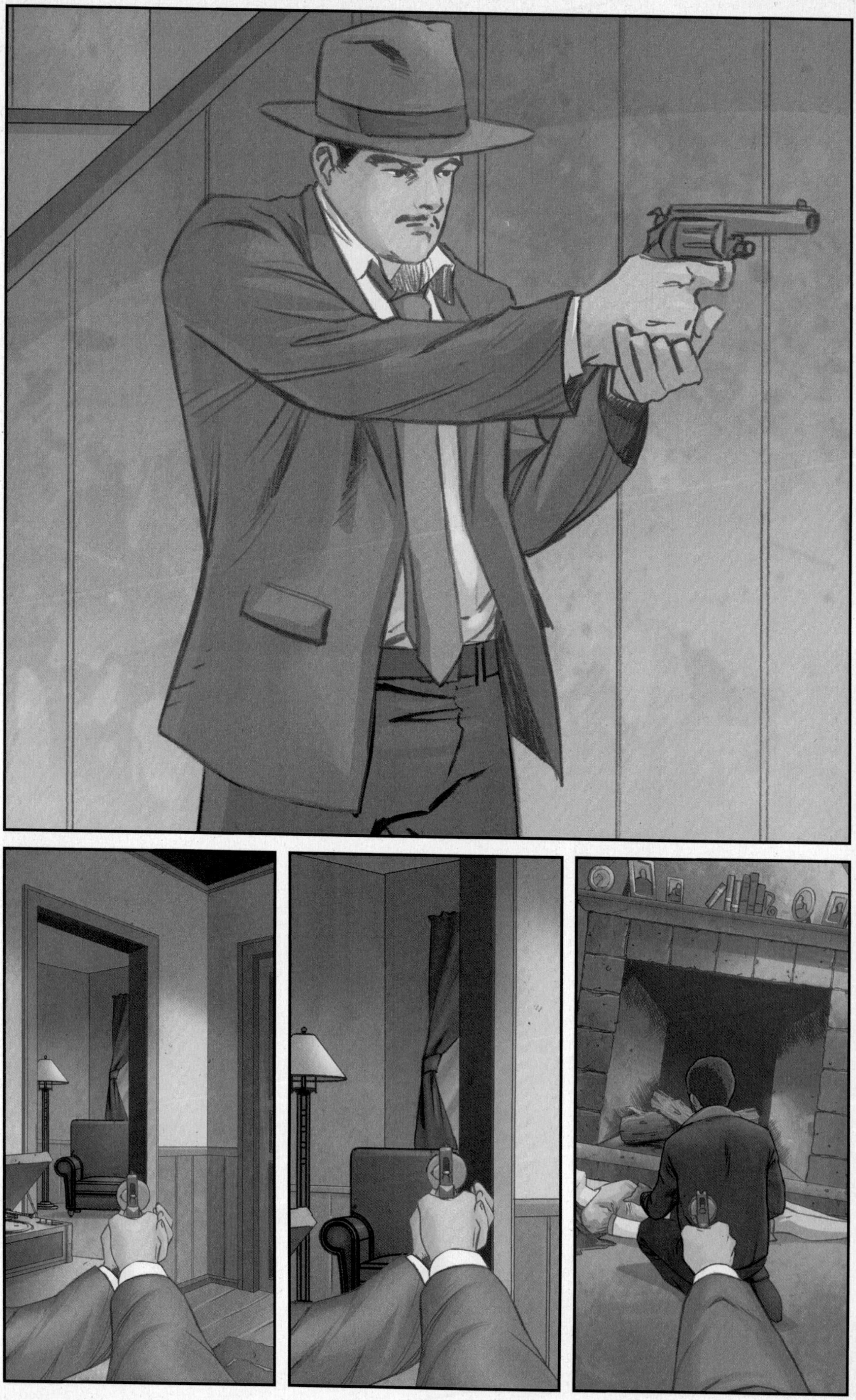

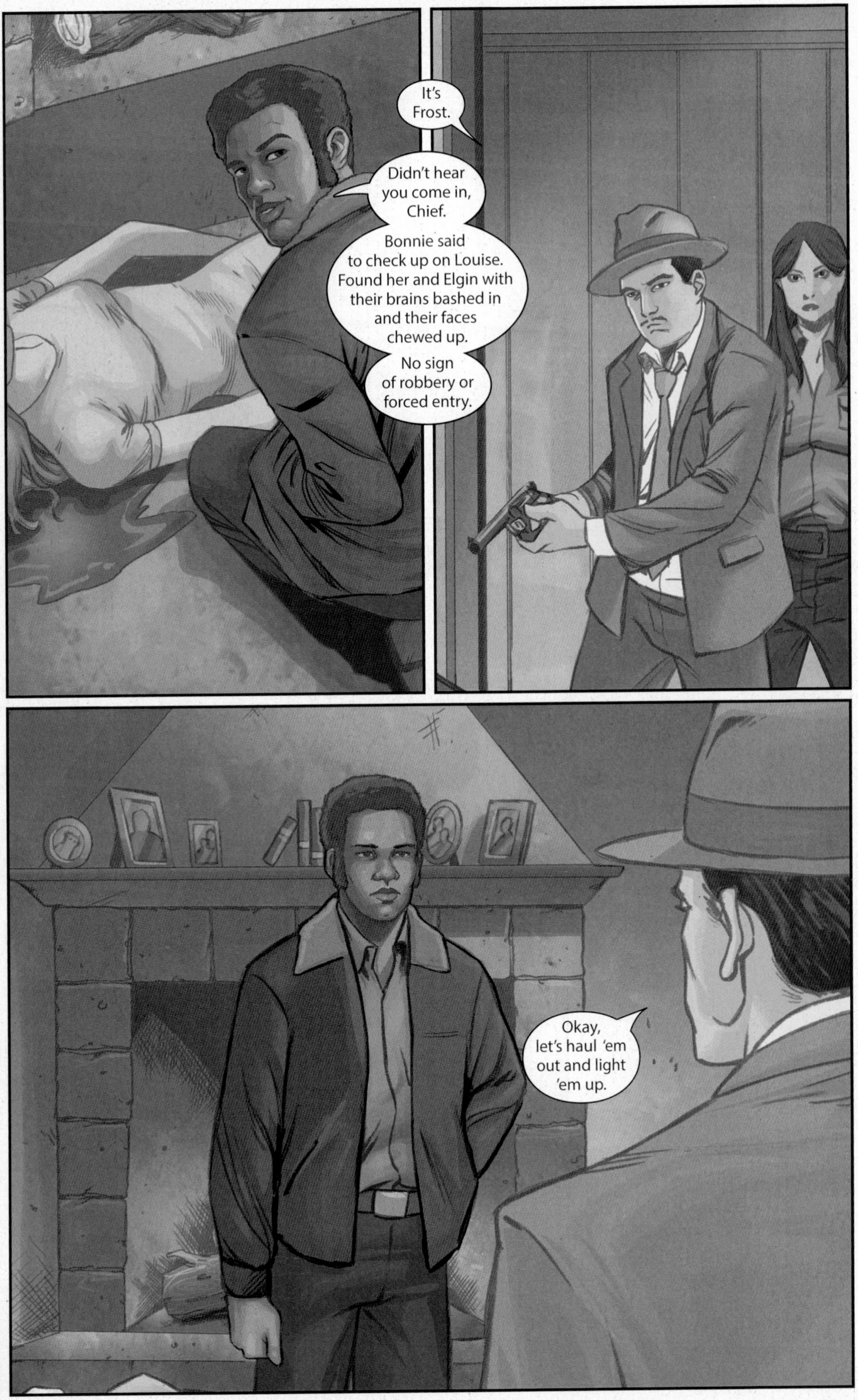
It's Frost.
Didn't hear you come in, Chief.
Bonnie said to check up on Louise. Found her and Elgin with their brains bashed in and their faces chewed up.
No sign of robbery or forced entry.
Okay, let's haul 'em out and light 'em up.

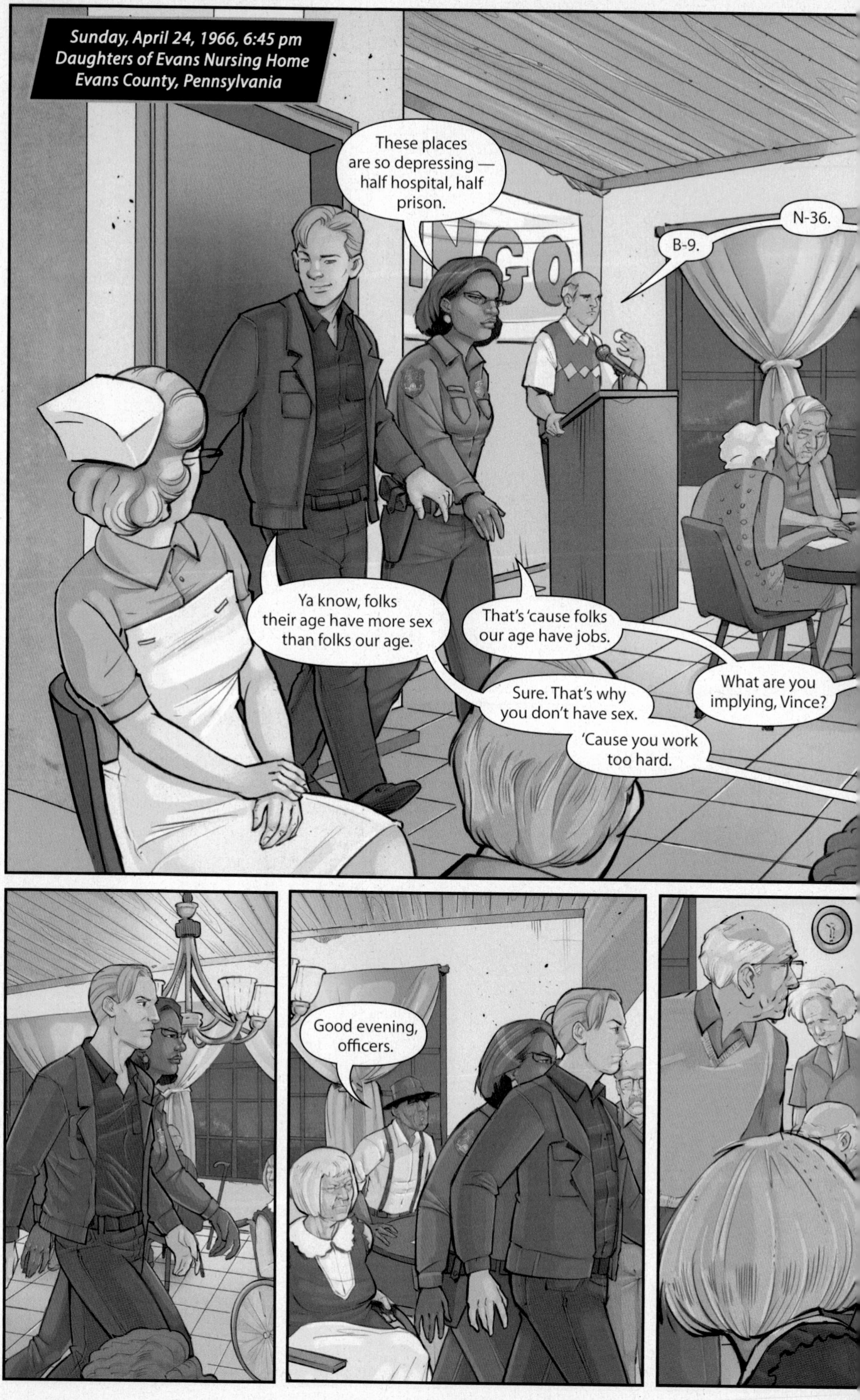
Sunday, April 24, 1966, 6:45 pm
Daughters of Evans Nursing Home
Evans County, Pennsylvania
These places are so depressing — half hospital, half prison.
B-9.
N-36.
Ya know, folks their age have more sex than folks our age.
That's 'cause folks our age have jobs.
What are you implying, Vince?
Sure. That's why you don't have sex.
'Cause you work too hard.
Good evening, officers.

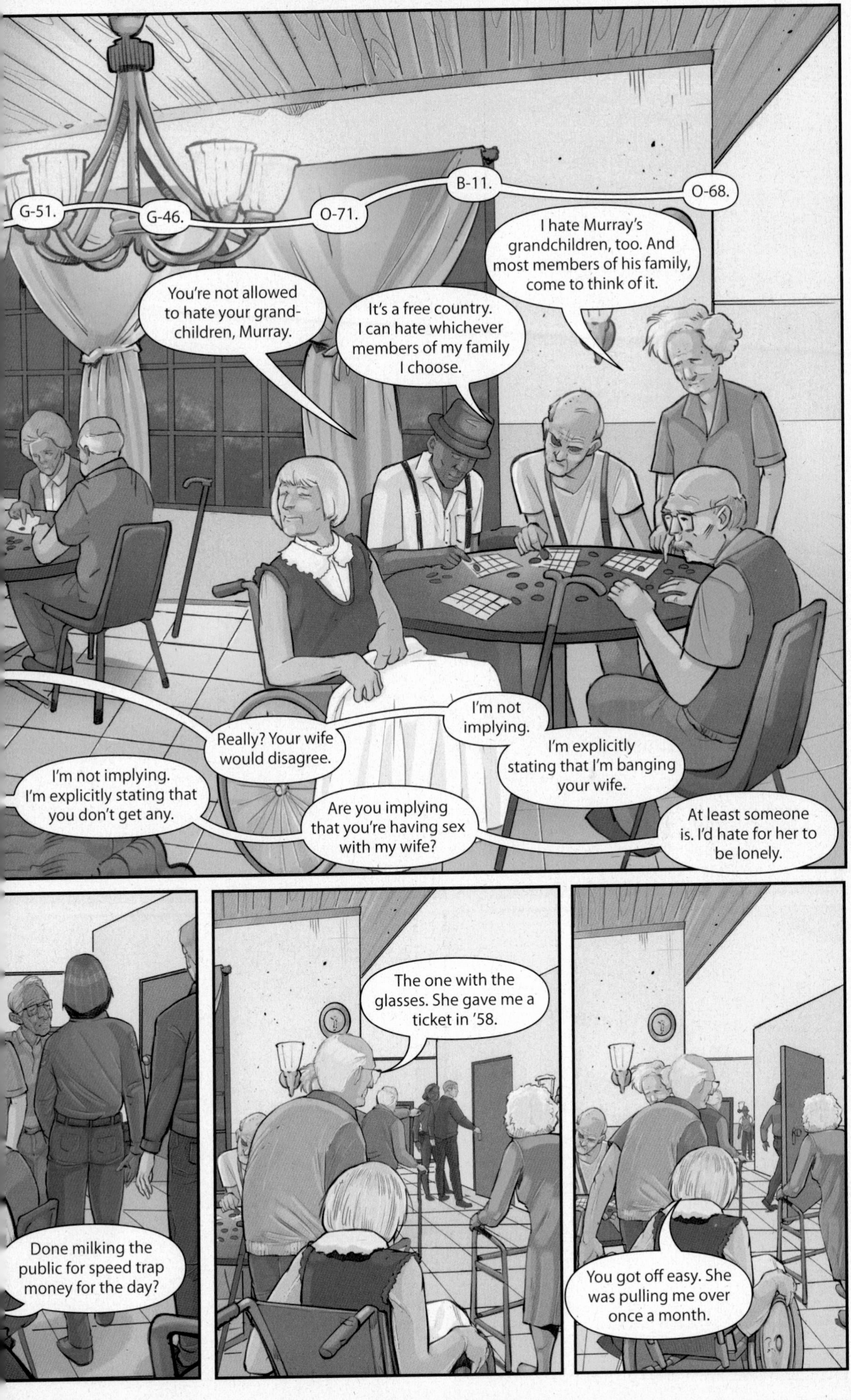
G-51.
G-46.
O-71.
B-11.
O-68.
You're not allowed to hate your grand-children, Murray.
It's a free country. I can hate whichever members of my family I choose.
I hate Murray's grandchildren, too. And most members of his family, come to think of it.
Really? Your wife would disagree.
Are you implying that you're having sex with my wife?
I'm not implying.
I'm explicitly stating that I'm banging your wife.
At least someone is. I'd hate for her to be lonely.
I'm not implying. I'm explicitly stating that you don't get any.
Done milking the public for speed trap money for the day?
The one with the glasses. She gave me a ticket in '58.
You got off easy. She was pulling me over once a month.

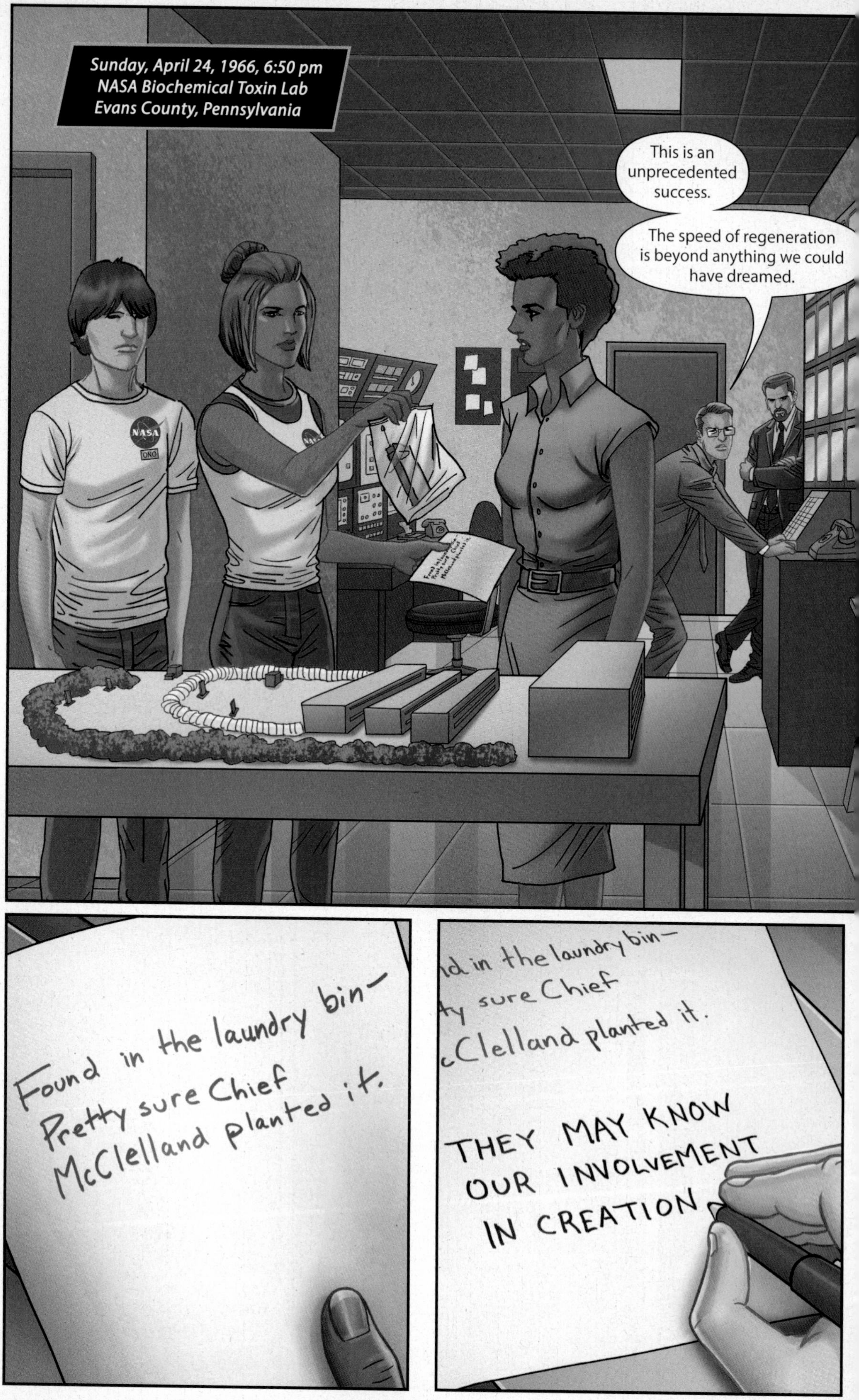
Sunday, April 24, 1966, 6:50 pm
NASA Biochemical Toxin Lab
Evans County, Pennsylvania
This is an unprecedented success.
The speed of regeneration is beyond anything we could have dreamed.
NASA
Found in the laundry bin-
Pretty sure Chief
McClelland planted it.
THEY MAY KNOW
OUR INVOLVEMENT
IN CREATION

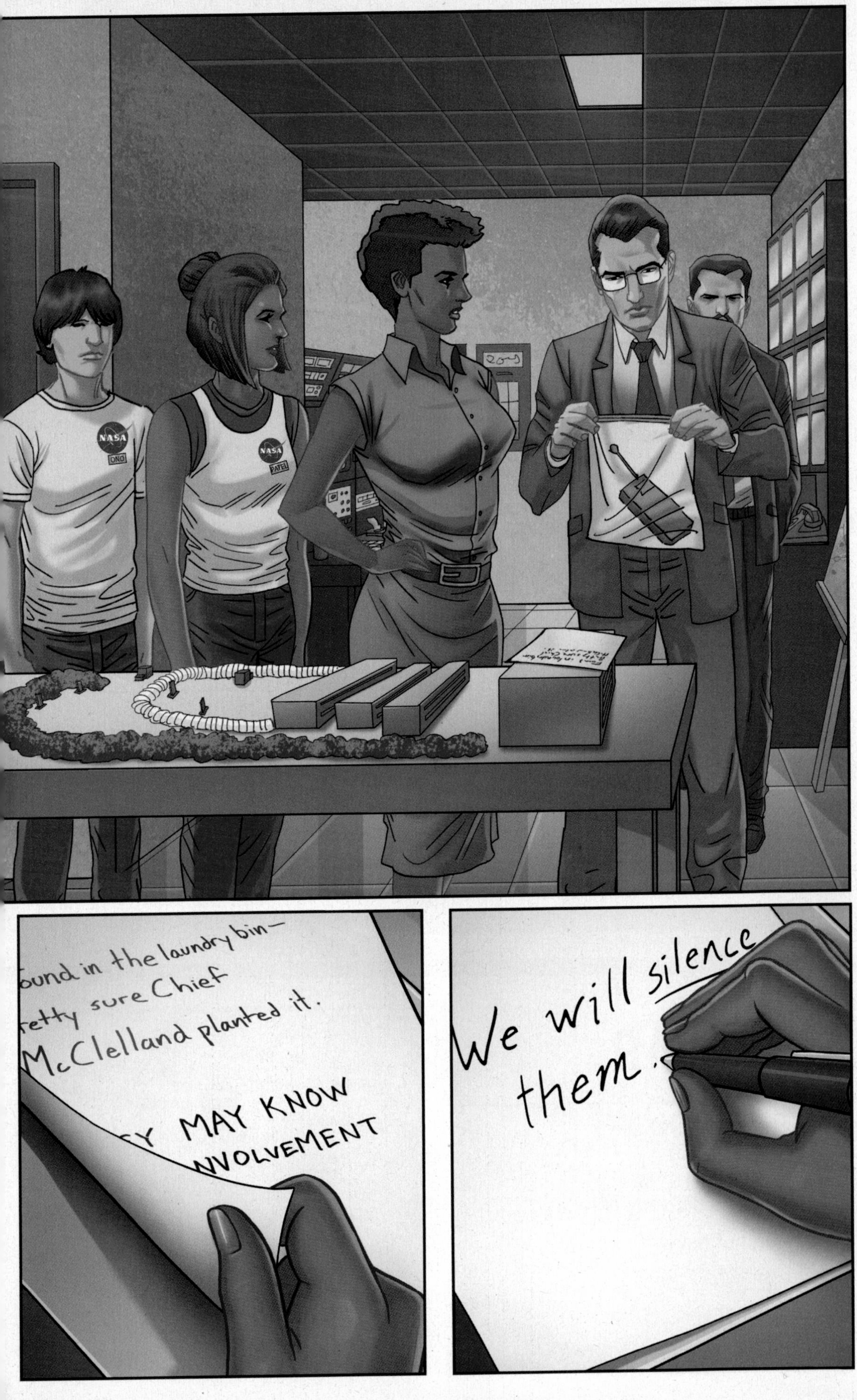
NASA
ONO
NASA
PATEL
ound in the laundry bin—
retty sure Chief
McClelland planted it.
Y MAY KNOW
NVOLVEMENT
We will silence them...

1960s Movements

CIVIL RIGHTS

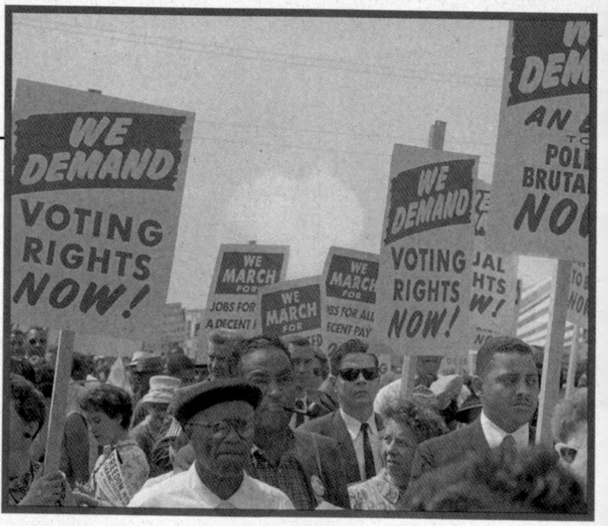

WE DEMAND
VOTING RIGHTS NOW!
WE MARCH FOR JOBS FOR A DECENT
WE MARCH FOR
WE DEMAND
VOTING RIGHTS NOW!
POLI BRUTA

POPULAR SLOGANS

"We shall overcome"

"Keep your eyes on the prize and hold on"

"Say it loud: I'm Black and proud"

"Ain't going to let nobody turn me round"

"Black is beautiful"

"Black power"

WOMEN'S LIBERATION

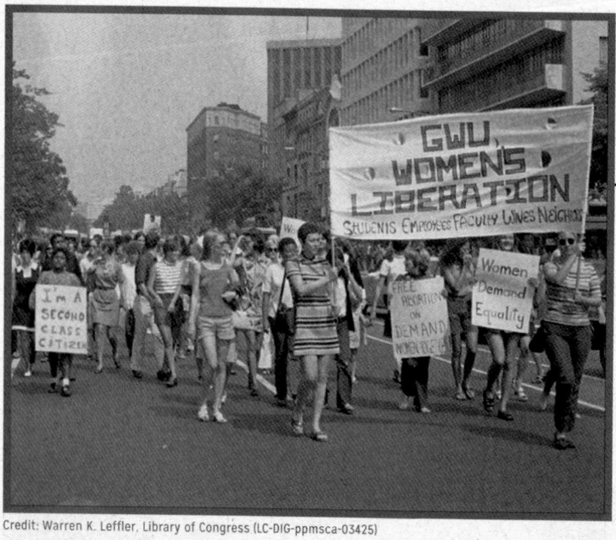

GWU
WOMENS
LIBERATION
STUDENTS EMPLOYEES FACULTY WIVES
I'm A SECOND CLASS CITIZEN
Women Demand Equality

Credit: Warren K. Leffler, Library of Congress (LC-DIG-ppmsca-03425)

POPULAR SLOGANS

"The Personal is Political"

"Sisterhood is Powerful"

"Equal Pay for Equal Work"

"Women Demand Equality"

"We're not beautiful. We're not ugly. We're angry."

ANTI WAR

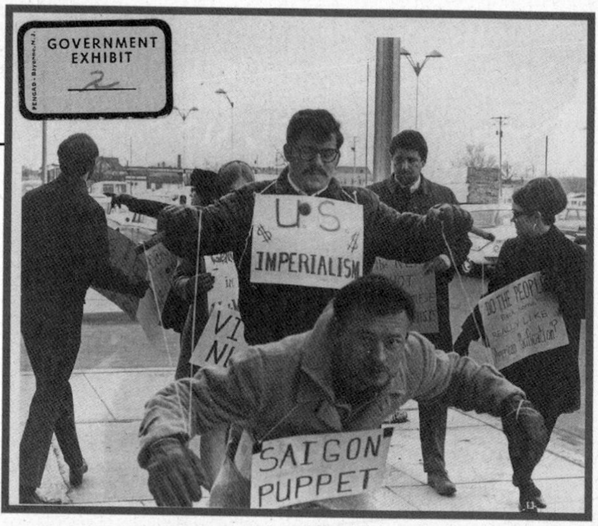

GOVERNMENT EXHIBIT
2
U S
IMPERIALISM
SAIGON PUPPET

POPULAR SLOGANS

"Hey, hey, LBJ,
how many kids did you kill today?"

"Draft beer, not boys"

"Hell no, we won't go"

"Make love, not war"

"Eighteen today, dead tomorrow"

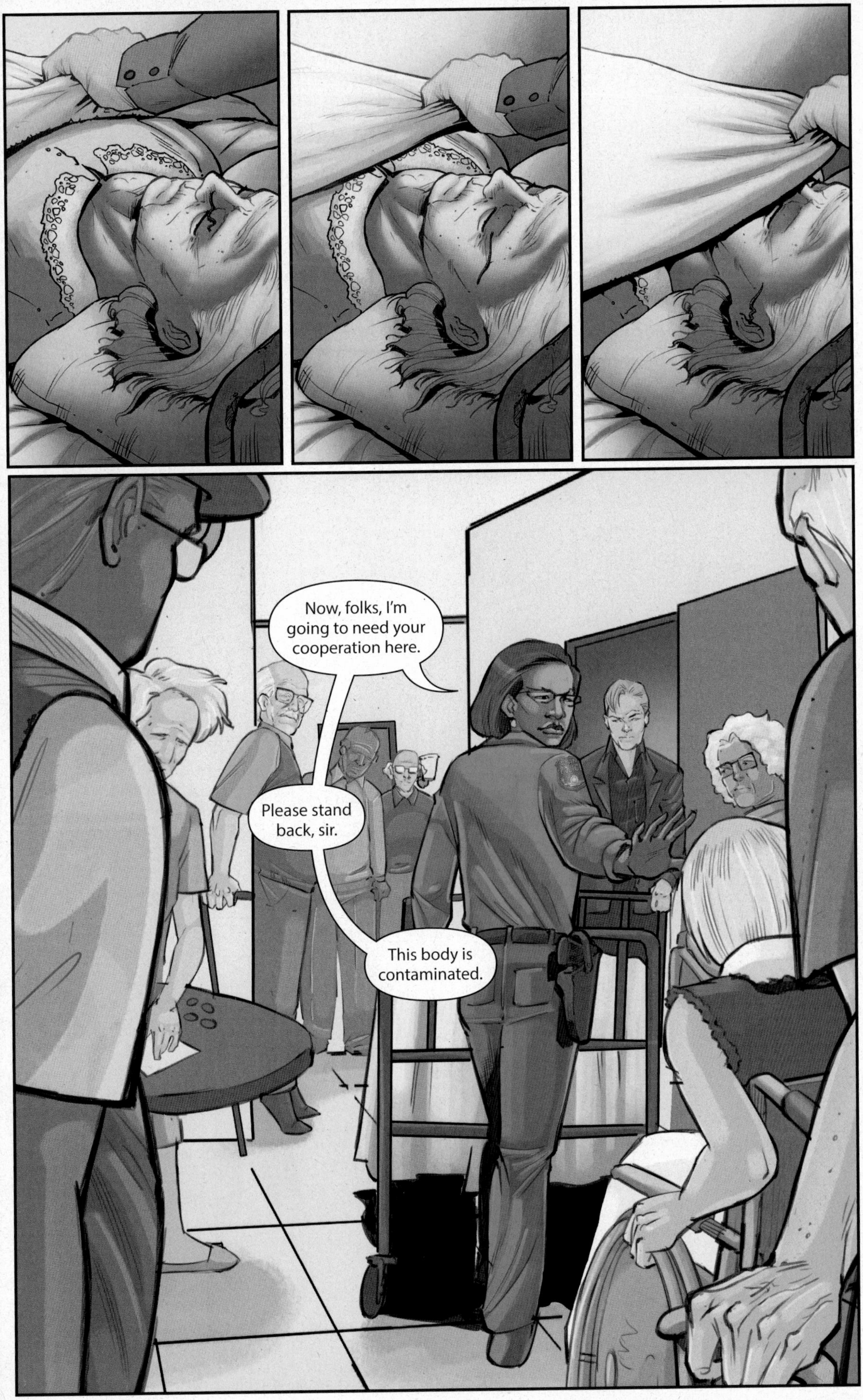
Now, folks, I'm going to need your cooperation here.
Please stand back, sir.
This body is contaminated.

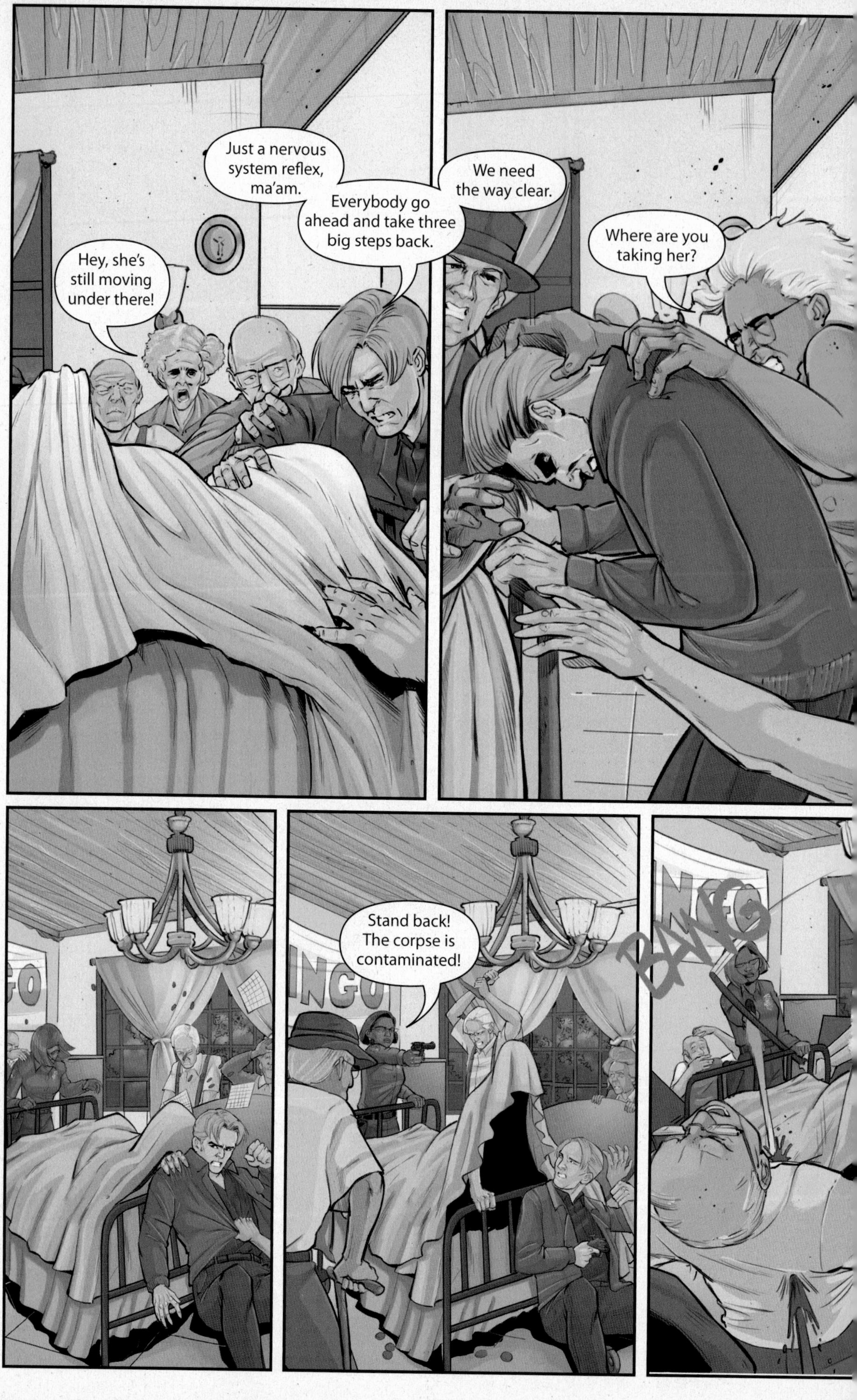
Hey, she's still moving under there!
Just a nervous system reflex, ma'am.
Everybody go ahead and take three big steps back.
We need the way clear.
Where are you taking her?
Stand back! The corpse is contaminated!
BANG

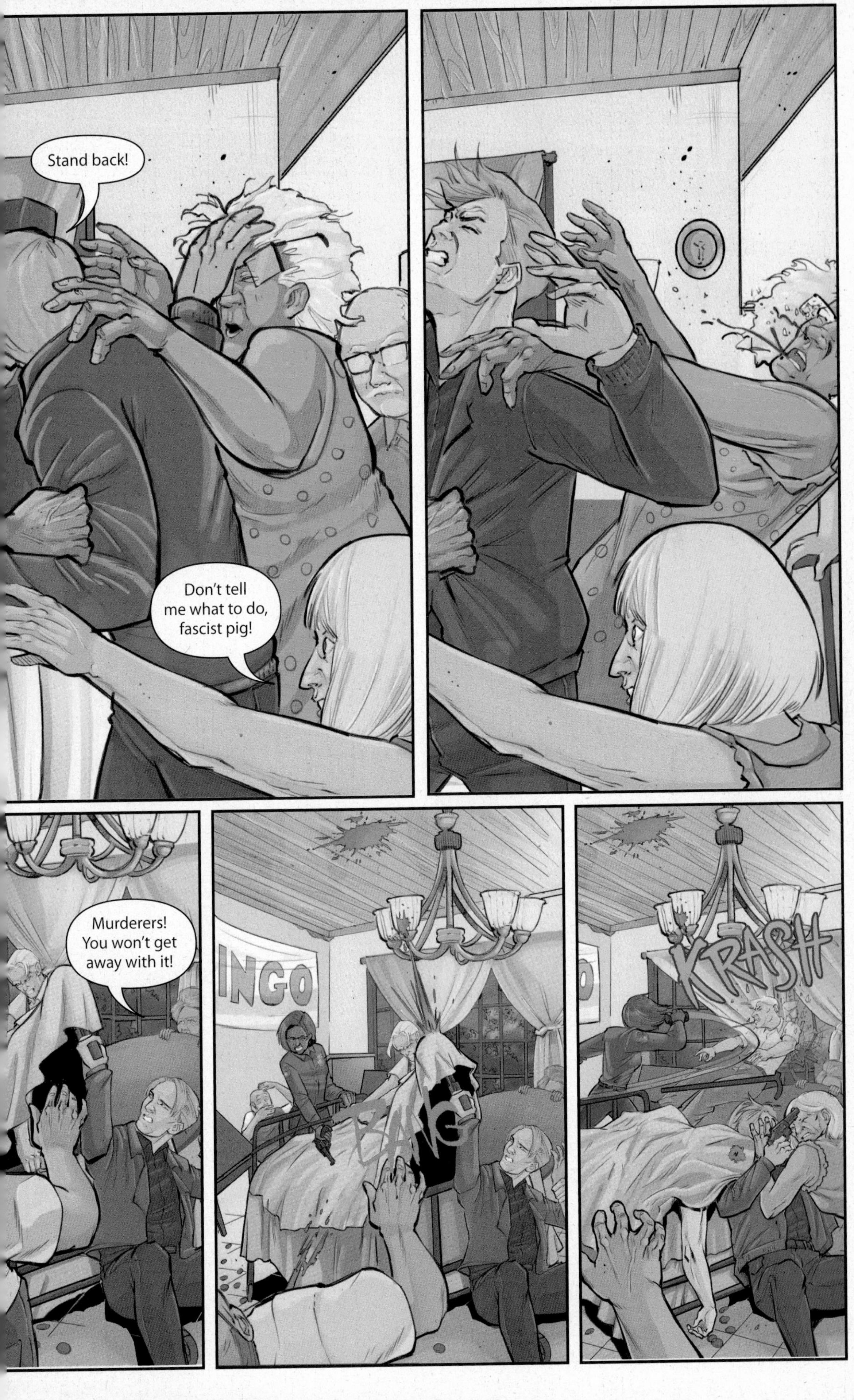
Stand back!
Don't tell me what to do, fascist pig!
Murderers! You won't get away with it!
INGO
BANG
KRASH

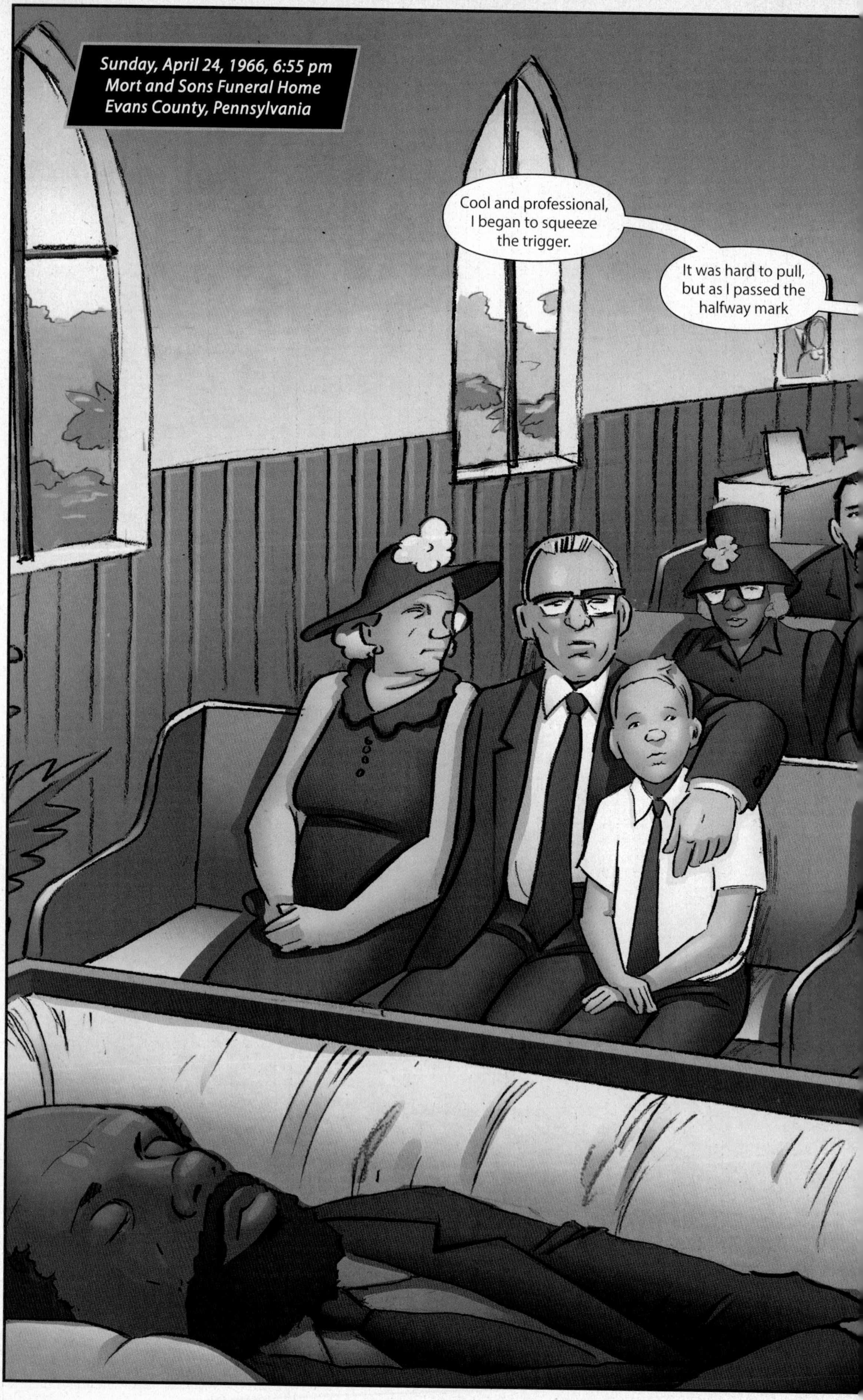
Sunday, April 24, 1966, 6:55 pm
Mort and Sons Funeral Home
Evans County, Pennsylvania
Cool and professional, I began to squeeze the trigger.
It was hard to pull, but as I passed the halfway mark

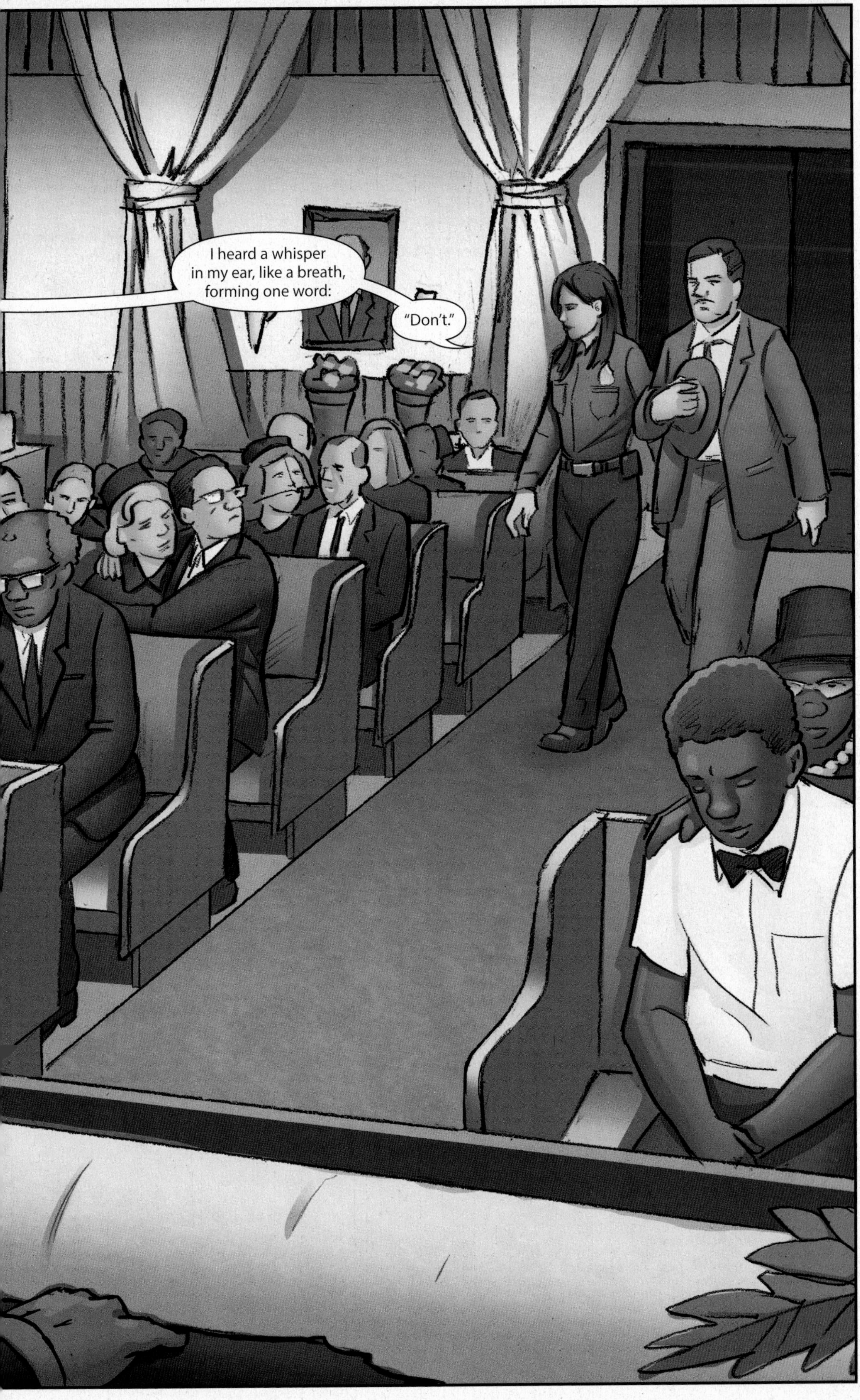
I heard a whisper in my ear, like a breath, forming one word:
"Don't."

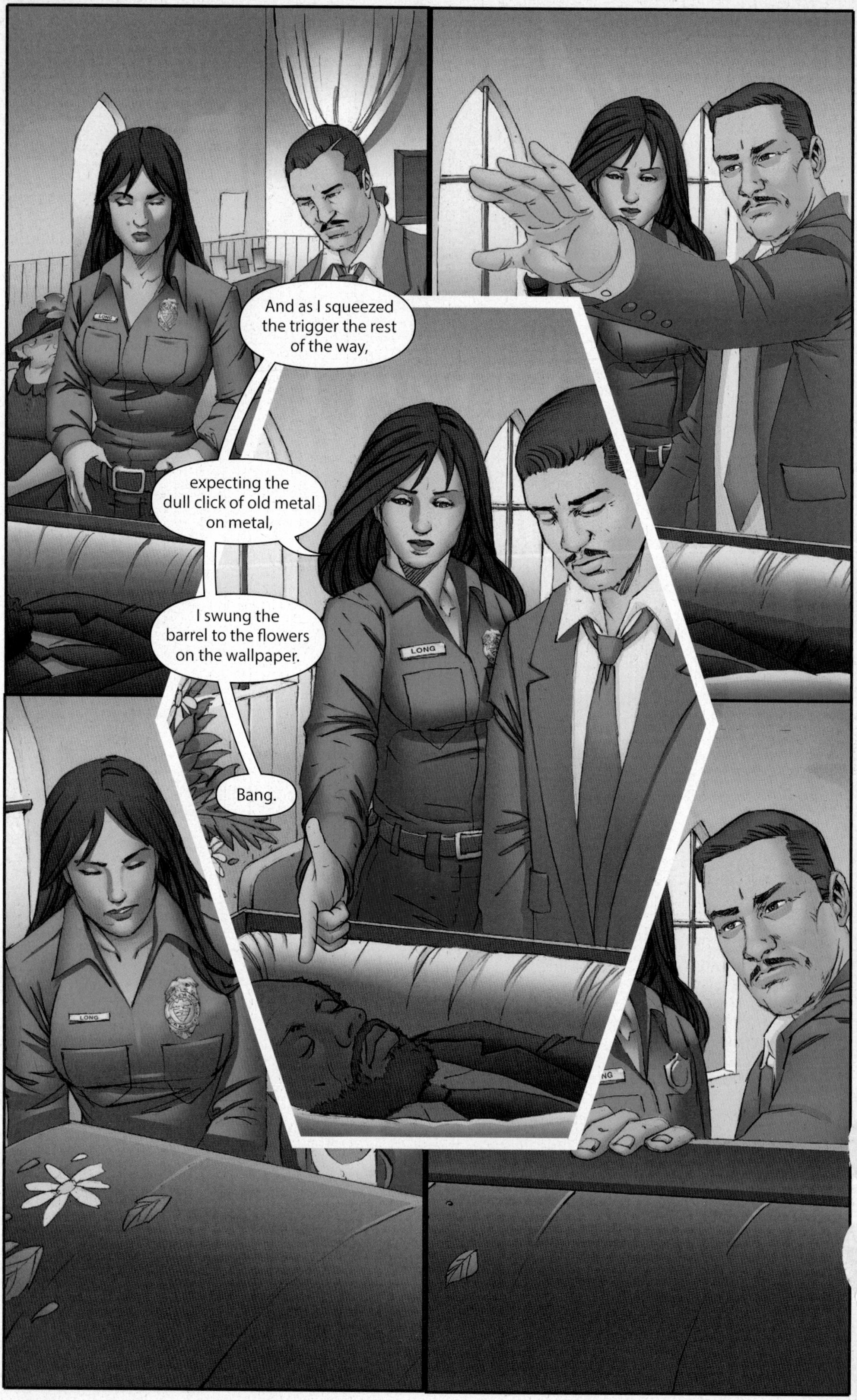

And as I squeezed the trigger the rest of the way,
expecting the dull click of old metal on metal,
I swung the barrel to the flowers on the wallpaper.
Bang.
LONG
LONG
LONG

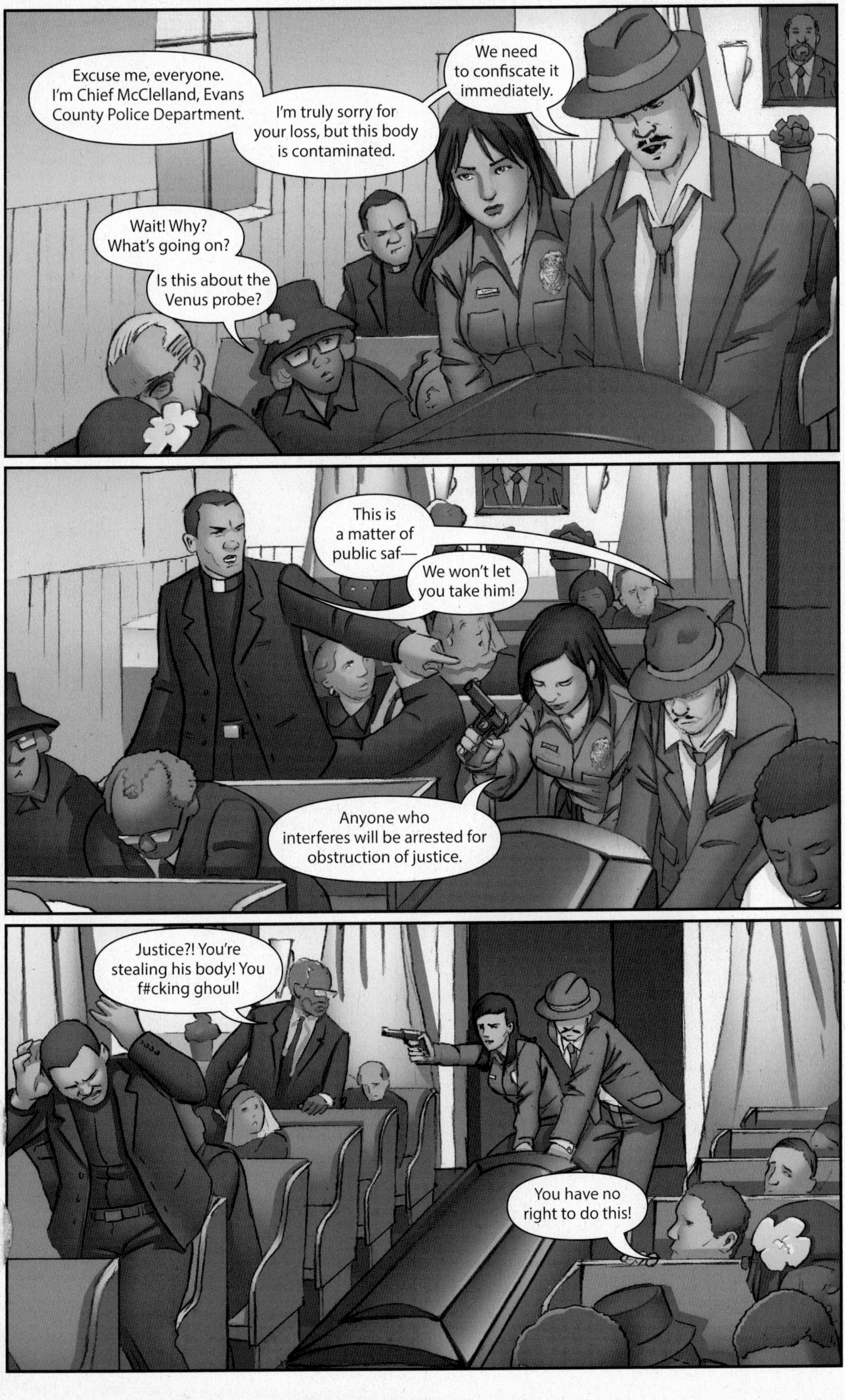
Excuse me, everyone. I'm Chief McClelland, Evans County Police Department.
I'm truly sorry for your loss, but this body is contaminated.
We need to confiscate it immediately.
Wait! Why? What's going on?
Is this about the Venus probe?
This is a matter of public saf—
We won't let you take him!
Anyone who interferes will be arrested for obstruction of justice.
Justice?! You're stealing his body! You f#cking ghoul!
You have no right to do this!

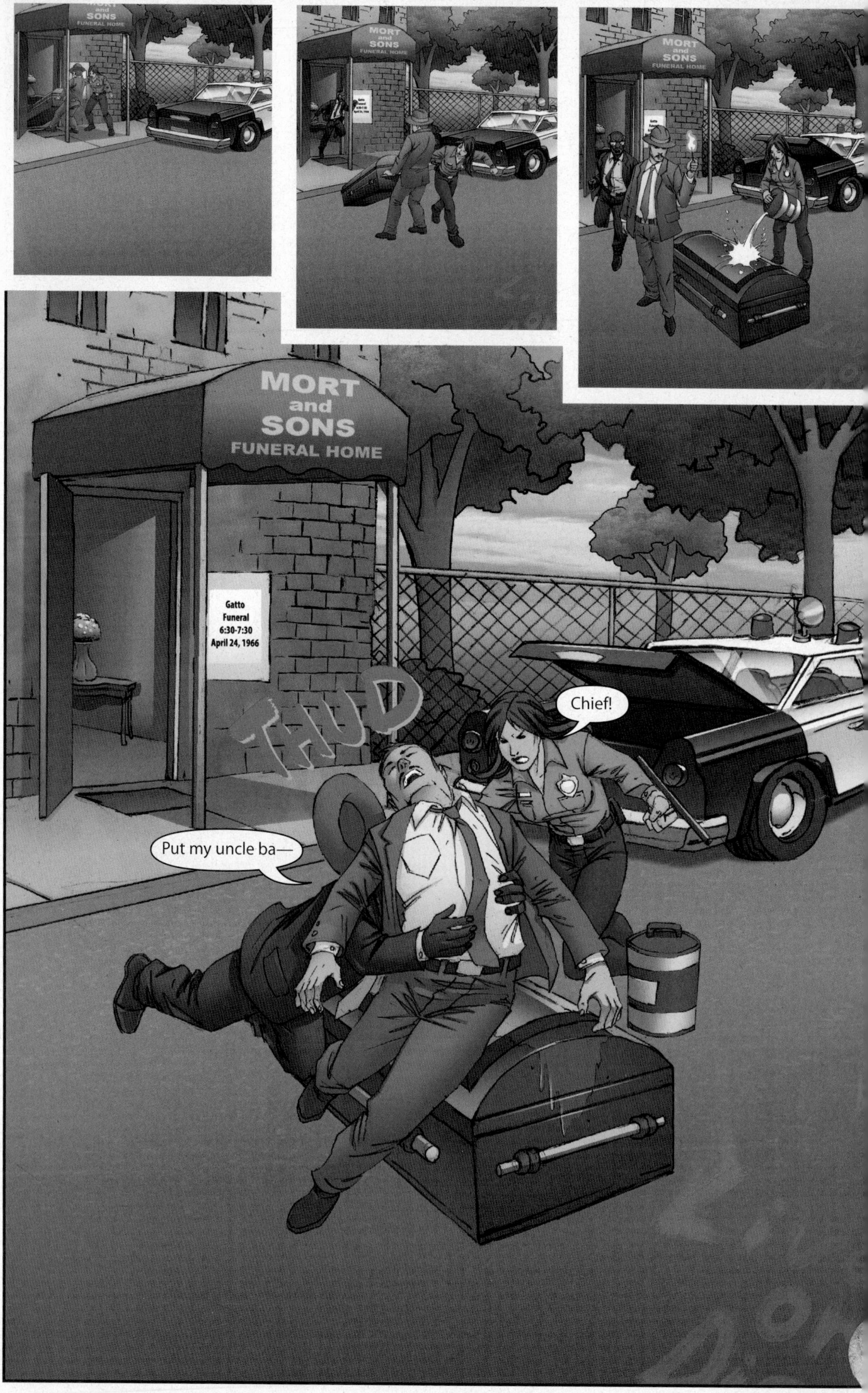
MORT and SONS FUNERAL HOME
Gatto Funeral 6:30-7:30 April 24, 1966
THUD
Chief!
Put my uncle ba—

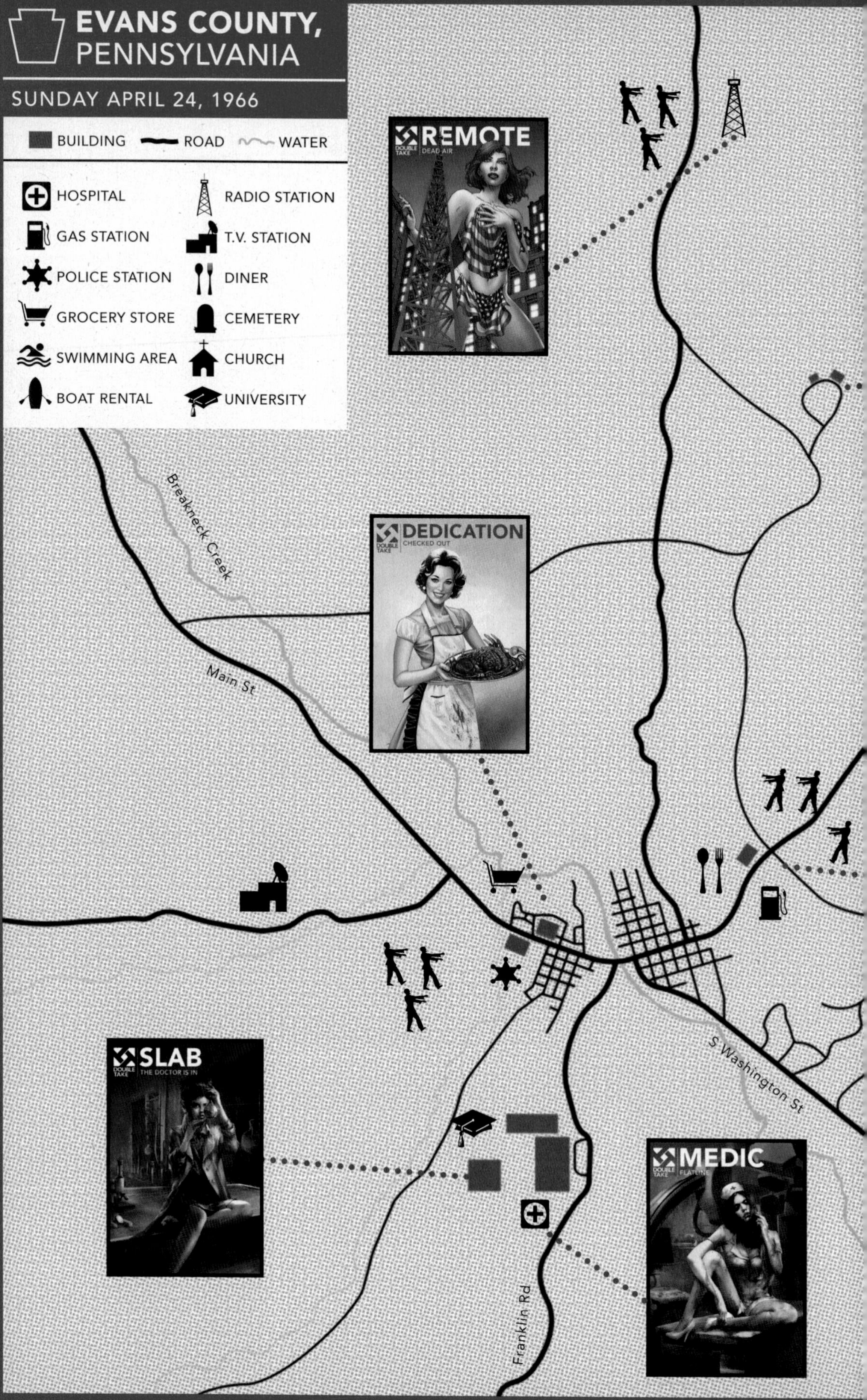
EVANS COUNTY, PENNSYLVANIA
SUNDAY APRIL 24, 1966
BUILDING
ROAD
WATER
HOSPITAL
GAS STATION
POLICE STATION
GROCERY STORE
SWIMMING AREA
BOAT RENTAL
RADIO STATION
T.V. STATION
DINER
CEMETERY
CHURCH
UNIVERSITY
DOUBLE TAKE REMOTE DEAD AIR
DOUBLE TAKE DEDICATION CHECKED OUT
DOUBLE TAKE SLAB THE DOCTOR IS IN
DOUBLE TAKE MEDIC FLATLINE
Breakneck Creek
Main St
S Washington St
Franklin Rd

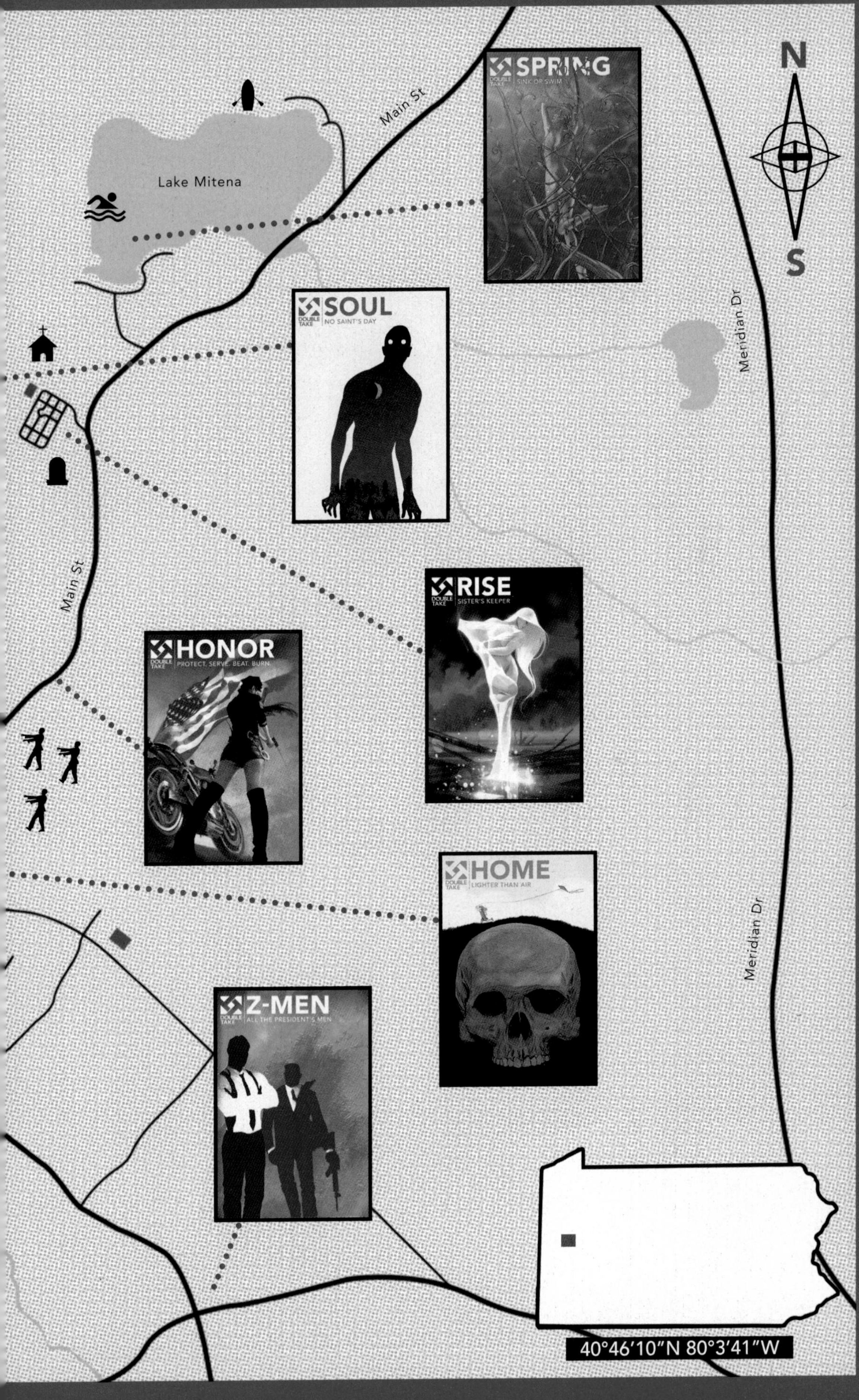

N
S
Main St
Lake Mitena
SPRING
DOUBLE TAKE
SINK OR SWIM
SOUL
DOUBLE TAKE
NO SAINT'S DAY
Meridian Dr
Main St
RISE
DOUBLE TAKE
SISTER'S KEEPER
HONOR
DOUBLE TAKE
PROTECT. SERVE. BEAT. BURN.
HOME
DOUBLE TAKE
LIGHTER THAN AIR
Meridian Dr
Z-MEN
DOUBLE TAKE
ALL THE PRESIDENT'S MEN
40°46′10″N 80°3′41″W

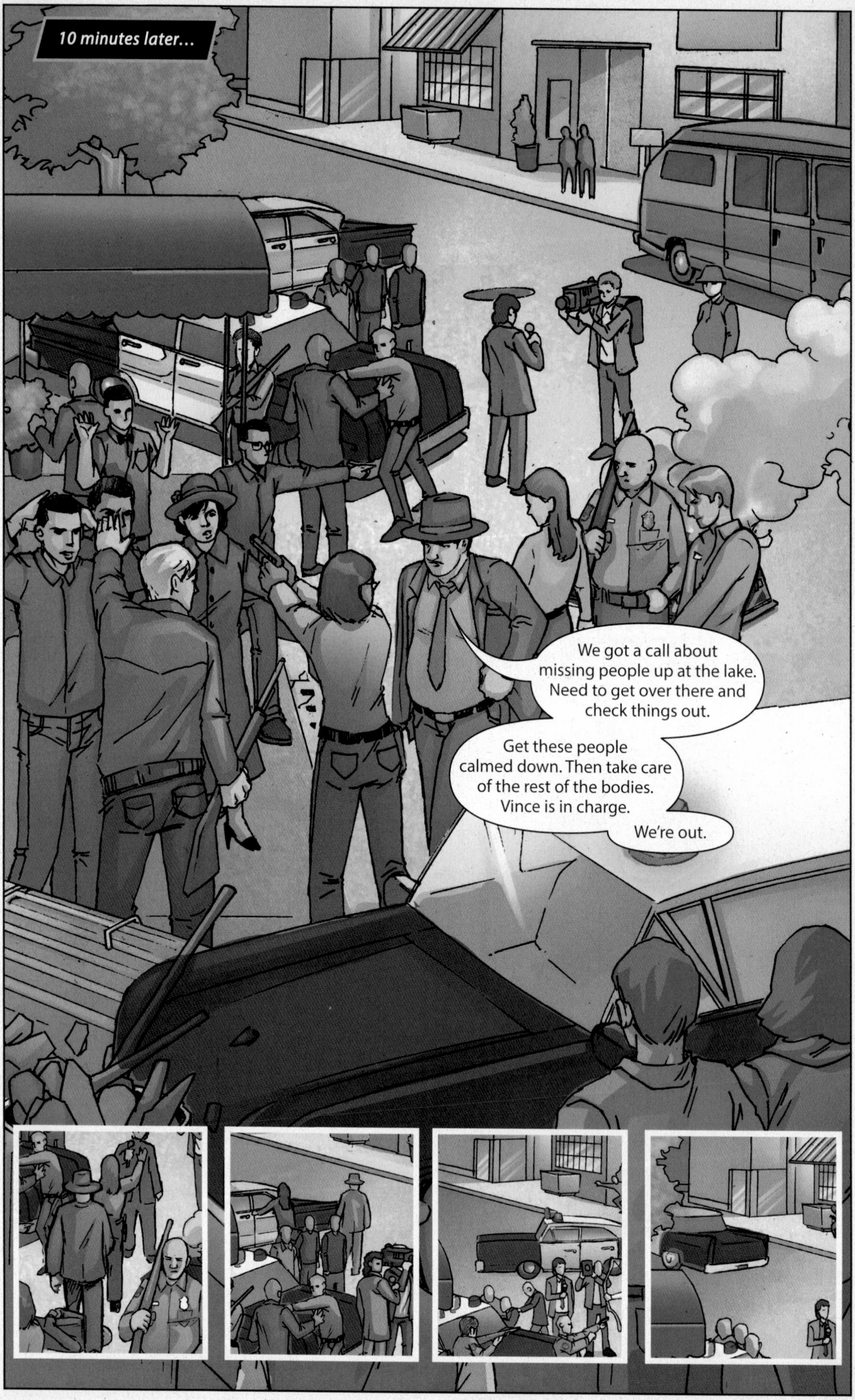
10 minutes later…
We got a call about missing people up at the lake. Need to get over there and check things out.
Get these people calmed down. Then take care of the rest of the bodies. Vince is in charge.
We're out.

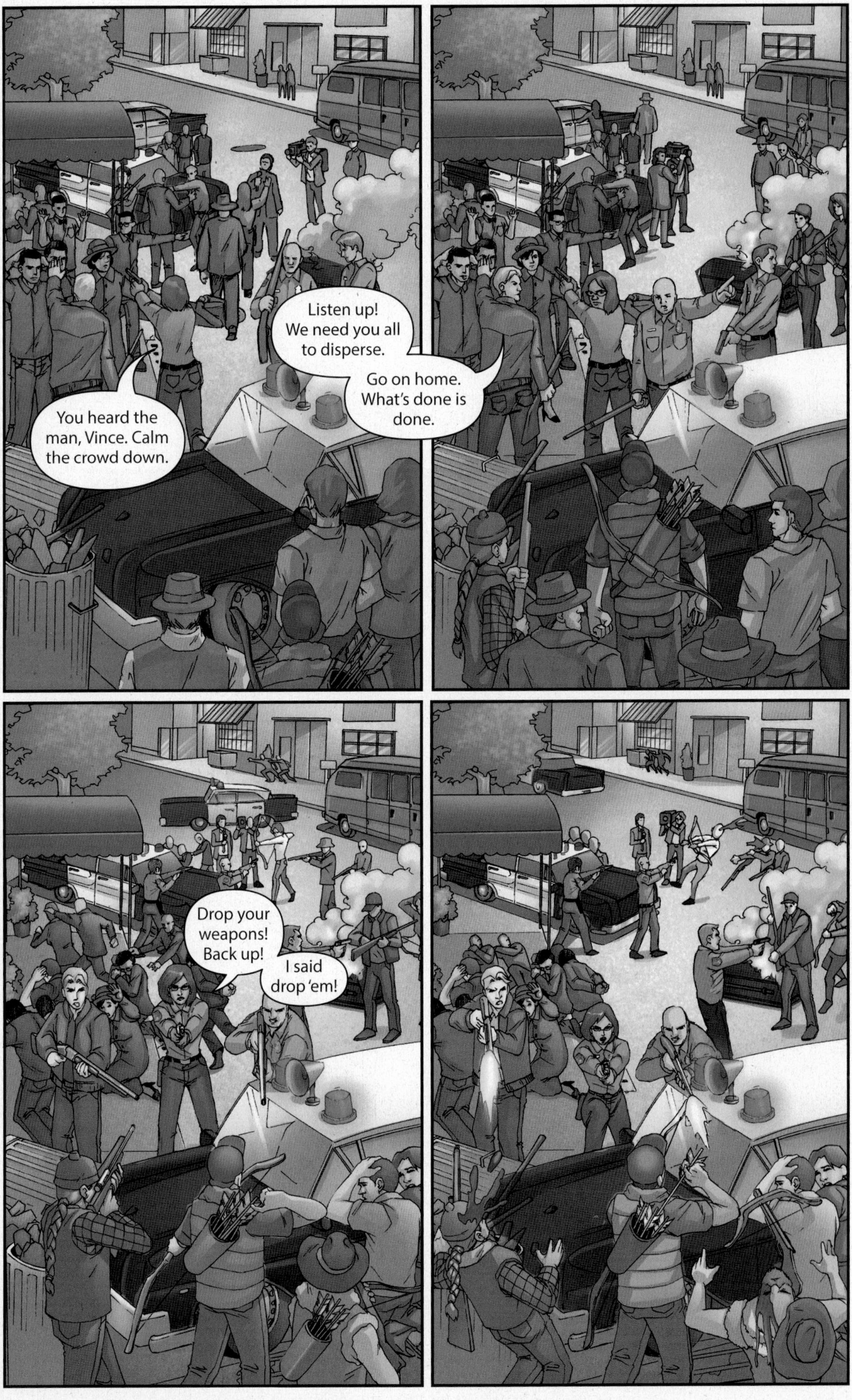
Listen up! We need you all to disperse.
You heard the man, Vince. Calm the crowd down.
Go on home. What's done is done.
Drop your weapons! Back up!
I said drop 'em!

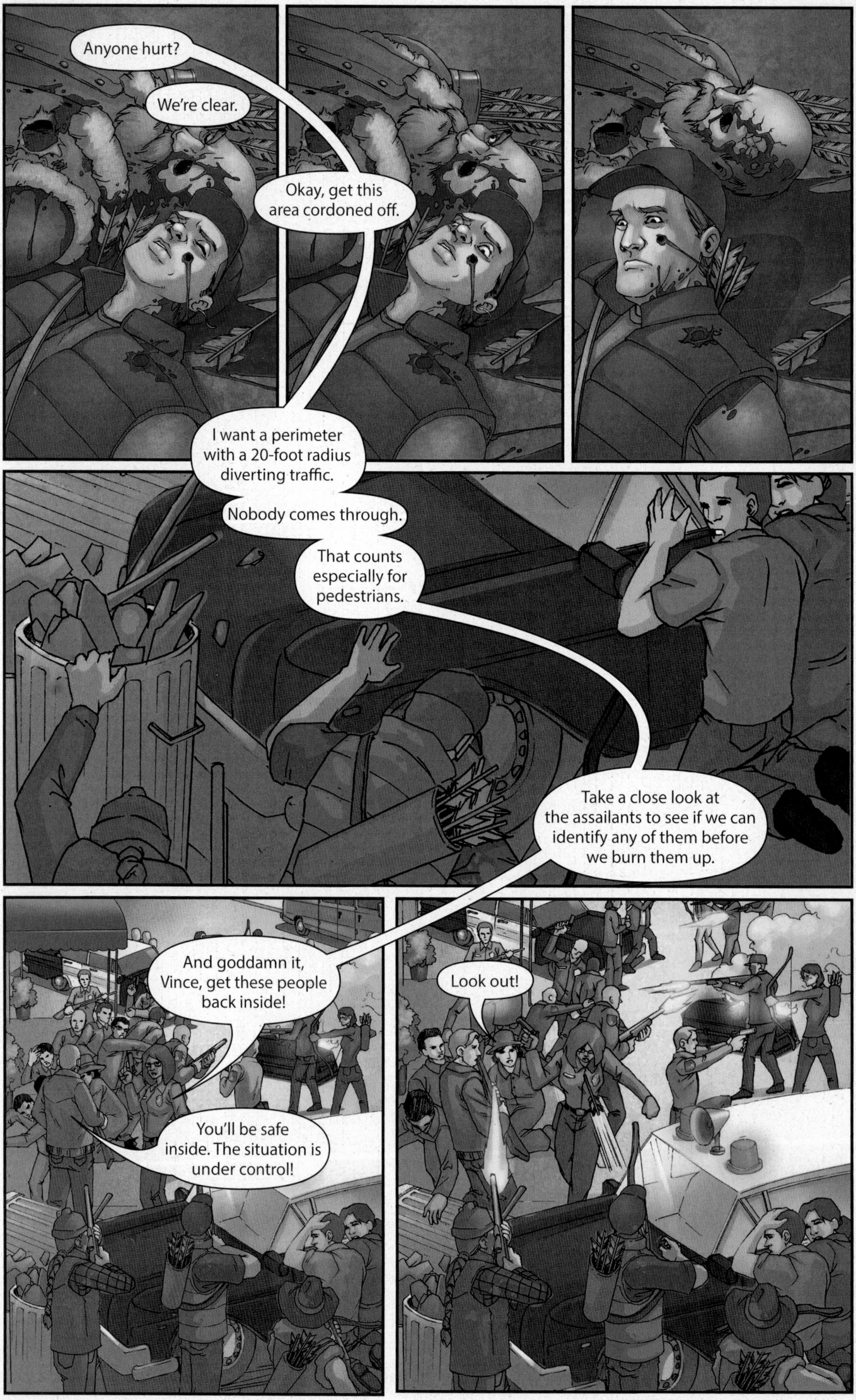
Anyone hurt?
We're clear.
Okay, get this area cordoned off.
I want a perimeter with a 20-foot radius diverting traffic.
Nobody comes through.
That counts especially for pedestrians.
Take a close look at the assailants to see if we can identify any of them before we burn them up.
And goddamn it, Vince, get these people back inside!
You'll be safe inside. The situation is under control!
Look out!

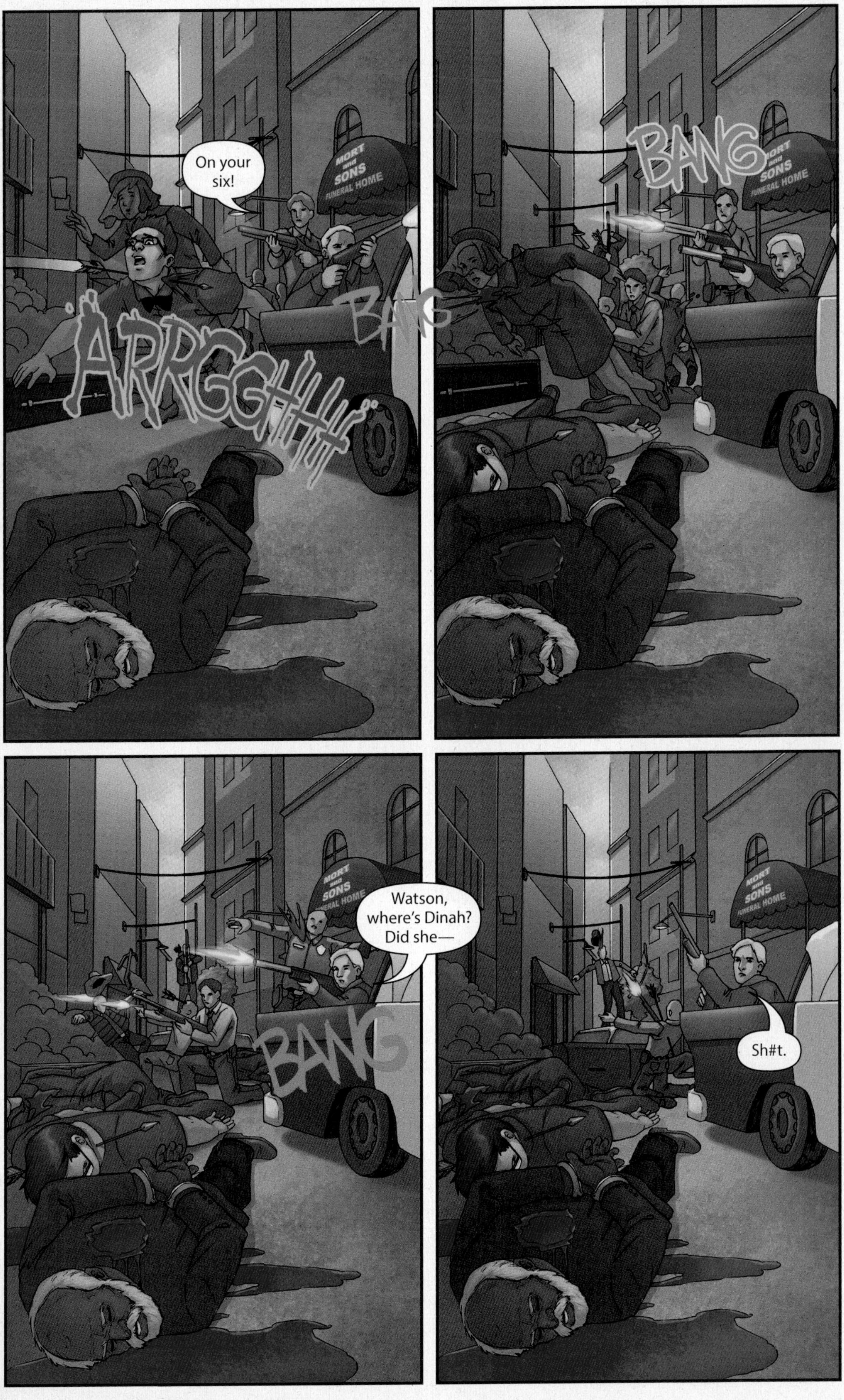
On your six!
MORT and SONS FUNERAL HOME
ARRGGHHH
BANG
BANG
MORT and SONS FUNERAL HOME
MORT and SONS FUNERAL HOME
Watson, where's Dinah? Did she—
BANG
MORT and SONS FUNERAL HOME
Sh#t.

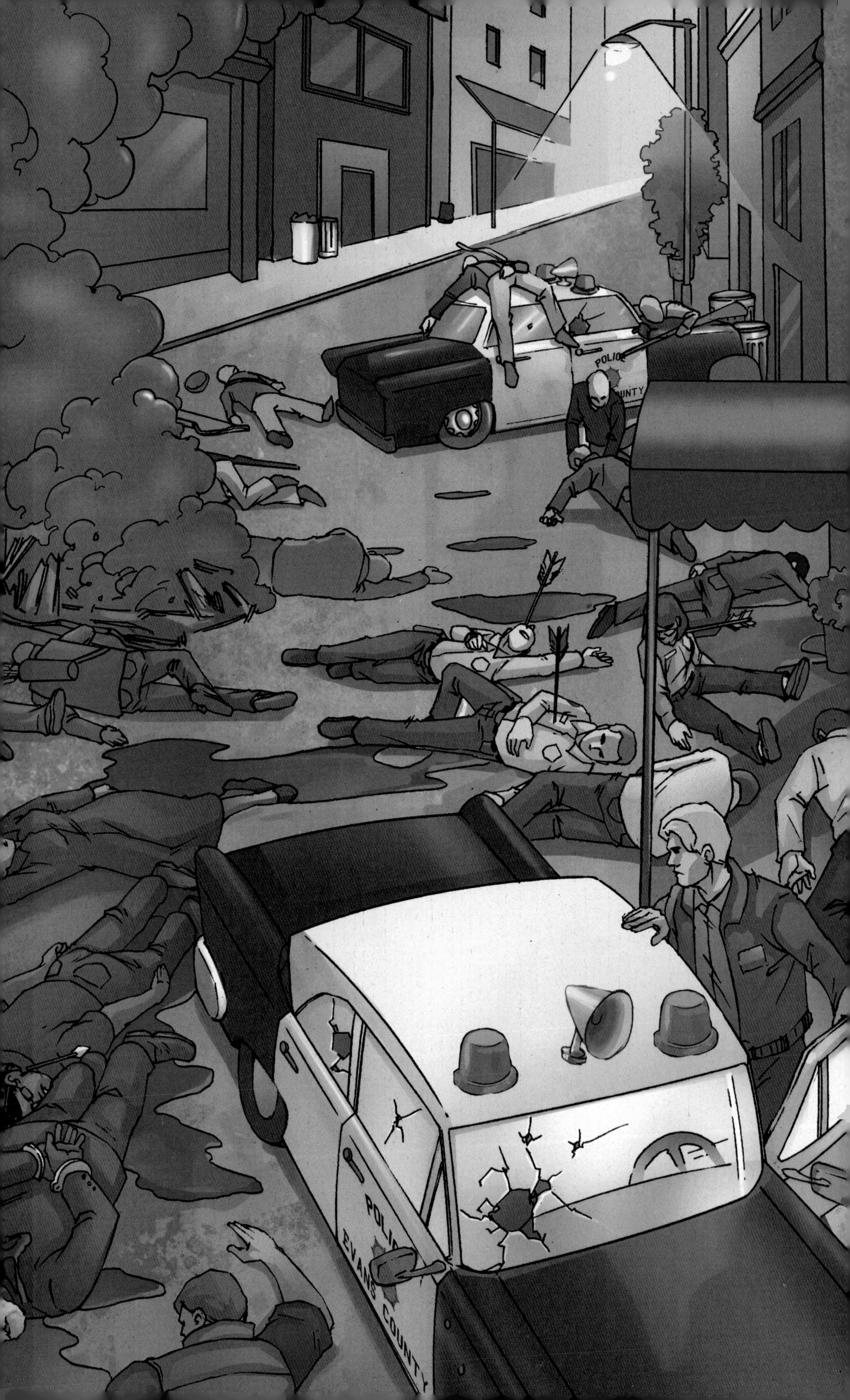
POLICE
EVANS COUNTY

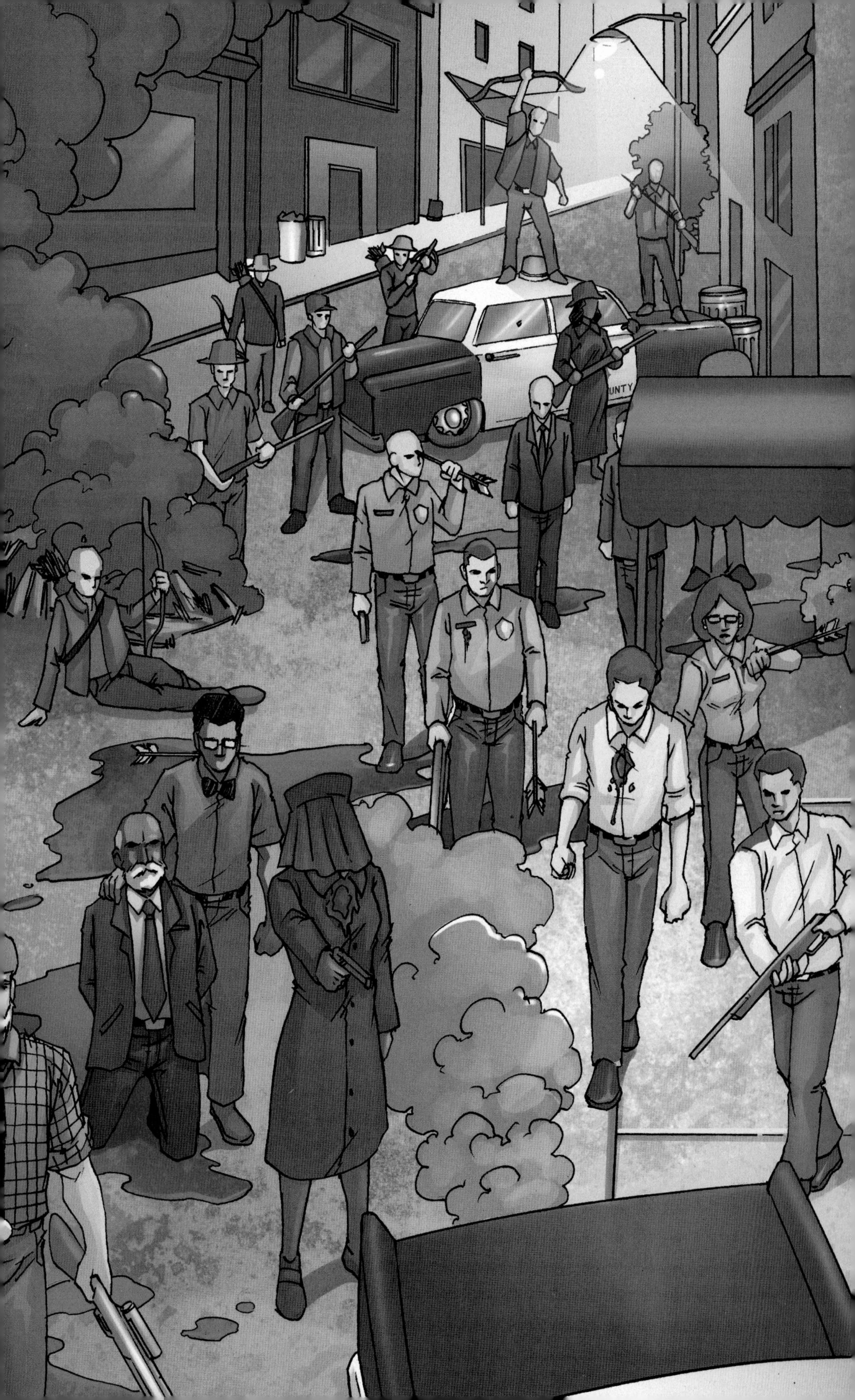

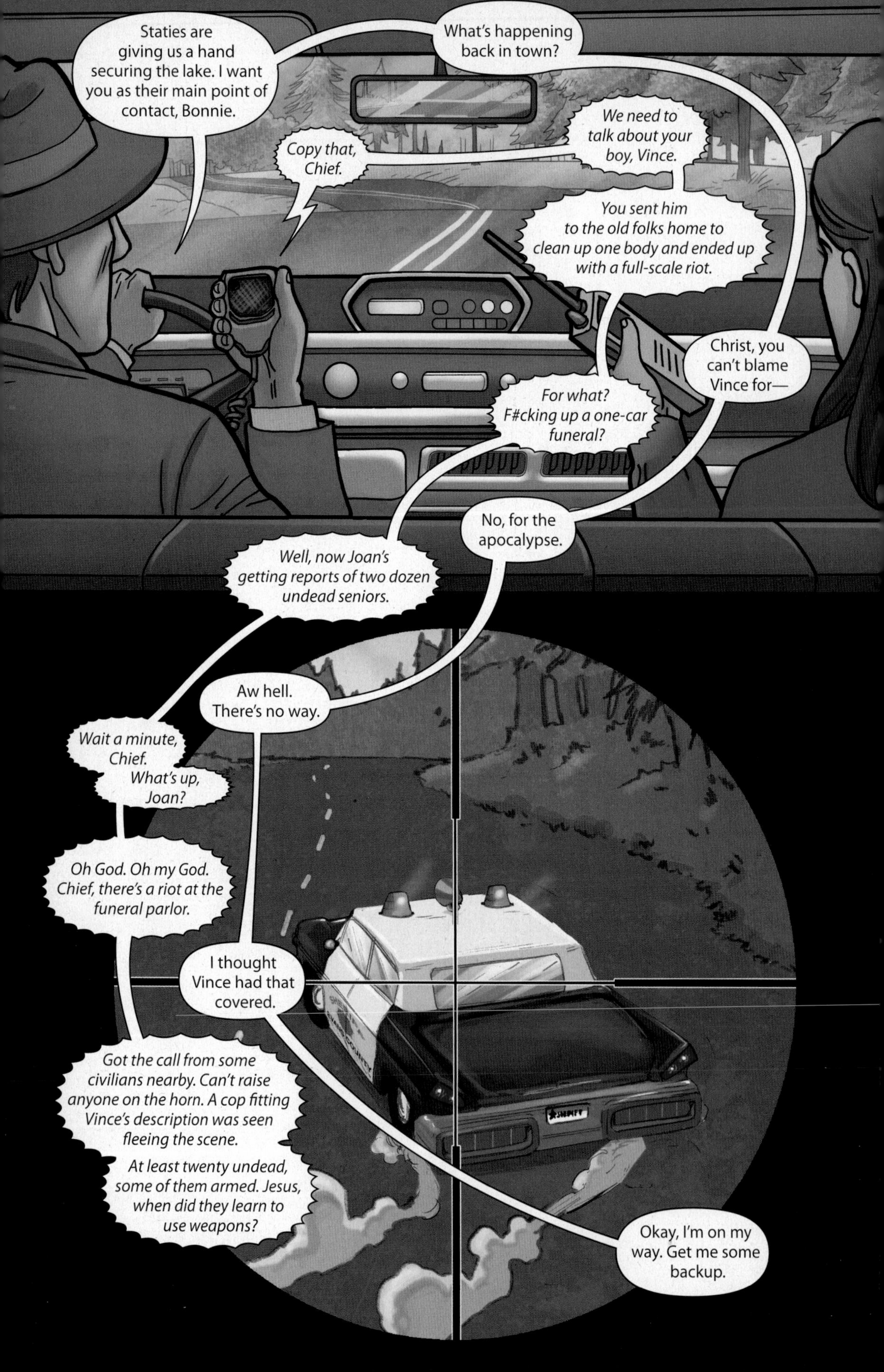
Staties are giving us a hand securing the lake. I want you as their main point of contact, Bonnie.
Copy that, Chief.
What's happening back in town?
We need to talk about your boy, Vince.
You sent him to the old folks home to clean up one body and ended up with a full-scale riot.
Christ, you can't blame Vince for—
For what? F#cking up a one-car funeral?
No, for the apocalypse.
Well, now Joan's getting reports of two dozen undead seniors.
Aw hell. There's no way.
Wait a minute, Chief.
What's up, Joan?
Oh God. Oh my God. Chief, there's a riot at the funeral parlor.
I thought Vince had that covered.
Got the call from some civilians nearby. Can't raise anyone on the horn. A cop fitting Vince's description was seen fleeing the scene.
At least twenty undead, some of them armed. Jesus, when did they learn to use weapons?
Okay, I'm on my way. Get me some backup.

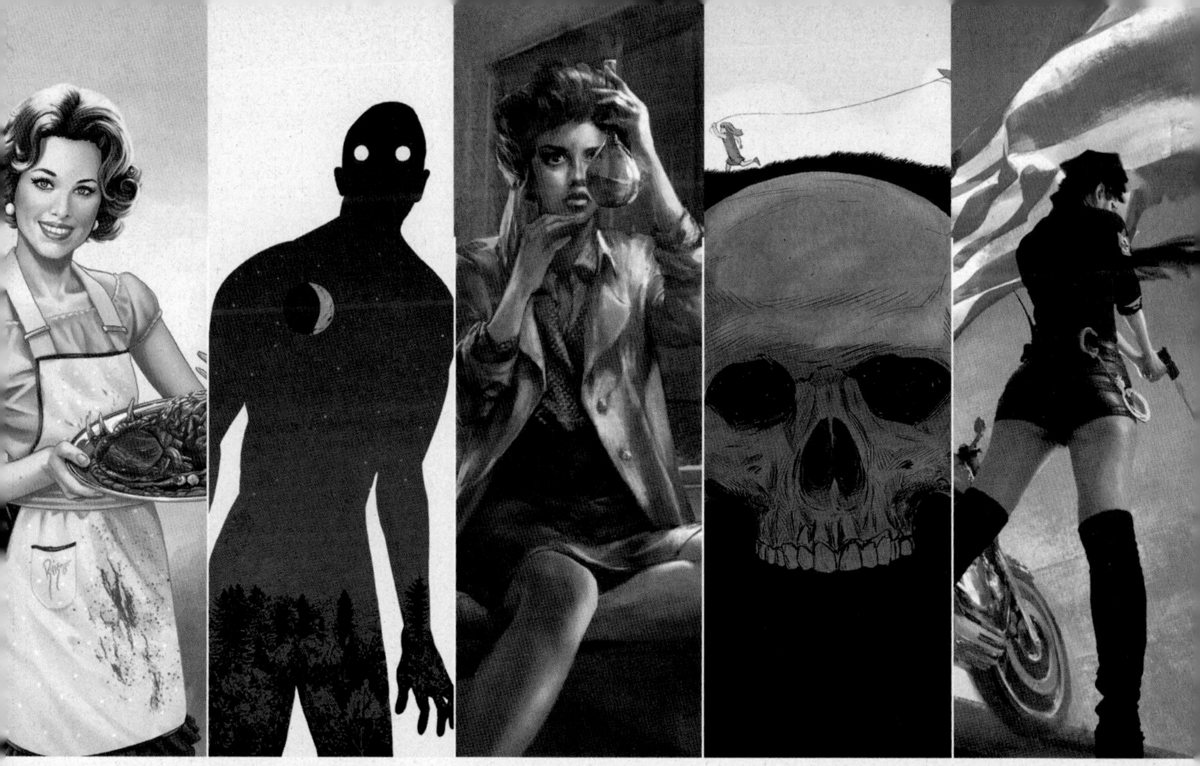

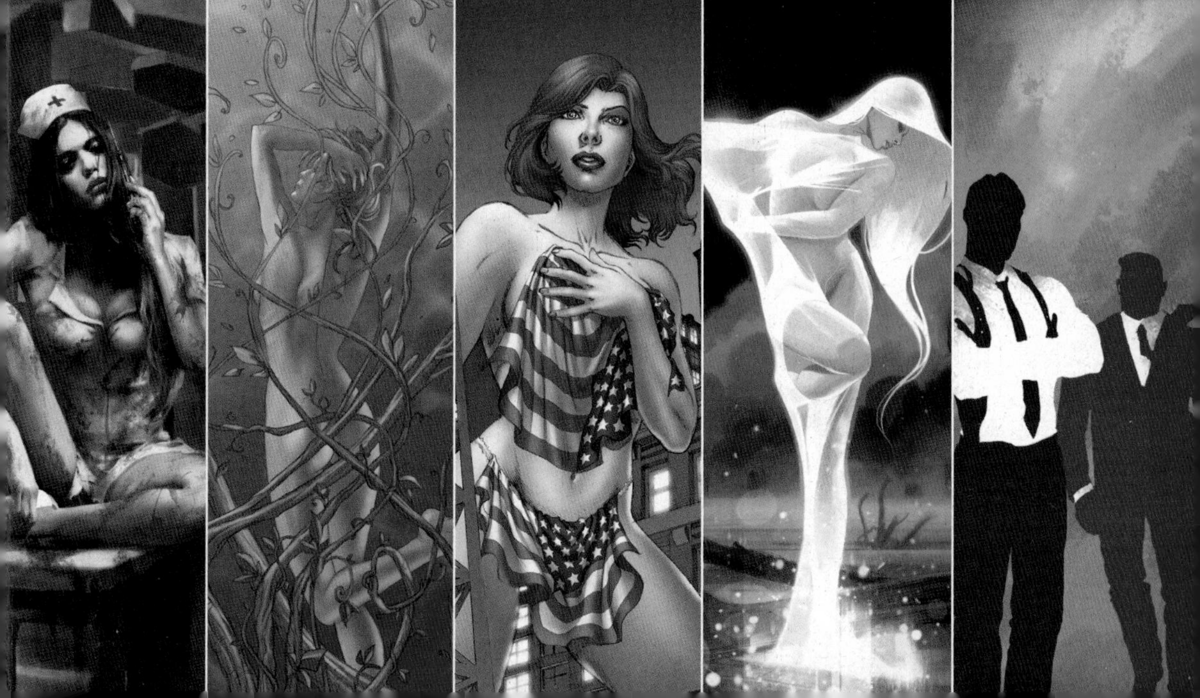

The Queen of Western Pennsylvania Lakes

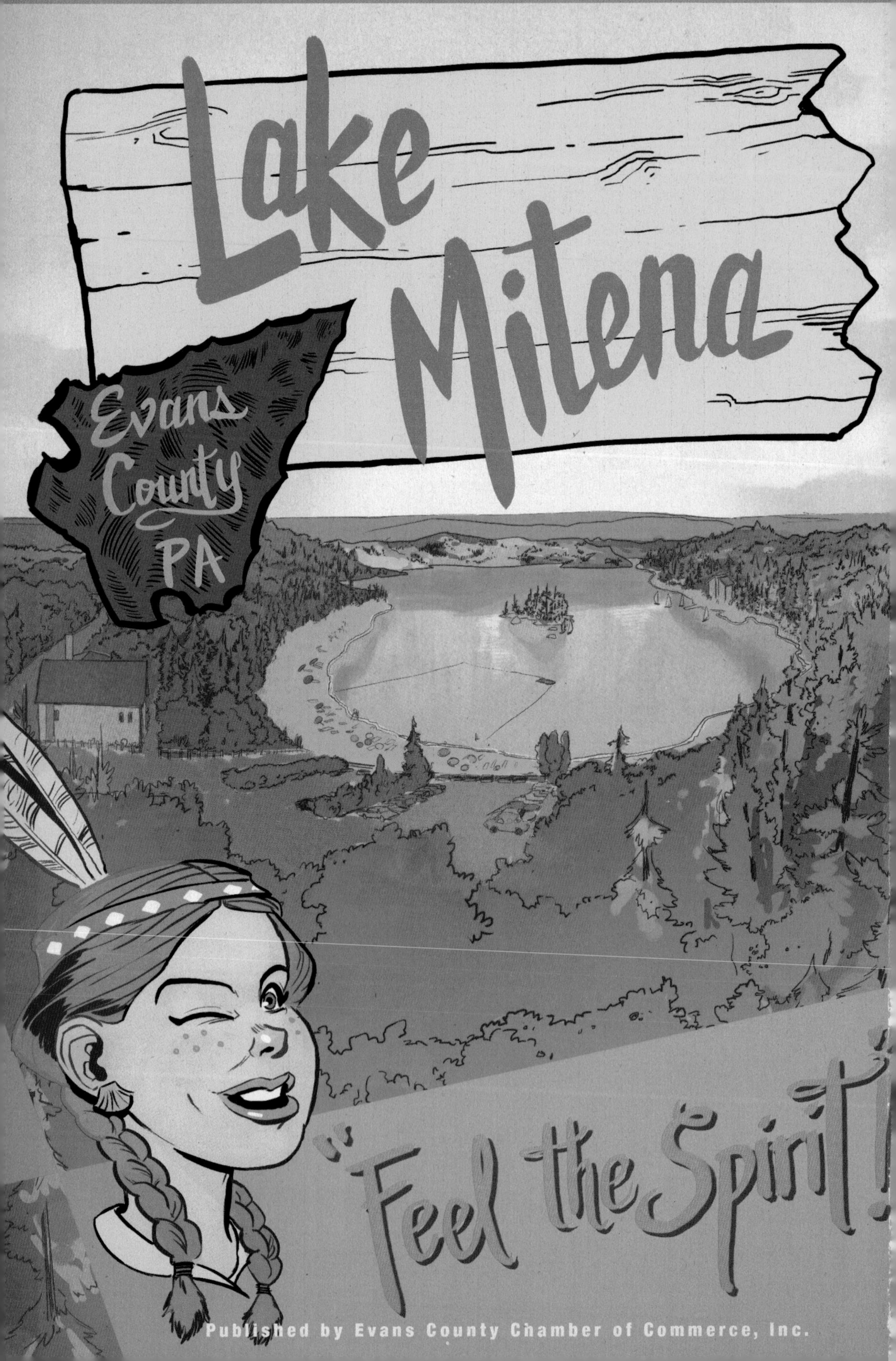
Lake Mitena
Evans County PA
"Feel the Spirit!"

Published by Evans County Chamber of Commerce, Inc.